£ 10

DICTIONARY
OF
NINETEENTH-CENTURY
IRISH WOMEN POETS

DICTIONARY
OF
NINETEENTH-CENTURY
IRISH WOMEN POETS

Anne Ulry Colman

KENNY'S BOOKSHOP

Published in Ireland by
Kenny's Bookshop and Art Gallery
High Street, Galway

Set in Palatino type and assembled by
Redsetter Limited, Dublin

Printed by
Betaprint, Clonshaugh, Dublin 17

Bound by
Kenny's Bindery, Salthill, Co. Galway

Designed by
Raymond Gunn

ISBN 0 906312 44 2

For my family:
Muriel Ulry, Justin and Branden Colman

and in memory of my father:
Clyde Ulry

ACKNOWLEDGEMENTS

This book owes a great debt of thanks to the many people whose time, efforts and encouragement went into its appearance in print. The Kenny family (Maureen, Tom, Des and Conor), without whose endless patience, guidance and enthusiasm this project might never have seen the light of day, and certainly would have been a lesser endeavour. Professor Kevin Barry, who valued the concept and demanded excellence. Siobhán Hutson, whose typing, filing, and organising kept me sane. Joan McBreen, Jane Pierce, and Anne Kennedy, who were the true midwives of this labour. Jack and Jean Gamble, whose knowledge of Ulster women was greatly appreciated. Medbh McGuckian, encouraged and understood the frustrations. J. J. Wilson and Helen Dunn, who taught me that recovery was the first step in hearing women's history. Maureen Clancy, Sheila Walsh, Louis Walsh, and Aebhgréine Cheavase, for their gracious hospitality and excellent memories. My special thanks to: Tadgh Foley, Riana O'Dwyer , Jody Allen-Randolph, Joe McBreen, Ann and John Ruane, Noreen O Curáin, Nano Pyne, Larry and Ethna Carey, Edward and Mary Lynch, Kay and Jim Westphal, Loretta Belgum.

Dead Women

You dead women in your graves,
You made beauty long ago;
But unceasing waters flow,
And great unattending waves
Carry all things that we know,
And they wither and grow old.
Are you nothing now but mould
Cold and brown?
You who were more bright than a crown
And amethyst and emerald
And all that gorgeous red and yellow gold.

Mary Devenport O'Neill
Prometheus and Other Poems
(1929)

'Always I have had mixed feelings about finding these women writers: on the one hand there has been the delight of discovering this treasure-chest; on the other hand, there has been the sadness, frustration, and anger, that such treasures ever should have been buried. And if it is difficult to separate the joy from the anger, so too has it been virtually impossible to separate the discovery from the burial. For there is no way of reclaiming these women . . . without wondering why they were lost.'

Dale Spender
Mothers of the Novel (London: Pandora, 1986)

CONTENTS

PREFACE

A proper nineteenth-century subtitle for this volume would be: a dictionary of women poets born during the period from 1800 to 1899; who wrote in the English language; who were born in Ireland, and who did not emigrate outside of the British Isles. This reference volume is intended to generate and to facilitate further research of the women writers fitting the criteria of that nineteenth-century subtitle. No attempt has been made to provide a literary or historical context for the period in which these women wrote, and critical analysis of the women's writings has been deliberately avoided. This volume uses the long century, defining a nineteenth-century woman poet as one born during the period from 1800 to 1899, but publishing before 1931.

Some of the poets included in this volume were multilingual authors, but only those works written in the English language are listed. Evidence of publications in languages other than English are included in the woman's biographical profile.

The nineteenth century was a period of intense emigration. A significant number of women who were born in Ireland emigrated to other countries, either before or after they began publishing. The question of emigrant women authors was settled by including those who were born in Ireland and began publishing in Ireland prior to emigrating. Only those works published in Ireland will be listed in the woman's bibliographical listing. Since Ireland was united with England in the nineteenth century, women who left Ireland to reside in England are included.

Sheer numbers became the determining factor regarding the stipulation of poetry as the exclusive genre. The number of women writing in all genres during the nineteenth century exceeded all expectations. Women born in the nineteenth century wrote in a variety of genres as it was not an era of specialization. Since the literary output of a writer cannot be accurately judged if all genres are not included, the published works in all genres are included in each bibliographical listing. In some cases this decision caused the inclusion of women who should not properly be classified as poets. 'M. E. Francis' (see listing under Mary Sweetman) is one such woman, a prolific novelist who wrote only a few poems.

This volume defines a poet as one who writes in a verse form or forms, so the women listed include hymnists, translators and writers of original verse. The marriage of poetry and music was fairly common in the nineteenth century, albeit more so in the first half of the century than the latter. The debate about whether verse translation is in itself poetry, assumes a particular importance for the era in which James Clarence Mangan was doing his original translations.

This study focuses on women born in Ireland. In rare instances, women born outside of Ireland have been included. Jessie Tulloch was born in Scotland to Irish parents, but she lived most of her life in Tipperary. Due to her extensive publishing record in Ireland she is included with her biographical information noting her Scottish birthplace.

The question of how to list each woman was specifically gender-related. Women had a decidedly larger number of possible names than men, and had a greater probability of seeking anonymity when publishing. Women were likely to have one or two married surnames in addition to their birth-names. They frequently published under a pseudonym, or initials, or place name, or an indication of social standing or gender, as evidenced by work published 'by a Lady'. The reasons for these masking devices varied, but women with multiple names were common. The married names of a substantial number of women are indeed better known than their birth names. Lady Gregory is barely recognizable as Isabella Augusta Persse, and Mrs S. C. Hall suffers the same anonymity as Anna Maria Fielding. Pseudonyms also overtook the maiden and married names of some women, such as 'Ethna Carbery', Anna Johnston MacManus, whose pseudonym appears on her grave marker. Other women published under both their maiden and married names. The possibilities for listing seemed endless. In the interest of consistency the primary listing is under the maiden name of each woman and a cross-referencing index is provided for married name or names, pseudonyms, names in religion, or initials.

The listings given for each woman author need little explanation beyond the following notations. Publishing information is divided into three sections. The major journals are listed, with the publication period given in general terms. Anthologies in which the poet's work may be found are included, and refers the reader to a separate listing of anthologies cited and consulted. A biographical reference section has been included, referring the reader to additional information, articles or volumes written about that poet.

The final listing is bibliographical, and contains a listing of all the works by that woman. All the recovered publishing information is included, although that may only be a title. Subsequent reprints, new editions, or retitled editions of the same volume have been noted as they were found. If a second edition was revised, or expanded, or illustrated, the difference between the first and second editions is noted. Brackets around the publication date indicate that the date was not printed in the volume, but the publication date has been ascertained from other sources.

INTRODUCTION

'This is not the book I started to write.
Half-way through my research, I changed my mind.'
Dale Spender, *Mothers of the Novel.*
(London and New York: Pandora, 1986)

In 1989, while driving Dale Spender from a speaking engagement to her friend's home in San Francisco, we spoke at length about her efforts in recovering British women novelists. Knowing of my interest in contemporary Irish women poets, she asked me about their predecessors. I found myself fumbling, and finally could only name six women. The seed was sown.

The book I intended to write was to have been a study of contemporary Irish women poets, focusing on their literary inheritance from Ireland's Anglophone foremothers. The project was to have been an influence study, but I quickly discovered that the previous influences were still unrecovered. Aside from A. A. Kelly's pioneering volume, *Pillars of the House*, the only anthology of poetry by Irish women was edited by Elizabeth Sharp, *Women's Voices: An Anthology of the Most Characteristic Poems by English, Scotch and Irish Women*, published in 1887. Biographical studies of nineteenth-century women were more plentiful, but the primary sources were not gender-specific: D. J. O'Donoghue, *The Poets of Ireland* , and Katharine Tynan, ed. *Cabinet of Irish Literature*. Compared with O'Donoghue, the contemporary biographical sources revealed a paucity of women writers, while the late nineteenth-century and early twentieth-century biographical sources, such as *Illustrious Irishwomen,* presented a mixed-bag of women writers, political figures, actors, and famous beauties. Obviously my study of contemporary women poets from a historical perspective would require first uncovering the historical perspective. So, 'half-way through my research, I changed my mind'.

Immediately three major gender-related myths emerged. A cursory glance at the reality of nineteenth-century Irish women's poetry left me wondering how these misconceptions ever came into being, let alone attained a firm validity. Nevertheless they are held to be truth, and need finally to be laid to rest.

1. Women only began writing in Ireland in the last fifty years.

2. There was little interest, prior to the mid-twentieth century, in literature by women, or in work about female writers.

3. Women writers who were active in the nineteenth-century were literary oddities, isolated and isolationist in their endeavours.

Regarding the first myth, there are in excess of four-hundred Irish women poets writing in English, whose birth-dates fall between 1800 and 1899. Their literary output ranges from a single poem in a single journal, to a single opus of 184 separate volumes of prose and poetry by Katharine Tynan. Tynan's literary output is atypical, yet the following list of authors and the number of volumes they published in all genres demonstrates an unexpected level of publishing activity:

Mary Sweetman ('M. E. Francis') published 58 volumes.
Rosa Mulholland (Lady Gilbert) published 50 volumes.
Isabella Augusta Persse (Lady Gregory) published 38 volumes.
Margaret Cusack (The Nun of Kenmare) published 35 volumes.
Clotilde Inez Mary Graves ('Richard Dehan') published 32 volumes.
Caroline Sheridan (Lady Norton) published 31 volumes.
Margaret Gibbons published 30 volumes.
Dora Sigerson (Mrs Clement Shorter) published 26 volumes.
Anna Maria Fielding (Mrs S. C. Hall) published 25 volumes.
Kathleen O'Meara ('Grace Ramsey') published 23 volumes.
Helena Walsh (Mrs Concannon) published 23 volumes.
Grace Little (Mrs Rhys) published 23 volumes.
Winifred Letts published 21 volumes.

This does not include reprints or new editions, which are given in the bibliographical listings for each of the women in this dictionary. The above list includes only those women with more than twenty volumes to their credit. The number of women who published between ten and twenty volumes is too lengthy to be listed here. Despite the first myth, Irish women were writing and publishing at a substantial rate.

As well as publishing in book form there were other publishing vehicles available in the nineteenth and early twentieth centuries. Monthly magazines flourished, and encouraged authors to submit poetry, prose essays, tales, short stories, travel pieces, serial novels, religious articles and non-fiction. Most notable in this promotion of women authors was the *Irish Monthly*, especially during the editorship of Father Matthew Russell. He deserves special accolades for his efforts in recording biographical information about the women he published. Often his Nutshell Biograms are the only source of biographical information about a woman writer. In the case of Ellen Mary Downing, Father Russell became insatiable in his biographical efforts, as evidenced by the five-part biography he published. He generally provided short biographical sketches, the format of his Nutshell biograms.

Regarding the second myth, that there was little interest in women's writings and in what we would now call feminist collections of literature and biography, consider the following list of titles, and their publication dates:

1877 *Illustrious Irishwomen.* A two-volume set of biographical information about famous Irish women from the nineteenth century. It includes authors, actresses, political figures, and famous beauties of the day. Edited by E. Owens Blackburne, the pseudonym of Elizabeth Owens Blackburne Casey, a poet in her own right.

1887 *Women's Voices: An Anthology of the Most Characteristic Poems by English, Scotch, and Irish Women.* Edited by Mrs William Sharp, whose husband wrote under the female pseudonym of Fiona Macleod.

1892 *Women Writers: Their Works and Ways.* An anthology, with literary analysis, by Miss C. J. Hamilton, another poet.

1904 *Notable Irishwomen.* Another volume by Miss C. J. Hamilton. This volume contains biographical information of authors, actresses, and beauties.

1919 *Women of Ninety-Eight.* Helena Walsh Concannon's work focuses on the wives, mothers, sisters, and sweethearts of the 1798 leaders. Helena Walsh is also listed in this dictionary.

1930 *Daughters of Banba.* Helena Walsh Concannon's second look at Irish womanhood is an overview of women from the Irish sagas to the Irish women poets of the eighteenth century. Feminist concerns are evident from the chapter titles: women of the castles, women of the cloister, women of the town, women of the country, women in exile, and the relationship between women and war.

These six works, specifically relating to women writers, show the interest in women's biographies and women writers. Readers were hungry for women's poetry and prose. Katharine Tynan again led the pack, being as popular as she was prolific. Ernest Boyd, writing about Tynan in *Ireland's Literary Renaissance* (New York: Alfred A. Knopf, 1922) couches his criticism of her later work with a reminder of her influence: 'It is difficult, when reading her later verse, to remember that until the arrival of W. B. Yeats, Katharine Tynan was held to be the young poet of the greatest promise in Ireland' (107). Boyd further concedes Tynan was 'the only important Catholic poet in Ireland' (112). Tynan's extensive literary contacts made her an integral and influential part of the late nineteenth-century literary scene. While earlier in the century, the women poets of *The Nation* were immensely popular and were given affectionate nicknames by their readers. These women were better known by the pseudonyms they used than by their true names.

The critical reception to women's poetry is found in the reviews of the *Irish Book Lover, Irish Monthly, Catholic Bulletin* and other periodicals, themselves waxing poetic in descriptions. Father Russell lamented the death of Frances Wynne for about two years in the *Irish Monthly*, and continued to use her poetry as a standard against which other poets were judged for an additional year. The small pamphlets produced by Maeve Cavanagh during the 1916 Rising sold out within days, if not hours, of their printing. A glance at the multiple editions, reprints and retitled issues of women's volumes gives an indication of the popular support. Particularly noteworthy are Frances Browne, with fifty-six editions of a single volume, and Nannie Lambert, with a total print run of 94,000 for *Ladies on Horseback*.

The influence wielded by these women is evidenced by accomplishments like those of Alice Milligan and Ethna Carbery (Anna Johnston) who edited one Northern newspaper, then founded and edited another. Margaret Cusack, the Nun of Kenmare, ran a successful publishing house while a cloistered nun of the Poor Clares Convent in Kenmare. It has been estimated that the Kenmare Publishing Company produced 200,000 volumes in a single decade.

The most comprehensive anthology, from the perspective of women writers, is still *The Cabinet of Irish Literature*, a four-volume set edited by Katharine Tynan and published in 1902-1903. Katharine Tynan's edition is a revision of the 1880 edition of the *Cabinet of Irish Literature* edited by Charles Read. It lists seventy-one women writers for the seventeenth to nineteenth centuries, a significant improvement in representation of women's writings from Read's original edition, and far better than *The Field Day Anthology of Irish Writing*

(Derry: Field Day Publications, 1991). Such a large percentage of deletions bears further examination. The entire group of late twentieth-century anthology editors clearly believed the second myth. John Montague, in the introduction to *The Book of Irish Verse* (New York: Macmillan, 1974) praises the contribution of women to Irish poetry: 'And here we should remark another aspect of early Irish poetry: it is the only literature in Europe, and perhaps in the world, where one finds a succession of women poets' (22). Unfortunately, Montague offers his readers not one example of Irish women's poetry from the nineteenth and early twentieth centuries. However, it would be unfair to ask the *Field Day* editors, or John Montague, to shoulder all the responsibility. Plainly stated, the research had not been done, and the mythical lack of interest in women authors and their writings had not been challenged. Women's poetry was widely anthologized in the nineteenth century, and collections excluding or marginalizing women are harder to find in their own era than today.

The third myth, that women writers were literary oddities, isolationist and isolated in their efforts, merits a return to the original listing of women and the large number of volumes they published. Beginning with these multiple volume authors, a pattern of literary dynasties and friendships emerges. Six key genealogical examples will suffice.

Mary Sweetman, 'M. E. Francis', was one of four sisters. Three of the four were to become authors. Elinor Mary Sweetman wrote poetry, and Agnes Sweetman, also Mrs Anthony Egerton Castle, was a novelist. Mary Sweetman married Francis Blundell, whose two sisters, Agnes and Margaret, were also authors. Mary Sweetman's daughter, Madge Blundell, wrote biographies and prose.

Dora Sigerson belongs to a particularly intricate web of literary figures. Her father was Dr George Sigerson, a writer and medical doctor. Her mother, Hester Varian Sigerson, was a novelist and the sister of Ralph Varian, a poet and editor of anthologies. Ralph Varian married Elizabeth Willoughby Treacy, a poet and Dora's aunt. Mary R. Varian, apparently the sister of Ralph, was another of Dora's aunts, and a poet. Hester Sigerson, Dora's sister, wrote poetry and prose. She became the editor of the *Weekly Freeman* children's literary section, under the pseudonym of Uncle Remus, following the death of the original Uncle Remus, Rose Kavanagh. Hester Sigerson married Donn Piatt, the son of John and Sophie Piatt, two American poets with extensive literary connections in America.

Katharine Tynan Hinkson is well-remembered, but her younger sister, Norah Tynan O'Mahony, has not fared so well. Even in Katharine's autobiographies (a lengthy, four-volume endeavour),

Norah is rarely mentioned. Yet Norah wrote one of the best of the 'chicken novels' of the late nineteenth and early twentieth centuries, *Una's Enterprise*. According to Norah, the way to financial independence, a good marriage, and true happiness, was through poultry. The plot is humorous, yet there were a series of novels with poultry themes during this period, indicative of an underlying socio-economic concern.

The four Furlong sisters, Alice, Mary, Katherine and Margaret, were neighbours and friends of the Tynans. Of the four sisters, Alice, Mary and Kate were all published poets. The fourth sister, Margaret, married the poet P. J. McCall. Being neighbours did not mean that the Tynan and Furlong relationships were without occasional animosity. Katharine Tynan apparently enjoyed the literary efforts of Alice Furlong, but of Mary's work Tynan states: 'From the age of fourteen Mary scribbled determinedly in spite of much good and unpalatable advice from editors' (*Cabinet* IV 241). Alice Furlong is also interesting as an example of the romanticised biographies of nineteenth-century women writers. There developed a persistent tale of Alice being so heart-broken by the failure of the 1916 Rising, and the subsequent executions, that she retreated into complete isolation in Tallaght, neither publishing, speaking nor writing another word in English. This romantic story of Furlong's life is unfortunately belied by her publishing record. Alice Furlong continued to publish in English as late as the June 1930 issue of the *Irish Monthly*.

Geraldine Plunkett was the author of a single volume, but she also edited and wrote an introductory memoir to the collected poems of her brother, Joseph Mary Plunkett. Geraldine was to become the mother of the late Eilís Dillon, and the grandmother of Eiléan Ní Chuilleanáin, a contemporary poet. Joseph Mary Plunkett married Grace Gifford, an occasional poet and artist, who became the sister-in-law of Geraldine.

Among the Northern writers the same kinds of literary friendships and kinships are found. Ruth and Celia Duffin, sisters from Belfast, co-authored two volumes of poetry, which were illustrated by a third sister, Emma. Celia Duffin went on to write a third volume, without Ruth, published under her married name of Celia Randall. The Duffin sisters were great friends of Helen Lanyon, another Belfast poet.

These political figures from the past may be memorable, but the literary women related to them by birth or marriage, are less recognizable now: Charles Stewart Parnell was the brother of Anna and Fanny Parnell. Daniel O'Connell was the father of Ellen O'Connell Fitzsimon. Jeremiah O'Donovan Rossa was married to Mary Jane Irwin, his 'little poetess wife'. John O'Leary was the brother of Ellen

O'Leary. Justin MacCarthy was the brother of Ely MacCarthy. William Smith O'Brien was the father of Charlotte Grace O'Brien.

The evidence of these ties of kinship and friendships simply does not support the third myth. Instead of isolated and isolationary women writers, there was a strong network supporting the literary endeavours of nineteenth-century women's poetry. This network, comprised of men and women, encouraged, promoted and published women writers. Irish women writers of the nineteenth-century were firmly in the mainstream of the literary activities. Particularly strong connections among the female writers also raises theories as to literary 'schools' among these women. Such speculation belongs to the critics and readers of this dictionary, which is intended to facilitate their efforts.

The diversity of subjects undertaken by the nineteenth-century women poets was surprising. Nationalism, religion and folklore as the basis for poetry were themes shared with their male contemporaries, but the body of feminist work they produced was startling. Discovering that women had been seriously engaged in writing themselves into history, particularly through volumes like *Illustrious Irishwomen* and *Notable Irishwomen*, went completely contrary to what I had read and heard about Ireland's literary foremothers. It made the ignorance of today regarding their existence even more poignant. Despite their best efforts they have been marginalized into a position outside history, or have been completely buried.

The women poets born from 1800 to 1899 were a diverse group, readily defying stereotypes and the myths that have since developed to entrap and obscure them. While some of their poetry was, and is, eminently forgettable, as a group they do not deserve the obscurity to which time and neglect have consigned them. Once the political verse is set aside, Nationalist or Unionist, the remaining poetry shows amazing commonality and maturity of themes. These are women who do not deserve to be forgotten.

By far the most unusual woman and most travelled woman of the nineteenth century was Kathleen Murphy. Her infrequent poetic contributions to journals were bolstered by travel articles, which she was eminently qualified to write. Although the first poem she published was in the March 1918 issue of *Studies*, it is a later prose piece, an autobiographical letter she provided for the 1952 *Capuchin Annual*, which captivates me. It is difficult to reconcile the modest and domesticated stereotype of womanhood, so commonly portrayed in regard to the late nineteenth- and early twentieth-century woman, with the self-sufficient and adventurous person of Kathleen Murphy from Birr.

'Dear Father Senan,

As to the autobiographical note; there is nothing whatever interesting about me except the fact that I have travelled more than anyone I ever met — indeed I believe I might justly claim to be Ireland's super-tramp! Intensely interested in ancient civilizations, I have visited nearly all the famous ruins of the world, including even those of the Khmers and the Incas. Not only have I climbed the Great Pyramid of Egypt and the Great Wall of China, but — a far rarer achievement — I have stood on the pillar of St Simon Stylites in Syria. I have seen pageants of all kinds, ranging from the wonderful carnival of Rio to the weird, colourful cremation ceremony of Bali; have been in a Lapp camp and an opium den; dined with a sheik in Morocco, and accompanied a meuzzin at sunset to the summit of a minaret when he chanted across the Sahara the impressive call to evening prayer. I succeeded in penetrating into the palace of the Shah of Persia to see the marvellous Peacock Throne; then, in a Peruvian port, had to submit to the humiliating experience of being treated as a mere piece of merchandise when I was hoisted by a crane on board a boat just like the cargo. Having lived alone in the stark simplicity of a jungle shack and in the tense atmosphere of a desert hut in Iraq while the tribes waged war against the Government, it seemed to me most luxurious to rest in peace when my sleeping apartment happened to be one of the rock tombs of Petra. Among memorable incidents I may mention finding myself locked inside the mausoleum of a Shogun in Japan; a narrow escape from being shot by a sentry in the fortress of Belgrade; and being nearly buried alive in Babylon. My volume of poems (published in 1932) won the First Prize in the Tailteann Literary Competition of that year, and I received the Papal decoration 'Pro Ecclesia et Pontifice' for religious poetry. I hope you will be able to select eighty words from the above. I must ask you to excuse me for not sending [a] photo. Very rarely in my life have I been photographed, and the only fairly modern one I possess represents me mounted on what I believe was the tallest camel in Africa. I am sure you would consider this far too unconventional to be published in *The Capuchin Annual*.

Sincerely yours, K. M. Murphy.'

GENERAL BIOGRAPHICAL
REFERENCE SOURCES

Brady, Anne M. and Brian Cleeve, editors. *A Biographical Dictionary of Irish Writers*. Mullingar: Lilliput, 1985.

Buck, Claire, editor. *Bloomsbury Guide to Women's Literature*. London: Bloomsbury, 1992.

Byrne, Art and Sean McMahon, editors. *Lives: 113 Great Irishmen and Irishwomen*. Swords: Poolbeg, 1990.

Cleeve, Brian, editor. *Dictionary of Irish Writers*. 3 vol. Cork: Mercier, 1969.

Deane, Seamus, general editor. *The Field Day Anthology of Irish Writing*. 3 vols. Derry: Field Day Publications, 1991.

The Dictionary of National Biography.

Hogan, Robert, editor-in-chief. *Dictionary of Irish Literature*. Westport, Connecticut, U.S.A.: Greenwood Press, 1979.

Keaney, Marian. *Westmeath Authors: A Bibliographical and Biographical Study*. Mullingar: Longford/Westmeath Joint Library Committee, 1969.

Kelly, A. A., editor. *Pillars of the House*. Dublin: Wolfhound, 1987.

McCarthy, Justin, editor-in-chief. *Irish Literature*. 10 vols. Philadelphia: John D. Morris and Co., 1904.

Maher, Helen. *Galway Authors*. Galway: Galway County Libraries, 1976.

————. *Roscommon Authors*. Roscommon: Roscommon County Library, 1978.

Newmann, Kate. *Dictionary of Ulster Biography*. Belfast: Institute of Irish Studies, The Queen's University, 1993.

O'Donoghue, D. J. *The Poets of Ireland*. Dublin: Hodges Figgis and Co.; and London: Henry Frowde, Oxford UP, 1912.

O'Kelly, Seamus G. *Sweethearts of the Irish Rebels*. Dublin: A1 Books, 1968.

O'Súilleabháin, Seán. *Longford Authors: A Biographical and Bibliographical Dictionary*. Mullingar: Longford/Westmeath Joint Library Committee, 1978.

Rafróidí, Patrick. *Irish Literature in English: The Romantic Period (1789-1850)*. 2 vols. Atlantic Highlands, New Jersey, U.S.A.: Humanities Press, 1980.

Read, Charles A. *The Cabinet of Irish Literature*. 4 vols. London: Blackie and Son, 1880.

Schlueter, Paul and Jane Schlueter, editors. *An Encyclopaedia of British Women Writers.* Chicago and London: St. James Press, 1988.

Thom's Irish Who's Who. Dublin: Alexander Thom and Co.; and London: Daniel O'Connor, 1923.

'Ulster Books and Authors: 1900-1953'. *Rann* 20 (June 1953): 55-73.

Weekes, Ann Owens. *Unveiling Treasures.* Dublin: Attic Press, 1993.

ANTHOLOGIES

A partial list of anthologies cited and consulted:

AE [George William Russell), editor. *New Songs: A Lyric Selection: Made by AE from Poems by Padraic Colum, Eva Gore-Booth, Thomas Keohler, Alice Milligan, Susan Mitchell, Seumas O'Sullivan, George Roberts, and Ella Young.* Dublin: O'Donohue and Co.; and London: A. H. Bullen, 1904.

Armitage, Evelyn Noble, editor. *Quaker Poets of Great Britain and Ireland.* London: William Andrews, 1896.

Brooke, Stopford A. and T. W. Rolleston, editors. *A Treasury of Irish Poetry in the English Tongue.* London: Smith, Elder and Co., 1900.

Browne, Stephen J., editor. *Poetry of Irish History.* Dublin and Cork: Talbot Press, 1927.

Connolly, Daniel, editor. *Household Library of Ireland's Poets.* New York: n.p., 1887.

Cooke, John, editor. *The Dublin Book of Irish Verse: 1728-1909.* Dublin: Hodges, Figgis and Co.; and London: Oxford UP, 1924.

Drury, T. W. E., editor. *Some Hymns by Irish Church Writers.* Dublin: Association for Promotion of Christian Knowledge, 1932.

Duffy, Charles Gavan, editor. *The Ballad Poetry of Ireland.* Dublin: James Duffy and Co., 1869.

Eyes of Youth: A Book of Verse by Padraic Colum, Shane Leslie, Viola Meynell, Ruth Lindsay, Hugh Austin, Judith Lytton, Olivia Meynell, Maurice Healy, Monica Saleeby, and Francis Meynell. Foreword by Gilbert K. Chesterton. London: Burns and Oates, 1912.

Fitzhenry, Edna C., editor. *Nineteen-Sixteen: An Anthology.* Dublin: Browne and Nolan, 1935.

Graves, Alfred Perceval, editor. *The Book of Irish Poetry.* Dublin: Talbot Press, n.d.

———, editor. *The Irish Song Book with Original Irish Airs.* 1894. Another edition: London: T. Fisher Unwin, 1914.

Gregory, Padraic, editor. *Modern Anglo-Irish Verse: An Anthology.* London: David Nutt, 1914.

Hayes, Edward, editor. *The Ballads of Ireland.* 2 vols. Edinburgh and London: Fullarton, Macnab and Co., n.d.

Lynd, Robert, editor. *Modern Poetry.* London: Thomas Nelson and Sons, 1939.

Kyle, Galloway, editor. *A Cluster of Grapes*. London: Erskine MacDonald, 1914.

Hoagland, Kathleen, editor. *1000 Years of Irish Poetry*. New York: Grosset and Dunlap, 1962.

Lover, Samuel, editor. *Poems of Ireland*. London: Ward, Lock and Co., [c.1895].

MacCarthy, Mary Stanislaus, editor. *A Birthday Book of the Dead*. Dublin: M. H. Gill, 1886.

MacDermott, Martin, editor. *The New Spirit of 'The Nation': or, Ballads and Songs by the Writers of 'The Nation'*. London: T. Fisher Unwin; and Dublin: Sealy, Bryers and Walker, 1894.

MacIlwaine, W., editor. *Lyra Hibernica Sacra*. Belfast: M'Caw, Stevenson and Orr, [1878].

Morton, David, editor. *The Renaissance of Irish Poetry: 1800-1930*. New York: Ives Washburn, 1929.

Paul, W. J., editor. *Modern Irish Poets*. Belfast: Belfast Steam-Printing Co., 1894.

Rhys, Grace, editor. *A Celtic Anthology*. London: Harrap, 1927.

Robinson, Lennox, editor. *A Golden Treasury of Irish Verse*. London: Macmillan and Co., 1925.

Seen By Five. Dublin: E. Ponsonby, 1912.

Sharp, E. A. and J. Matthay, editors. *Lyra Celtica: An Anthology of Representative Celtic Poetry*. Edinburgh: John Grant, 1924.

Sharp, Mrs William, editor. *Women's Voices: An Anthology of the Most Characteristic Poems by English, Scotch and Irish Women*. London: Walter Scott, 1887.

Sparling, H. Haliday, editor. *Irish Minstrelsy*. London: Walter Scott, [1887].

Sullivan, A. M. and T. D. Sullivan, editors. *Irish Readings*. Dublin: M. H. Gill and Son, 1913.

Sullivan, T. D., editor. *Emerald Gems*. Dublin: n.p., 1885.

Taylor, Geoffrey, editor. *Irish Poets of the Nineteenth Century*. London: Routledge and Kegan Paul, n.d.

Tynan, Katharine, editor. *The Wild Harp: an Anthology*. London: Sidgwick and Jackson, 1913.

Varian, Ralph, editor. *The Harp of Erin: Book of Ballad Poetry and of Native Song*. Cork: Francis Guy, 1869.

Walsh, Thomas, editor. *The Catholic Anthology: The World's Great Catholic Poetry*. New York: Macmillan Co., 1927. Revised edition, with additional poems: New York: Macmillan Co., 1942.

Walters, L. D'O., editor. *Irish Poets of To-Day*. London: T. Fisher Unwin, 1921.

Welsh, Charles, editor. *The Golden Treasury of Irish Songs and Lyrics.* 2
vols. New York, Dodge Publishing, 1907.

White, Albert Clement, editor. *A Little Book of Irish Verse.* London:
Heath, Cranton and Ouseley, [1917].

Yeats, William Butler, editor. *A Book of Irish Verse.* [1895]. London:
Methuen and Co., 1920.

DICTIONARY
OF
BIOGRAPHY
AND
BIBLIOGRAPHY

A

ADAM, Una
A single poem by Una Adam appeared in the *Irish Monthly*, March 1896 issue.

ADAMS, Mary Jane
Born: 1840, in Ireland
Died: 1902, in America
First married name: Mrs Alfred S. Barnes
Second married name: Mrs Mary Adams

Although she published as Mary Jane Adams, her maiden name may have been Mathews. She was born in Ireland, but emigrated with her family to America while she was still a child. Her first husband was a Brooklyn publisher, and her work was published only in America, except for one volume which has a shared U.K. imprint.

Bibliography:
Sonnets and Songs. New York and London: Putnam, 1901.

ADDEY, Louisa
Louisa Addey contributed twice to the *Irish Monthly* during the period 1896 to 1899.

AGNEW, Sarah
Bibliography:
Resource of Melancholy. Larne (Co. Antrim): 1839.

AKERS, Elizabeth Chase
Born: 1832
Died: 1911
Pseudonym: Florence Percy

Bibliography:
Rock Me to Sleep, Mother. London: Sampson Low and Co., 1883.
Queen Catherine, Rose and Other Poems. Dublin: n.p., 1886.

ALEXANDER, Eleanor Jane
Born: circa 1870
Died: 1939

Eleanor was the daughter of Cecil Frances Humphreys Alexander (see listing under Cecil Humphreys) and William Alexander, Primate of All Ireland. Following her mother's death, Eleanor became her father's companion and the biographer for both her parents. Her extensive biography of William Alexander, into which she incorporates the biographical details of her mother, includes autobiographical excerpts from a manuscript her father had begun to write, but never completed. This dual-voiced memoir is Eleanor's major literary effort. She was declared a Member of the Order of the British Empire in 1918, and is listed as residing at Hampton Court Palace, Middlesex, in 1923. Eleanor Alexander's poetry appeared in the *Times* and the *Spectator*.

Anthologized in: Graves, and Gregory.

Bibliography:
Lady Anne's Walk: a Sketch of Lady Anne Beresford. London: Edward Arnold, 1903. Another edition: 1904.
The Rambling Rector. London: Edward Arnold, 1904.
The Lady of the Well. London: Edward Arnold, 1906.
Primate Alexander, Archbishop of Armagh: a Memoir. London: Edward Arnold, 1913. Another edition: 1914.

ALLEN, Harriet
Born: 4 November 1831
Died: 9 March 1861
Married name: Harriet Johnston

Harriet Allen's name is occasionally given as Haidee, which was probably her preferred diminutive. She was the daughter of Robert Allen, from Kilkenny. Harriet became the first wife of William Johnston, MP for South Belfast, and a leader in the Orange Order. The couple had four children. Harriet's *Lays of the Lost One* was originally published on her husband's Downshire Protestant Press. Her work reportedly appeared in *Irish Penny Readings*.

Bibliography:
Lays of the Lost One, and Other Poems. Downpatrick: Downshire Protestant Press, 1858.

ANDERSON, Helen
Born: in Belfast
Married name: Mrs W. H. Patterson

Helen was the daughter of John Crossley Anderson, of Belfast. Her marriage to the eminent antiquarian, W. H. Patterson, also of Belfast, made Helen the daughter-in-law of Mary Elizabeth Ferrar Patterson (see listing under Ferrar). Helen was an accomplished musician. The Patterson's residence was Sydenham, Belfast.

Anthologized in: MacIlwaine.

APJOHN, Rebecca Helena
Born: 1841
Married name: Mrs Maurice Charles Hime

Rebecca was the youngest daughter of John Apjohn, Professor of Chemistry at Trinity College. In 1887, she married Dr Maurice Charles Hime, a classical scholar and educationalist. Rebecca moved to Londonderry, where her husband was the Headmaster of Foyle College, a position he retained until his retirement in 1896. Rebecca was Dr Hime's second wife, and through her husband she was acquainted with Sophie A. M. James (see listing) who had written a memorial poem to Mary Hime, Maurice's first wife.

Bibliography:
Brian Boru, and the Battle of Clontarf. London: Simpkin, Marshall & Co.; and Dublin: Sullivan Bros., 1889.
Christmas Roses: a Volume of Occasional Verses. With Maurice Charles Hime. London: J. and A. Churchill; and Dublin: Hodges, Figgis and Co., 1930.

ARCHER, Edna Eileen
Edna Archer contributed a single poem to *Green and Gold*, in 1922.

ARMSTRONG, Florence A.
Bibliography:
Wayside Forget-me-nots. Belfast: William Strain, 1908.

ARMSTRONG, Florence C.
Born: 18 March 1843

Florence was the daughter of William Armstrong (the elder), and a sister to William Armstrong (the younger). Both Williams were medical doctors in Sligo, and the family resided at Collooney, Co. Sligo. Florence's father was physician to the Sligo Fever Hospital during the Famine. She seems to have left Sligo at an early age, but her destination and later life remain a mystery.

Bibliography:
The King in His Beauty, and Other Hymns. London: A. Richardson, W. Wells Gardner, 1875.
The Sunny South. London: n.p., 1880.
Sisters of Phaeton. London: Ward and Downey, 1890.

ARNOLD, Charlotte
Charlotte and her sister, Henrietta, were residents of Lismore, Co. Waterford.

Bibliography:
Village Lyrics. With Henrietta Arnold. London: 1877. Another edition: 1878.
Tales of My Father's Fireside. Collected and edited. London: Provost and Co., 1879.

ARNOLD, Henrietta
Henrietta and her sister Charlotte, were residents of Lismore, Co. Waterford.

Bibliography:
Village Lyrics. With her sister, Charlotte. London: 1877. Another edition: 1878.

ARRESTI, Rose
Nine poems by Rose Arresti were published in the *Irish Monthly* from 1904 to 1907.

ARTHUR, Charlotte
Charlotte Arthur published in *The Irish Statesman*, in addition to her two volumes of poetry. The introduction to *Dreams and Trees* briefly acknowledges George William Russell (AE).

Bibliography:
Dreams and Trees. Dublin: Wood Printing Works, 1925.
Poor Faun. New York and London: G. Putnam's Sons, 1930.

ATTERIDGE, Helen
'An Irish lady who has contributed largely to Catholic periodicals' (O'Donoghue 15).

Bibliography:
Foremost If I Can. Golden Mottoes Series. London: Cassell and Co., 1886.
Butterfly Ballads and Stories in Rhyme. London: J. Milne, 1898.
Bunty and the Boys. London: Cassell and Co., 1888.
The Bravest of the Brave, and The Story of a Soldier, a Donkey and a Doll. London: Cassell and Co., 1900.
Fluffy and Jack (Godfrey and Hilda). London: Cassell and Co., 1900.
The Mystery of Master Max, and The Shrimps of Shrimpton. London: Cassell and Co., 1900.
To School and Away. London: Cassell and Co., 1900.
Uncle Silvio's Secret. London: Cassell and Co., 1900.
At the Sign of the Silver Cup. London: B. Herder, [1927].
The Old-World House. London: Catholic Truth Society, 1929.
Madonna: a Poem. London: n.d.

B

BAISS, Grace
Grace Baiss contributed two poems to the *Irish Monthly*; the first in 1880 and another in 1889.

BALFE, Kathleen Mary
Pseudonym: G. Bernoville

A total of six poems by Kathleen Mary Balfe appeared in the *Irish Monthly*, from 1898 to 1907. Kathleen edited volumes of religious prose.

Bibliography:
Thoughts of St Teresa for Every Day. Edited. 1923.
Thoughts of St John of the Cross for Every Day. Edited. 1924.
Thoughts of St Augustine for Every Day. Edited. 1926.
The Jesuits . . . an Abridged Translation. Edited. 1937.

BARLOW, Jane
Born: 1857, in Clontarf
Died: 17 April 1917, at St Valerie, Bray, Co. Wicklow
Pseudonym: Antares Skorpios, and Felix Ryark

Jane was the eldest daughter of Reverend James William Barlow, later Vice-Provost of Trinity College, Dublin. She was educated at home, and was 'frail in body and slight in build' (Obituary). Jane Barlow achieved greater popularity for her novels than for her poetry. Almost her entire life was spent at The Cottage, Raheny, a thatched house located on the Dublin Road. Hill-walking appears to have been her favourite recreational activity. She received an honorary D.Litt. from Trinity College. Jane was a friend and admirer of Sarah Purser, the artist, with whom Jane was a regular correspondent.

Jane Barlow was a frequent contributor to *Dublin University Review*, from 1886 to 1917, and also contributed to *Dana*.

Anthologized in: Brooke/Rolleston, *Cabinet* IV, Cooke, Graves, and Gregory.

Biographical References:
Obituary. *Irish Book Lover* 8 (June/July 1917): 141-2.

Bibliography:
History of a World of Immortals Without God: Translated from an Unpublished Manuscript in the Library of a Continental University (Antares Skorpios). Dublin: William McGee, and London: Simpkin, Marshall, 1891.
Bog-Land Studies. London: T. Fisher Unwin, 1892. Second edition, revised and enlarged: London: Hodder and Stoughton, 1893. Third edition: 1894.
Irish Idylls. London: Hodder and Stoughton, 1892. Another edition: 1893. Illustrated, eighth edition: 1898.
The Land of Elfintown. 1894.
The Battle of the Frogs and Mice; in Verse. From the Greek of Homer. (A metrical version of the 'Batrachomyomachia'). London: Methuen, 1894.
Kerrigan's Quality. London: Hodder and Stoughton, 1894. Another edition: New York: Dodd, Mead, 1894.
The End of Elfintown. London: Macmillan, 1894.
Maureen's Fairing and Other Stories. Iris Library Series. London: J. M. Dent and Co., 1895.
Strangers at Lisconnel: a Second Series of Irish Idylls. London: Hodder and Stoughton, 1895. Another edition: New York: Dodd, 1895. Reprinted: 1896.
Mrs Martin's Company. Iris Library Series. London: J. M. Dent and Co., 1896.
A Creel of Irish Stories. London: Methuen, 1897.

From the East Unto the West. London: Methuen, 1898.

From the Land of the Shamrock. London: Methuen, 1900. Reprinted: 1901.

Ghost-Bereft: With Other Stories and Studies in Verse. London: Smith, Elder and Co., 1901.

The Founding of Fortunes. London: Methuen, 1902. Another edition: New York: Dodd, Mead, 1902.

By Beach and Bog-Land. London: T. Fisher Unwin, 1905.

Irish Neighbours. London: Hutchinson and Co., 1907.

The Mockers. London: George Allen and Sons, 1908.

Irish Ways. London: George Allen and Sons, 1909. Another edition: 1911.

Mac's Adventures. London: Hutchinson and Co., 1911.

Flaws. London: Hutchinson and Co., 1911.

Doings and Dealings. London: Hutchinson and Co., 1913.

Between Doubting and Daring. Oxford: B. H. Blackwell, 1916.

In Mio's Youth. London: Hutchinson and Co., 1917.

BARNARD, Charlotte Alington
Born: 23 December 1830
Died: 30 January 1869, in Dover, and buried in St James's Cemetery
Married name: Mrs Charles Barnard
Pseudonym: Claribel

Charlotte Barnard married Charles Cary Barnard on 18 May 1854. She was known as a musician, and as a writer of popular songs and ballads. Charlotte studied music from Mr W. H. Holmes, and had singing lessons from a variety of instructors. She is reported to have started writing and composing about four years after her marriage. Her husband credits her with writing about one hundred ballads during the period from 1858 through 1869. In James Stephens' memoir, *Reminiscences*, he incorrectly makes a reference to 'Claribel', the pseudonym of Charlotte Barnard, when he should have said 'Christabel', the pseudonym of Mary McCarthy. Mary McCarthy was the woman to whom Stephens intended the reference.

Bibliography:
Fireside Thoughts, Ballads, etc. London: J. Nisbet and Co., 1865.

Verses and Songs. London: J. Nisbet and Co., [1870]. Printed for private circulation.

Thoughts, Verses, and Songs. London and Edinburgh: J. Nisbet and Co., 1877.

BARRAS, May Violet
During the period from 1910 to 1913, thirteen poems contributed to the *Irish Monthly* were written by May Violet Barras.

BARRY, Alice Frances
Born: 1861
Died: 1951

One of Alice Barry's poems appeared in the July 1892 edition of the *Irish Monthly*.

Bibliography:
A Singer in the Outer Court. London: n.p., 1889.
Arrows; a Collection of Songs and Verses. London: Simpkin, Marshall and Co., 1901.
Last Poems. London: Hove, 1952.

BARRY, M. A.
'A lady of this name wrote a good deal of verse for the *Cork Southern Reporter* in the earlier half of the nineteenth century. Eight of her pieces are in *Echoes from Parnassus,* selected from the original poetry of the *Southern Reporter*, Cork, 1849' (O'Donoghue 20).

BARRY, Mary Jane
A single poem in the *Irish Monthly*, September 1888 issue, is attributed to Mary Jane Barry.

BARTOLINI, Louisa Grace
Louisa Bartolini was born in Dublin to an Italian family. She wrote two volumes of poetry, both in the Italian language, which were printed and distributed in Italy. She may have eventually emigrated to Firenze, Italy.

BATTERSBY, C. Maud
C. Maud Battersby was a Protestant poet, and probably from the North. She wrote memorial verses for Sarah Geraldina Stock (see listing) and Cecil Frances Humphreys (see listing).

Bibliography:
Gaspar; or, the Story of a Street Arab. London: George Cauldwell, [1891].
Seven Times in the Fire: a Story of France in Revolution Times. London: R. T. S., [1892].

Twilight and Dawn; Hymns, Fragments and Poems. London: Partridge;
and Dublin: Cambridge and Co., 1899.

BATTERSBY, Hannah S.
Bibliography:
Home Lyrics. Second edition. London: Ward, Lock, and Tyler, 1876.

BEAMISH, Florence F.
Florence Beamish was a native of Cork. Her poems occasionally
appeared in *Duffy's Fireside Magazine.*

Anthologized in: Hayes.

BECK, Ellen
Pseudonym: Magdalen Rock

Ellen Beck, under her pseudonym, was among the most consistent
contributors to the *Irish Monthly,* where a total of ninety poems were
published from April 1890 to December 1921. Her work also appeared
in *Carmina Mariana* and *Green and Gold.* O'Donoghue believed her to
be 'a schoolmistress in the North of Ireland'. Reverend Matthew
Russell, in his introductory memoir to *Rose Kavanagh and her Verses,*
recalls the close friendship between Rose Kavanagh (see listing) and
Ellen Beck. Beck wrote a commemorative poem for Kavanagh, 'White
Rose of Green Tyrone'.

BELL, Marguerite
Bibliography:
Where Shamrocks Grow. Belfast: Davidsson and McCormick, 1909.

BENN, Miss
Married name: Mrs John F. Hodges

Miss Benn was the sister of George Benn, a Belfast historian. She
became the wife of Dr John Frederick Hodges (1815-1899), Professor
of Agriculture at The Queen's College, Belfast, and a published poet.
Miss Benn was a popular hymnist, and is included in *Hymns for Christian Worship.*

BENTLEY, Bessie
A single contribution was made by Bessie Bentley to the August 1899
issue of the *Irish Monthly.*

BLACK, Ivy Kirwan
Ivy Kirwan Black contributed two poems to the *Irish Monthly*, in 1922 and in 1923.

BLACK, Josephine Macauley
Married name: Mrs Josephine Black
Pseudonym: J. M. M.

One poem by Mrs Black appeared in the *Irish Monthly*, in 1873. She also wrote prose pieces for that same periodical, including one tale set during the Zulu war. Josephine Black published only her translations in volume form.

Bibliography:
Stephanie. Translated from the French of L. F. Veuillot: 1882. Another edition: 1883.
The Coiner's Cave. Translated from W. Herchenbach. 1887.
As Good as Gold. Translated from W. Herchenbach. 1890.

BLACKALL, Elizabeth
Bibliography:
Psalms and Hymns, and Spiritual Songs. [1835]. Another edition: Dublin: 1857.

BOND, Alessie
Born: 8 January 1841, at Ballee, Co. Down
Married name: Mrs. Henry Faussett

Alessie was a daughter of Reverend W. Bond, the Rector of Ballee. She married Reverend Henry Faussett, of Edenderry Parsonage, Omagh, Co. Tyrone, in 1875.

Anthologized in: MacIlwaine, and Paul.

Bibliography:
Thoughts on Holy Words. Printed privately: 1867.
The Triumph of Faith, and Other Poems. Dublin: George Herbert, 1870. Another edition: London: 1870.
The Cairns of Iona, and Other Poems. Dublin: George Herbert, 1873.
Leaves. Dublin: George Herbert, 1873.
Rung In; and Other Poems. Belfast: M'Caw, 1880.
From Quiet Ways. Dublin: Charles, 1882.
The Gathering-Place and Other Poems. Dublin: Church of Ireland

Printing and Publishing, 1898.

BOND, Eliza L.
Only a single reference to Eliza L. Bond exists, which states she was one of the *Nation* poets.

BORRELL, Laura B.
Bibliography:
Ye Tale of Ye Star, and Other Poems. Dublin: Browne and Nolan, 1861.

BOURKE, Hannah Maria
Bibliography:
O'Donoghue, Prince of Killarney; a Romance in Seven Cantos. Dublin: William Curry, 1830.
The City of the Star; or, Second Coming of Christ: A Religious Poem in Ten Cantos. Dublin: n.d. (Dedicated to Queen Victoria).

BOYLAN, Teresa C.
Born: 29 June 1868, in Kilbrook
Died: 19 August 1943, in Kilbrook, and buried in Cloncurry Cemetery
Married name: Teresa C. Brayton
Pseudonyms: T. B. Kilbrook

Teresa Boylan was born in the townland of Kilbrook, to Hugh Boylan and the former Elizabeth Downes. She was the fifth of six children, three boys and three girls. Her parents were farmers, and their farmhouse stood about three hundred yards east of the Cloncurry Cemetery, near the road. Teresa was trained as a teacher, and she was assistant-teacher to her sister, Elizabeth, at the Newtown National School before she emigrated. Teresa began publishing poetry under the pseudonym of T. B. Kilbrook. She emigrated to America at the age of twenty, in 1888, although one source suggests the date of her emigration should be 1894.

After emigrating, Teresa lived first in Boston, then Chicago, and lastly in New York. It was in New York that she met and married Richard Brayton, a French-Canadian. Her husband was an executive of the New York Municipal Revenue Department, and their marriage was a happy one. She returned to Ireland for regular visits, becoming a friend and supporter to those involved with nationalistic politics, particularly some of the 1916 Easter Week Rising leaders. Following the death of her husband, in 1932, she returned to live in Ireland permanently. She lived first with a sister in Bray, then in North Strand on Waterloo Avenue. In 1941 she moved a final time, back to the family farmhouse in Kilbrook, where she died two years later in the same room in which she had been born.

Teresa Boylan published volumes in both Ireland and America. She was a frequent contributor to journals on both sides of the Atlantic: *Irish Monthly, The Nation, Irish Fireside, Weekly News, Westmeath Independent, Westmeath Examiner, Young Ireland, Boston Pilot,* and the *Young Folk's Paper.*

Biographical Reference:
Flynn, James. 'Teresa Brayton, 1868-1943.' *Capuchin Annual* (1961): 189-205.

Bibliography:
The New Lodger. Catholic Truth Society Pamphlet, no. 1157. Dublin: Catholic Truth Society, [1933].
Christmas Verses. Dublin: At the Sign of the Three Candles, 1934.
The Old Bog Road. Sheet Music. Words by Teresa Brayton, and music by Madeleine King O'Farrelly. Dublin: Walton, [1957].

BOYLE, Emily Charlotte
Married name: Countess of Cork and Orrery

Emily Charlotte Boyle was the second daughter of the First Marquess of Clanricarde. She married the Earl of Cork and Orrery in 1857.

Bibliography:
Memories and Thoughts, in Verse. London: G. Bell and Sons, 1886.
The Orrery Papers. Edited. 2 vols. London: Duckworth and Co., 1903.

BOYLE, Lillie
The *Irish Monthly* published one poem in November 1930, by Lillie Boyle.

BOYLE, Mary Louisa
Born: November 1810
Died: 7 April 1890, in Chelsea

Mary Louisa Boyle was the daughter of Admiral Sir Courtenay Boyle, the son (but not heir) to the Seventh Earl of Cork and Orrery. She was a socially adept woman, who counted Tennyson, Dickens, Browning and Landor among her friends. Mary Boyle is unique for her talent in writing and publishing biographical catalogues of the portraits contained in the homes of her aristocratic friends. O'Donoghue states that she 'was a frequent contributor to the annuals, etc., during the thirties, and wrote one of the best poems in 'The Tribute', a collection of pieces edited by the Marquis of Northampton in 1837'. Her address was Oakley Street, Chelsea, at the time of her death.

Biographical References:
Boyle, Courtenay (Sir), and (Lady) Muriel S. Boyle. *Mary Boyle: Her Book.* London: John Murray, 1901.

Bibliography:
The State Prisoner; a Tale of the French Regency. 2 vols. London: Saunders and Otley, 1837.
The Forester; a Tale of 1688. 3 vols. London: Longmans and Co., 1839.
The Bridal of Melcha; a Dramatic Poem. London: Henry Colburn, 1844.
My Portrait Gallery, and Other Poems. London: privately printed, 1849.
An Imperfect Narrative of the Gay Doings and Marvellous Festivities Holden at Althorp . . . on the Occasion of My Lord, John Poyntz, Viscount Althorp, Completing His Twenty-first Year. London: C. Whittingham, 1857.
Woodland Gossip: Being a Free and Easy Translation from the German. 1864. Another, illustrated edition: London: 1865.
Tangled Weft; Two Stories. London: Elder and Co., 1865. Another edition: 1866.
Biographical Catalogue of the Portraits at Hinchingbrook. London: Victoria Press, 1876.
Biographical Catalogue of the Portraits at Longleat in the County of Wilts, the Seat of the Marquis of Bath. 1881. Another, illustrated edition: 1882.
Biographical Catalogue of the Portraits at Panshanger, the Seat of Earl Cowper. 1885.
The Court and Camp of Queen Marian; By a Contemporaneous Historian . . . Done into English from the original Marianese by a Bungler. London: Emily Faithfull, c.1890.
Mary Boyle; Her Book. Boyle, Courtenay and Muriel S. Boyle, editors. London: John Murray, 1901. Another edition: 1902.

BRADY, Charlotte Westropp
Charlotte Brady was probably a sister of Sir Francis William Brady, an amateur musician, occasional poet, and barrister.

Bibliography:
Christian Songs. Music by Sir F. W. Brady. London: n.p., 1894.

BRETT, Sister M.
Sister M. Brett was a member of the Poor Clares Convent, Harold's Cross, Dublin. She was primarily a writer of hymns, and her work appears in *Hymns and Devotions*, edited by Reverend James A. Nowlan (Dublin: 1885).

BREW, Margaret W.
Margaret Brew was a contributor of poetry to the *Irish Monthly*, where five of her poems appeared between December 1886, and April 1889.

Bibliography:
The Burtons of Dunroe. 3 vols. London: Tinsley, 1880.
The Chronicles of Castle Cloyne. 3 vols. London: Chapman and Hall, 1885.

BROWNE, Dorothy
Dorothy Browne contributed three poems to the *Irish Monthly*, from 1918 to 1923.

BROWNE, Frances
Born: 16 January 1816, in Stranorlar, Co. Donegal
Died: 25 August 1879, in London

There appears to be great confusion about the spelling of her name, Brown or Browne, with Browne being the more consistent spelling. She is frequently referred to as 'The Blind Poetess of Donegal'.

Frances Browne was the seventh of twelve children born to the village postmaster in Stranorlar. Blinded as the result of smallpox at age eighteen months, her early education was achieved by listening to her siblings recite their lessons. Frances next attended a local school, conducted by a Mr. McGranahan, where her classmates included Isaac Butt, and William MacArthur, later Lord Mayor of London. Throughout her life Frances concentrated on developing her memory to compensate for her lack of sight. She was soon able to quote long passages of poetry by Scott, Byron and Pope. In exchange for doing their household chores, Frances's brothers and sisters read to her, a steady stream of books. Her talent for poetry developed early, beginning with rewriting the Lord's Prayer in verse form at age seven. Her first poem appeared in the Belfast *Northern Whig*, and was sent to that publication by a friend, without Frances's knowledge.

Sir Robert Peel granted her an annual pension of £20 in 1844, after reading her first collection of poetry. Frances used a portion of her early income to train one of her sisters as an amanuensis. This sister became Frances's devoted companion for many years. In 1847, the sisters moved to Edinburgh, where Frances succeeded in making a living by writing. Her mentor in Edinburgh was John Wilson, a professor of moral philosophy, who wrote under the pseudonym of Christopher North. With Wilson's assistance, she was hired by *Chamber's Magazine*.

A gift of £100 from the Marquis of Lansdowne made possible a move to London, where she furthered her literary career. She wrote essays, reviews, poetry, stories, and all manner of prose. Her death, at age sixty-three, was the result of a heart ailment.

Mrs Newton Crosland's 1895 volume, *Landmarks of a Literary Life*, provides this verbal portrait of Frances Browne:

> The first thing that struck me in Frances was her very exquisite figure, set off to advantage by a simple but well-fitting dress. She was just about, or but slightly above, the middle height, and a painter or sculptor would have delighted in the lines of beauty that were revealed in her movements. I remember also thinking she would have been handsome but for the darkened vision, and the most disfiguring vestiges of the fell disease which had afflicted her. She moved with such ease that it was difficult at first — and until some little incident was evidence of it — to believe in her infirmity. Her memory was most retentive, and her mind singularly receptive, for she seemed fairly well acquainted with the topics of the day and its current publications.

Frances Browne is largely remembered for *Granny's Wonderful Chair and its Tales of Fairy Times*, a collection of stories for children, which went through several editions before passing out of print and being forgotten. In 1904, Frances Hodgson Burnett brought the stories back to life under the title *The Story of the Lost Fairy Book*, and the collection enjoyed another half-century of popularity.

She was a contributor to: *Northern Whig, Irish Penny Journal, The Athenaeum, Hood's Magazine, The Keepsake*, and *Chamber's Journal*.

Anthologized in: *Birthday*, Hayes, MacIlwaine, and Sparling.

Biographical References:
'The Blind Girl of Donegal'. *Irish Book Lover* 8 (December/January 1916-1917): 49-51.
Russell, Matthew. 'Our Poets, No. 29: Frances Browne'. *Irish Monthly* 24 (May 1896): 262-8.

Bibliography:

The Star of Atteghei, The Vision of Schwartz; and Other Poems. London: Edward Moxon, 1844.

Lyrics and Miscellaneous Poems. Edinburgh: Sutherland and Knox, 1848.

The Ericksons: The Clever Boy; or, Consider Another (Two Stories for My Young Friends). Edinburgh: Paton and Ritchie, 1852. Another edition: *Tales for the Young*. 1855.

Pictures and Songs of Home. London: T. Nelson and Sons, 1856.

Granny's Wonderful Chair, and its Tales of Fairy Times. Illustrated by Kenny Meadows. London: Griffith and Farran, 1857. Another edition, illustrated by Marie Seymour Lucas: [1891]. Reissued: [1896]. Another edition: [1900]. Another edition, with introduction by Frances Hodgson Burnett: *The Story of the Lost Fairy Book*. London and New York: McClure, Phillips and Co., 1904. Another edition, introduced by Dollie Radford, with illustrations by Dora Curtis: London: J. M. Dent and Co.; and New York: E. P. Dutton and Co., [1906]. Another edition, illustrated in colour by W. H. Margetson: London: Hodder and Stoughton, 1908. Another edition: London: S. W. Partridge and Co., 1909. Another edition: *Lords of the Castles, and Other Stories From Granny's Wonderful Chair . . . With Composition Exercises*: London: A. and C. Black, 1909. Another edition, abridged, and illustrated by A. A. Dixon: London: Blackie and Son, [1912]. Another edition: London and Glasgow: Collins, 1924. Another edition, illustrated by 'Decies': London: G. T. Foulis and Co., 1925. Another edition, illustrated by Charles Folkard: London: 1925. Another edition: Collins's 'Lion' Series: London and Glasgow:[1925]. Another edition, illustrated by R. B. Ogle: London: [1926]. Another edition: Toronto and London: Letchworth, [1927]. Another edition, of the first three chapters only: London: [Brodie Books, 1927]. Another edition, edited by H. A. Treble: Edinburgh and London: Oliver and Boyd, [1938]. Another edition: *The Story of Fairyfoot From Granny's Wonderful Chair*. Lower Chelston: Gulliver Books, [1943]. Another edition, 'retold' and revised: Silver Torch Series: Glasgow: Collins, 1947. Another edition, illustrated by Sylvia Green: [London]: Roger Ingram, 1948. Another edition, a reissue of the 1912 edition: London and Glasgow: Blackie and Son, [1955].

Our Uncle the Traveller's Stories. London: W. Kent, 1859.

The Young Foresters. 1860. Magnet Stories, no. 45. London: Groombridge and Sons, [1864].

My Share of the World: an Autobiography. London: Hurst and Blackett, 1861.

The Castleford Case. 3 vols. London: Hurst and Blackett, 1862.
The Orphans of Elfholm. London: Groombridge [1862].
The Hidden Sin. 3 vols. London: n.p., 1866. Published anonymously.
The Exile's Trust, a Tale of the French Revolution, and Other Stories.
    London: Leisure Hour, [1869].
My Nearest Neighbour, and Other Stories. London: R.T.S., [1875].
The Dangerous Guest; a Story of 1745. London: R.T.S., [1886].
The Foundling of the Fens. London: R.T.S., [1886].
The First of the African Diamonds. London: R.T.S., [1887].

BROWNRIGG, Annie E.

Annie Brownrigg specialized in translations of German-language poets.

Bibliography:
Translations. Dublin: Alexander Thom, 1862.

C

CADDELL, Cecilia Mary
Born: 1814, in Harbourstown, Co. Meath
Died: 11 September 1877, in Kingstown, and buried in the family
    vault, Stamullen Churchyard.

Cecilia was the second daughter of Richard O'Ferrall Caddell, of Harbourstown, near Balbriggan, Co. Meath. Her mother was the Hon. Pauline, sister of Viscount Southwell, of an old Gormanston Catholic family, 'which, while clinging to the old faith, has had the knack of clinging also to the old homestead and the old family estates' (Russell 773). She was born into a family of acknowledged social position, and wrote to fulfill her intellectual needs coupled with an abundance of leisure time. Cecilia was particularly noted as a benefactor of orphanages. Her own health deteriorated as the result of devoted attendance to her parents during their final illnesses, according to Matthew Russell. Her father died 3 January 1856, and her mother died on 5 May of that same year. Cecilia never regained her health, and was an invalid for twenty years until her death in 1877.

Cecilia Mary Caddell was primarily a novelist and short story writer. She wrote some hymns, which were anthologized in the collections of Orby Shipley, particularly in *Lyra Messianica*, 1864. Cecilia Caddell was a frequent contributor to the *Irish Monthly, Lamp, Month,* and *Catholic World.* Her first contribution to the *Irish Monthly* was in 1874.

Biographical References:
'Cecilia Mary Caddell: A short biographical note'. *Irish Monthly* 44 (March 1916): 202-3.
Russell, Matthew. 'Cecilia Caddell'. *Irish Monthly* 5 (December 1877): 772-4.

Bibliography:
Flower and Fruit; or, the Use of Tears. Dublin: Duffy, 1856.
A History of the Missions in Japan and Paraguay. 2 pts. London: Burns and Lambert, 1856.
Marie; or, The Workwoman of Liege. New York: Kennedy, 1856. Another edition: *Hidden Saints: Life of Soeur Marie, the Workwoman of Liege.* London: T. Richardson, 1869.
Home and the Homeless. 3 vols. London: T. C. Newby, 1858.
The Martyr Maidens of Ostend. 1858.
Never Forgotten; or, the Home of the Lost Child. London: Burns, Oates, and Co., 1871.
Blind Agnese; or, the Little Spouse of the Blessed Sacrament. Second edition: Dublin: Duffy, 1856. Fifth edition: 1873. Another edition: [1887]. Another edition: New York: Kennedy, 1888. Other editions issued in French and Italian.
Nellie Netterville. London: Burns, Oates and Washbourne, [1867]. Another edition: New York: Catholic Publication Co., 1878.
Hidden Saints: Life of Marie Bonneau de Miramion. London: T. Richardson; and New York: H. H. Richardson, 1870. Another edition: London: Art and Book Co., 1893.
Wild Times. London: Burns, Oates and Washbourne, 1872.
Summer Talks About Lourdes. London: Burns and Oates, 1874. Another edition: London: Burns and Oates, 1897.
The Cross in Japan. London: Burns and Oates, 1904.
Lost Genevieve. London: Burns, Oates and Washbourne, n.d.
The Miner's Daughter. London: Burns, Oates and Washbourne, n.d.
A Pearl in Dark Waters. London: Burns, Oates and Washbourne, n.d.
Father de Lisle: a Story of Tyborne. London: Burns, Oates and Washbourne, n.d.
Blanch Leslie. London: Burns, Oates and Washbourne, n.d.

Minister's Daughter. London: Sadlier, n.d.
Little Snowdrop. London: Burns, Oates and Washbourne, n.d.
Tales for the Young. London: Burns, Oates and Washbourne, n.d.

CAIRNS, Christina Victoria
Christiana is an alternative spelling of her name.

Bibliography:
Fugitive Poems. London: Jones and Causton, 1860.

CALCOTT, J. Berkeley
Born: 1823

J. Berkeley Calcott was eleven years old when *Stanzas* was first published.

Bibliography:
Stanzas. Dublin: George Folds, 1834. Another edition: 1837.

CALLANAN, Helena
Born: circa 1864, in Cork

The *Irish Monthly* refers to Helena Callanan as, 'The Frances Brown of the South' (13: 108). Helena was a blind poet and she was a resident or associate of the Asylum for the Blind, Infirmary Road, Cork, as that address follows her name in her second volume. She was a frequent contributor to the *Irish Monthly*, with eleven poems published from August 1879 to April 1896.

Anthologized in: Sullivan.

Bibliography:
Gathered Leaflets. Cork: Purcell, 1885.
Verses, Old and New. Cork: Eagle Works, 1899.

CANNING, Charlotte
Charlotte Canning is listed as an Irish poet in O'Donoghue's *The Poets of Ireland* without any further biographical details. The British Museum Catalogue lists her as Charlotte Canning of Eastcourt.

Bibliography:
Wood-Notes, a Collection of Original Poems, Together with the Siege of Cirta, an Opera. London: n.p., 1850.

CAREW, Miss
Married name: Mrs William A. Rafferty
Pseudonyms: Frank Pentrill, and Mrs Frank Pentrill

Miss Carew lived in the Dublin area, and was a constant contributor to various Catholic journals, generally under a pseudonym. Her pseudonyms are confusing, for she uses both the male and female (Mr and Mrs) titles with the name Frank Pentrill. In addition to poetry, she also wrote short stories, essays and travel articles. From January 1882, to March 1899, seventeen of her poems appeared in the *Irish Monthly*.

Bibliography:
Lina's Tales. Dublin: Gill, 1885.
Odile: a Tale of the Commune. Dublin: Gill, 1886.
The Catholic Child's Hymn Book. Dublin: Gill, 1888.

CAREY, Elizabeth Sheridan
Elizabeth was the daughter of William Paulet Carey, and the former Miss Lennon, of Grafton Street in Dublin. William Carey was an engraver, writer, nationalist and artist, but he was perhaps best known as an art critic and connoisseur. Elizabeth's uncle was Mathew Carey, the journalist who later gained fame in America. Elizabeth came from a Protestant family, and it is stated in her volume that she converted to Catholicism. She was a frequent contributor to periodicals and annuals, most regularly to *Bentley's Miscellany*.

Bibliography:
Ivy Leaves; or, Offerings in Verse. London: privately printed, 1837.

CARRINGTON, Judith
A single poem by Judith Carrington is in the *Irish Monthly*, issue of September 1919.

CASEY, Elizabeth Owens Blackburne
Born: 10 May 1845, in Slane, Co. Meath
Died: April 1894, in Dublin
Pseudonym: E. Owens Blackburne

There is some dispute about the dates for Elizabeth Owens Blackburne, with 1848 being the alternative birthdate, and 1892 as another possible date of death.
  Elizabeth was the daughter of Andrew Casey, and the former Miss Mills. At about eleven years of age, she lost her sight, and remained

blind until treatments by Sir William Wilde restored her vision. After moving to London in 1873 or 1874, her literary career was first successful and then declined, leaving her in poverty. In later life Elizabeth was receiving assistance from the Royal County Fund. After returning to Dublin she burned to death in an accident shortly before her fifty-ninth birthday.

Elizabeth Casey was better known as a novelist than a poet. She was also the author of an early feminist encyclopaedia, *Illustrious Irishwomen*, a two-volume set.

Anthologized in: *Emerald Gems*.

Biographical References:
Sillard, P. A. 'A Notable Irish Authoress'. *New Ireland Review* 27 (August 1907): 369-72.

Bibliography:
A Woman Scorned. 3 vols. London: Tinsley, 1876. Another edition: London: A. H. Moxon, [1887].
Illustrious Irishwomen. 2 vols. London: Tinsley, 1877.
The Way Women Love. 3 vols. London: Tinsley, 1877.
A Bunch of Shamrocks. London: Newman and Co., 1879. Another, Seaside Library edition: New York: Munro, 1879. Another edition: 1883.
Molly Carew. 3 vols. London: Tinsley, [1879].
The Glen of Silver Birches. 2 vols. London: Remington and Co., 1880. Another edition: New York: Harper, 1881. Another, abridged edition: Warsaw, 1883.
My Sweetheard When a Boy. Moxon's Select Novelettes, no. 1. London: [1880].
As the Crow Flies. Moxon's Select Novelettes, no. 4. London: [1880].
The Love that Loves Always. London: F. V. White and Co., 1881.
The Heart of Erin: an Irish Story of To-day. 3 vols. London: Sampson Low, 1882. Another, Seaside Library edition: New York: Munro, 1882. Another edition: 1883.
Con O'Donnell, and Other Legends and Poems for Recitation. London: n.p., 1890.

CAULFIELD, Sophia Frances Anne
Died: circa 1900

Sophia Caulfield was the daughter of 'an author of various pamphlets on religious and political subjects' (O'Donoghue 65). Her uncle was the second Earl of Charlemont, a prominent political figure. Sophia was living in Bath at the time of her death.

Bibliography:
Desmond, and Other Poems. London: Longmans and Co., [1870].
Avenele, and Other Poems. London: Longmans and Co., 1871.
By Land and Sea; and, Ben, a Rough Diamond. London: Cassell and Co., [1880].
Needlework; an Encyclopaedia of Plain and Fancy Needlework. With Blanche C. Saward. (Caulfield wrote those parts pertaining to plain sewing, textiles, dressmaking, appliances and terms). London: L. Upcott Gill, 1881. Another edition: 1882.
A Directory of Girls' Societies. London: n.p., 1886.
The Lives of the Apostles, Their Contemporaries and Successors. London: Hatchards, [1887].
Restful Work for Youthful Hands. London: Griffith, Farran and Co., 1888.
True Philosophy. London: Hatchards, 1888.
House Mottoes and Inscriptions; Old and New. London: Elliott Stock, 1902. Another edition, new and revised with illustrations: London: Elliott Stock, 1908.
The Home Nurse. (Formerly *Sick Nursing at Home*). Third edition revised and enlarged: London: Elliott Stock, 1903.
The Voice of the Fathers. London: S. C. Brown and Co., 1905.
The Prisoners of Hope; a Series of Twenty-six Lectures. (Part One was the only part completed). London: Marshall Bros., [1909].
The Dawn of Christianity in Continental Europe, and the Planting of the Order of Knights of the Hospital of St John of Jerusalem in England. London: Elliott Stock, [1909].

CAVANAGH, Maeve
Married name: Maeve Cavanagh MacDowell

Maeve Cavanagh's married name is sometimes spelled McDowell. Her *Passion Flowers* was dedicated to her two brothers: 'Jack, lost at sea in the North Atlantic Ocean, 2 November 1913; and Ernest, murdered by English Military on the steps of Liberty Hall, Dublin, Easter Tuesday, 1916'. Ernest Cavanagh was a cartoonist for *The Irish Worker*, and Maeve wrote the verse captions for his work. Ernest was unarmed and standing on the steps of Liberty Hall when he was shot by the British military. *Sheaves of Revolt*, is dedicated to 'The President (Countess De Markievicz) and the Boys of Na Fianna Eirinn'.

R. M. Fox, in *Rebel Irishwomen*, states that Maeve Cavanagh was proclaimed as 'the poetess of the Revolution', by James Connolly. She served on the first committee of the Gaelic League, and was involved with that organization in Dublin, Sligo and Derry. Her first poems appeared in *The Peasant*, edited by W. P. Ryan. By the time she returned from Derry to Dublin she was already well known as a writer. Her involvement with the labour movement brought her into contact with James Connolly and Jim Larkin, and she was a frequent contributor to the *Irish Worker*. Fox also notes that Cavanagh's poem, 'Ireland to Germany', was 'solemnly quoted by the Chief Secretary in the House of Commons as indicating the existence of a German plot'. During the 1916 Rising, Maeve carried Connolly's message, 'we fight at noon', to the Waterford volunteers. Returning from Waterford to Dublin, she was arrested and brought before court, where she refused to give an account of her movements during the entire Easter week of 1916. She did manage to be reimbursed for the money stolen from her purse while she was being interrogated. In total, her home was searched three times by the British. *A Voice of Insurgency*, was published on Christmas Eve 1916, and sold out within twenty-eight days of being issued.

In 1921 she married Cathal MacDowell, one of the 1916 Volunteers. Thereafter she generally published under the name Maeve Cavanagh MacDowell. She attributed Thomas Davis, James Clarence Mangan and Wolfe Tone with being her poetic influences, naming Wolfe Tone as her favourite. Maeve was responsible for the recovery of Catherine Anna Parnell's lost manuscript, *The Tale of the Great Sham*. While cleaning out her sister's house following Sarah's death in December 1959, Maeve found Anna Parnell's manuscript in a brown envelope among her sister's papers.

Thirty-six of Maeve Cavanagh's poems are found in the *Catholic Bulletin*, April 1923 to April 1938.

Anthologized in: Browne and Fitzhenry.

Biographical References:
Fox, R. M. *Rebel Irishwomen*. Dublin: Talbot Press, 1935.

Bibliography:
Sheaves of Revolt. Dublin: City Printing Works, 1914.
A Voice of Insurgency. Dublin: privately printed, 1916.
A Ballad for Rebels. Dublin: privately printed, c. 1916.
Passion Flowers. Dublin: privately printed, 1917.
Soul and Clay. With portrait and introduction by F. R. Higgins. Dublin: W. H. West, printed for private circulation, [1917].

Irish Songs of the Month. Dublin: 1932.
Ireland to Germany. Dublin: Shan-van-Vocht, n.d.
Thomas Ashe. Dublin: privately printed, n.d.

CHRISTIAN, Emily M.
Emily M. Christian contributed two poems to the *New Ireland Review* issues of December 1897 and March 1898.

CHRISTIE, Mary Jane
Born: Castlebar, Co. Mayo
Married name: Mary Jane Serrano

Mary Jane Christie emigrated to America in 1849, apparently at an early age. She was best known as a translator of prose works from the Portuguese and Spanish languages. Her only volume of poetry, *Destiny; and Other Poems,* was published in New York in 1883.

CLARE, Gertrude
A single contribution to the November 1888 *Irish Monthly* is credited to Gertrude Clare.

CLERKE, Ellen Mary
Born: 26 September 1840, in Skibbereen, Co. Cork
Died: 2 March 1906, in London

Ellen was a daughter of John William Clerke, and his wife, the former Miss Deasy, who was a sister of Lord Justice Deasy. Ellen was eighteen months older than her sister, Agnes Mary Clerke, who became one of Europe's foremost astronomers and non-fiction writers. The Clerke family moved to Dublin in 1861, then on to Queenstown, in 1863. Winters were spent abroad by the family: Rome in 1867 and 1868, Naples in 1871 and 1872, Florence from 1873 through 1876. Given the family's penchant for wintering in Italy, it is not surprising that Ellen Clerke was fluent in Italian, and was a noted translator of that language. She wrote a great many 'versified translations' of Italian poetry for Dr. Garnett's *History of Italian Literature.* Ellen also wrote articles in the German and Arabic languages. She was a member of the Manchester Geographical Society, and contributed articles to their *Journal.* Ellen preferred geology to her sister's study of astronomy, although she was reasonably well versed in astronomy. Her article in Volume 15 of *Observatory* combines two of her talents, astronomy and the Arabic language. In that article she explores the possibility of Arabian astronomers having knowledge of Algol, an advanced mathematical process.

Ellen was primarily a religious poet, and Lady Huggins calls her 'a devoted and exemplary Catholic'. The last twenty years of her life she wrote a weekly leader for the *Tablet*, largely a report of Church activities in foreign lands. Ellen was a gifted musician, and particularly adept at the guitar. Her death is reported to have followed a short, unspecified illness.

Anthologized in: Mrs. Sharp.

Biographical references:
Huggins, Lady. *Agnes Mary Clerke and Ellen Mary Clerke; an Appreciation*. Printed for private circulation, 1907.

Bibliography:
The Flying Dutchman, and Other Poems. London: Satchell and Co., 1881. Another edition: 1882.
Jupiter and His System. London: Edward Stanford, 1892.
History of Italian Literature. R. Garrett, 1898. Ellen provided the versified English translations of Italian poetry.
Fable and Song in Italy. London: Grant Richards, 1899.
Flowers of Fire. London: Hutchinson, 1902.

COGHLAN, Edith N.
Born: Lislee, Courtmacsherry, Co. Cork

Edith was the eldest daughter of Heber Coghlan, a writer. Her mother died when Edith was four years of age and she was very attached to her father, who nurtured her poetic talents. She is reported to have had a great affinity for animals, and for gardening. Edith lived in France for part of her life, and she contributed regularly to the weekly newspapers in Cork and Dublin.

Anthologized in: Paul.

COLTHURST, E.
Born: Cork

Miss E. Colthurst was born in Cork, but lived at Danesfort, Killarney for most of her life. She wrote little prose in comparison to her multiple volumes of poetry. She was associated with Reverend Edward Nagel and his controversial evangelical mission to Achill, although the specifics of her association are unclear. The majority of her work was published anonymously.

Bibliography:
Emmanuel, a Poem by a Lady. Cork: John Bolster, 1833.
Life, a Poem. Cork: John Bolster, 1835. Another edition: Dublin and
    Achill: 1845.
Home, a Poem. Cork: John Bolster, 1836.
Futurity, a Poem. Cork: John Bolster, 1837.
Futurity Continued. Cork: John Bolster, 1838.
Loyalty, a Poem. Cork: John Bolster, 1838.
Lays of Erin. 1839.
The Storm, and Other Poems. Liverpool: 1840.
Innisfáil; or, the Irish Scripture Reader. 1841.
Irrelagh; or, the Last of the Chiefs. 1849.
Love and Loyalty. London: 1851.
Memories of the West, a Poem. London: 1854.
Tales of Erin. London: Wright, n.d.

CONDON, Lizzie G.
Born: 1857, in Waterford
Pseudonyms: L. G. C., Lizzie, and Alice

Lizzie was the daughter of Thomas William Condon, a minor poet
from the Waterford area. Her single volume of poetry was published
when she was fifteen years of age.

Bibliography:
Killeeny of Lough Corrib, and Miscellaneous Poems. Dublin: McGlashan
    and Gill, 1872.

CONNOLLY, Mary E.
Mary Connolly was a contributor to the *Irish Monthly* from September
1894, to August 1900. Five of her poems and several prose stories were
published therein.

CONNOLLY, Susan H.
The *Irish Monthly* published Susan Connolly's work in three issues:
September 1890, February 1891 and July 1891.

COONEY, Mary
Born: Clonmel
Married name: Mary Locke

Mary Cooney emigrated to America in 1879. She married the poet John Locke in 1881, and thereafter resided in New York. Mary was a frequent contributor to journals such as the *Shamrock, Flag of Ireland,* and *Irishman.* Only one of her volumes was published in the United Kingdom.

Bibliography:
In Far Dakota. London: Allen and Co., 1890.

CORBET, Mary
One poem in the *Irish Monthly,* January 1906 edition, appears under Mary Corbet. It probably was a typographical error, and the name should have been spelled as Corbett, for subsequent poems did appear in the *Irish Monthly* by a Mary Corbett.

CORBETT, Mary
A total of six poems appear by Mary Corbett in the *Irish Monthly,* October 1906 to January 1910. See the note concerning a typographical error under Corbet, Mary.

CORRY, Helen M.
Married name: Mrs Thomas Corry

Helen was the wife of Thomas H. Corry, a noted botanist. She was widowed around 1886, when her husband accidentally drowned in Lough Gill. Her only volume was published in conjunction with her husband, and contains a memoir and portrait of Thomas.

Bibliography:
Dual Songs. Belfast: William Mullan and Son, 1887.

COSTELLO, Louisa Stuart
Born: 1815, in Ireland
Died: 24 April 1870

Louisa Stuart Costello must have begun writing at an early age, as she was only twenty years old when her second volume, *Specimens of the Early Poetry of France,* was published. Her first volume of poems was printed for private circulation and thus far has been untraceable. Only vague references to the existence of a first volume appear and the title is not noted in these references. Louisa's elusive first volume attracted the attention of Thomas Moore, who influenced her work and was supportive of Louisa's literary ambitions. Her second volume, published in 1835, was dedicated to Thomas Moore.

Bibliography:
Specimens of the Early Poetry of France. 1835.
Memoirs of Eminent Englishwomen. 1844.
Falls, Lakes and Mountains of Wales. 1845.

COVENEY, Mary
Name in Religion: Sister Mary
Pseudonym: Moi-Même

Sister Mary Coveney was a nun of the Presentation Convent in Carlow. She contributed verses regularly in the *Cork Examiner*. As Moi-Même, she published three poems in the *Catholic Bulletin*, January to November, 1911.

Bibliography:
Poems of the Past. Dublin: M. H. Gill and Son, 1890. Second edition: 1911.

COWAN, Charlotte
Born: Belfast
Died: October 1902
Married name: Charlotte Jobling
Pseudonym: Irish Molly

Charlotte Cowan was the daughter of an Irish father and an English mother. She married a Mr Jobling, then moved to England, where they stayed until his death. Charlotte subsequently returned to Ireland.

Paul records that she had an unusual style of writing her poetry, writing the last verse first, then the first verse, and filling in the middle verses last. She was an ardent patriot, with a 'great disgust for party politics', and was 'of the opinion that Ireland's enemies do not all live outside our own green isle' (Paul 85).

Charlotte Cowan was a constant contributor to numerous papers and journals, especially the *Weekly Irish Times*, which published over 200 of her poems. She published a total of more than 800 poems and 150 songs, all as single submissions to periodicals. She contributed two poems to *Hibernia*, in May and June 1883, and won the 1893 Rondeau Competition.

Anthologized in: Paul.

COX, Eleanor Rogers
Born: 1865, at Enniskillen

Her name is spelled as Elanor in Gregory's anthology. She emigrated to America, where her later volumes and poems were published. Only one volume of poetry was published in Ireland, although her work strongly features Irish themes.

Anthologized in: Graves and Gregory.

Bibliography:
A Hosting of Heroes, and Other Poems. Dublin: Sealy, Bryers and Walker, 1911.

CRAWFORD, Sophia
Married name: Mrs Abraham Crawford

Sophia Crawford was better known as a novelist and short story writer than as a poet.

Bibliography:
Stanzas. London: T. C. Newby, 1830.
Stanzas on Hearing Broadhurst Sing John Anderson. n.p.: [1850].
The Lady of the Bedchamber. 2 vols. London: T. C. Newby, 1850.
The Double Marriage. 3 vols. London: T. C. Newby, 1852.
Lismore. 3 vols. London: T. C. Newby, 1853.
The Story of a Nun. 3 vols. London: T. C. Newby, 1855.
Early Struggles. 3 vols. London: T. C. Newby, 1857.

CROMIE, Helen C.
Married name: Mrs Helen Mollan

Helen contributed two poems to the *Irish Book Lover* in November 1911, and February 1912.

Bibliography:
Ruth Erford's April Days. London: Blackie and Sons, [1899].

CULHANE, Kate
Pseudonym: Louisa Bride

Kate Culhane was a frequent contributor to *The Nation*, *Weekly News*, and *Young Ireland*, under her pseudonym.

Anthologized in: *Emerald Gems*.

CUMMINGHAM, Jane
Married name: Mrs Jane Cummingham

Bibliography:
Mystagogue, a Poem. Dublin: privately printed, 1851.

CUSACK, Margaret
Born: 6 May 1829, in Dublin
Died: 5 June 1899, in England
Name in Religion: Sister Mary Francis Clare, Mother Clare

Margaret Cusack rose to fame as 'The Nun of Kenmare'. Her parents were Samuel and Sarah Cusack, a substantial, Episcopalian couple from York Street, Dublin. Samuel Cusack was a medical doctor who worked at the Dispensary of Coolock, north of Dublin, specializing in obstetrics. He was dedicated to providing medical services for the poor. The Cusack family believed their ancestors had lived continuously in Ireland since the early thirteenth century. Margaret's mother, the former Sarah Stoney, considered herself to have come from a landlord ascendancy family, but her assertion is questioned by one of Cusack's biographers. Margaret's uncle, James Cusack, was a professor of Surgery at Trinity College.

Samuel Cusack contracted cholera from one of his patients, resulting in a slow physical decline into incapacity. Sarah Cusack, whose own health was precarious, left her husband in the care of some family friends, took the two children, Margaret and Samuel, to live with her wealthy relatives in Exeter, England. 'Grannie Baker', Margaret's great-aunt, provided Margaret with an excellent education, including enrolling her in a fashionable boarding school. Margaret's upbringing was somewhat unconventional, as she had an excellent education and substantial personal freedom, both physical and intellectual. She also had the funds to allow her independence. About 1844, Samuel Cusack's health reached a critical stage, and Margaret travelled alone, without family approval, back to Ireland to assess her father's condition. She saw her father comfortably settled in the care of his sister and her husband in Co. Wicklow.

Margaret was later engaged to Charles Holmes, the son of an Anglican minister in Exeter. Margaret's fiancee may also have been a minister, although that remains speculation. A short time after they became engaged, Margaret again journeyed to Ireland to visit her father. While she was gone, Charles fell victim to a sudden fever and died. Margaret's grief was compounded by the death of her father shortly thereafter. In the early 1850s she joined the Anglican sisterhood established by Edward Pusey. Pusey was attempting to reform the Church of England by reinstating certain traditions and institutions which had disappeared after the Reformation. The convent community established by Pusey was never fully acceptable to either the High Church or the Protestant community, and Cusack left the Protestant sisterhood after a very few years.

She converted to Catholicism on 2 July 1858, and was confirmed a short time later by Cardinal Wiseman. Margaret added Anna to her name following her religious conversion. She then entered the Christian Sisters of Penance, a religious community in Staffordshire, England. Finding the order too restrictive, Cusack travelled to Ireland and became Sister Mary Francis Clare, entering the Poor Clares Convent in Newry on 2 July 1859. When the Mother Abbess and six nuns left the Newry convent to establish the Poor Clares convent at Kenmare, Co. Kerry, Sister Mary Francis was among that group. In Kenmare she wrote a considerable number of texts on Irish history and established Kenmare Publications, which she personally controlled.

Sister Mary Francis Clare was an extremely outspoken nun, her letters concerning Irish causes appeared frequently in Irish, American and Canadian periodicals. She was the first to establish a Famine Relief Fund when Kerry farmers began to experience difficulties in the 1870s. Her fund received support from both Anna and Fanny Parnell, prior to their own efforts in the area of famine relief. The Nun of Kenmare's fund proved very effective, with no administrative costs. The money was sent immediately after receipt to the parish priests and local ministers for distribution to those in need. Her relief fund maintained a non-denominational stance, with funds going to Protestant and Catholic congregations. Donations were also solicited from both Catholics and Protestants alike. As a special inducement to the Catholics from whom she requested donations, Sister Mary Francis Clare promised that the nuns would pray for those who donated, saying the Office of the Dead throughout the year for any deceased subscribers.

On a visit to Knock, Sister Mary Francis believed herself to have been miraculously cured of her persistent rheumatism. She conceived of a plan to open a convent and vocational school for women in Knock. In 1882 permission was granted and the Convent of St Joseph of the Ave Maria opened, with Mother Clare at the helm. Her new order in Knock created hostility within the Church in Ireland and she found herself enmeshed in the ecclesiastical politics of the age. Her venture in Knock ended, reportedly due to political in-fighting. She was subsequently invited to open a new community in Nottingham, England. Pope Leo XIII granted permission for the new St Joseph's Sisters of Peace in 1884, at a personal meeting with Mother Clare in Rome. Shortly after her return to Nottingham she was sent on a tour of America to raise funds for the Nottingham community. In Jersey City, New Jersey, she established the American branch of St Joseph's Sisters of Peace, in 1885. In America she found herself enmeshed again in the politics of the Catholic hierarchy. The persis-tence of these problems led her to resign from her position as Mother General, in 1888.

After leaving the Catholic church she lived with relatives in Leamington. Several sources indicate that she may have returned to the Catholic faith on her deathbed and received the last rites, although it is impossible to substantiate this claim.

Anthologized in: MacIlwaine.

Biographical References:
Cusack, Mary Francis. *The Nun of Kenmare: an Autobiography.* London: Jonah Child, [1888].
Cusack, Mary Francis. *The Story of My Life.* London: Hodder and Stoughton, 1891.
Davis, Eugene. 'Irish Contemporary Celebrities 3: Sister Mary Cusack'. *Shamrock* 17: 76-7, 91-2, 105-7.
Eagar, Irene Ffrench. *The Nun of Kenmare.* Cork: Mercier Press, 1970.
McCarthy, Philomena. *The Nun of Kenmare; the True Facts.* Killarney: Killarney Printing Works, 1989.
O'Neill, Margaret Rose. *The Life of Mother Clare.* Seattle: Sisters of St Joseph of Peace, 1990.
'The Nun of Kenmare: Sketch of Sister Mary Francis Clare'. *Donahoe's Magazine* 5 (1881): 194, 257-8.

Bibliography:
Miraculous Cure at Assisi. Translated. [1867].
An Illustrated History of Ireland; From the Earliest Period. London: Longmans, 1868.
The Patriot's History of Ireland. Kenmare: Kenmare Publishing, 1869.
The Student's Manual of Irish History. London: Longmans, Green and Co., 1870.
Ned Rusheen. London: Burns and Oates; and Boston: Donahoe, 1871. Another edition: London: Gill, 1880.
The Life of Saint Patrick, Apostle of Ireland. London: Longmans, Green

and Co., 1871.

A History of the Kingdom of Kerry. London: Longmans, Green and Co., 1871.

The Liberator (Daniel O'Connell); His Life and Times, Political, Social and Religious. London: Longmans, Green and Co., 1872. Another edition, expanded and with an essay on the future of Ireland: London: John G. Murdoch, [1877].

The Life of St Aloysius Gonzaga, of the Society of Jesus. 1872.

Advice to Irish Girls in America. New York: n.p., 1872.

The Pilgrim's Way to Heaven. Second edition: 1873.

The Book of the Blessed Ones. Books for Spiritual Reading Series. London: Burns, Oates and Co., 1874.

The Life of Father Mathew, the People's Soggarth Aroon. Dublin: 1874.

Woman's Work in Modern Society. Kenmare: Kenmare Publishing, 1874.

Devotions for Public and Private Use at the Way of the Cross. London: R. Washbourne, 1875.

A History of the City and County of Cork. Cork: Francis Guy; and Dublin: McGlashan and Gill, 1875.

Jesus and Jerusalem; or, the Way Home. Third edition: 1875.

The Speeches and Public Letters of the Liberator, with Preface and Historical Notes. 2 vols. Kenmare: Kenmare Publishing, 1875.

In Memoriam Mary O'Hagan, Abbess and Foundress of the Convent of Poor Clares, Kenmare. London: Burns and Co., 1876.

The Lives of St Columba and St Bridget. Dublin: Kenmare Series of the Lives of the Irish Saints, 1877.

Tim O'Halloran's Choice; or, From Killarney to New York. London: Burns and Co., 1877.

The Trias Thaumaturga; or, Three Wonder-Working Saints of Ireland. London: J. G. Murdoch, [1877].

A History of the Irish Nation. London: J. G. Murdoch, [1877].

A Nun's Advice to her Girls. Third edition. Kenmare: Kenmare Publication Agency, 1877.

Good Reading for Girls. London: Burns, Oates and Co.; and Dublin: Gill, 1877.

The Life and Times of Pope Pius IX. Kenmare: Kenmare Publishing, 1878.

The Life of the Most Rev. Joseph Dixon DD, Primate of All Ireland. Dublin: 1878.

The Apparition at Knock: with the Depositions of the Witness Examined by the Ecclesiastical Commission Appointed by His Grace the Archbishop of Tuam, and the Conversion of a Young Protestant Lady by a Vision of the Blessed Virgin. London: Burns and Oates; and

Dublin: M. H. Gill, [1880].

The Case of Ireland Stated; a Plea for My People and My Race. Dublin: M. H. Gill and Son, 1880; New York: P. J. Kennedy, 1881.

Cloister Songs. London: Burns; and Dublin: Gill, 1881.

Three Visits to Knock. Dublin: W. H. Gill and Son; and London: R. Washbourne, 1882.

Prayers and Other Devotions for Times of Public Calamity or Pestilence. Dublin: M. H. Gill and Son; and London: R. Washbourne, 1883.

Devotions for Pilgrims to Knock. Dublin: M. H. Gill; and London: R. Washbourne, 1883.

A Souvenir of Knock. Dublin: Gill and Son; and London: R. Washbourne, [1883].

A Patriot's History of Ireland. Dublin, 1885.

The Question of To-day. Chicago and New York: Belford, Clarke and Co., [1887].

The Nun of Kenmare; an Autobiography. London: Jonah Child, [1888]. Reissued: London: Hodder and Stoughton, 1889. Another edition: Boston: Ticknor, 1889.

Life Inside the Church of Rome. London: Hodder and Stoughton, 1889.
  The Story of My Life. London: Hodder and Stoughton, 1891.
  A Remarkable Book and Two Remarkable Relics. London: Marshall Bros., 1892.

What Rome Teaches. London: Marshall Bros., 1892.

The Black Pope; a History of the Jesuits. London: Marshall, Russell and Co.; and Brighton: D. B. Friend and Co., [1896].

His Yarn and Another Story. London: Marshall, Russell and Co., [1897].
  Is There a Roman Catholic Church? London: Marshall, Russell and Co.; and Brighton: D. B. Friend and Co., 1897.

Revolution and War; The Secret Conspiracy of the Jesuits in Great Britain. London: Swan Sonnenschein and Co., 1910. Second edition: London: George Allen and Co., 1913. Another revised edition: London: Stanley Paul and Co., 1913.

Franciscan Rhymes Culled from the Little Flowers of St Francis. Dublin: 1932.

The Tripartite Life of St Patrick. Translated from the original Irish by W. M. Hennessy.

Spouse of Christ. n.d.

The Morning Sacrifice. Music composed to words by the Rev. J. Ryan, n.d.

St Agnes Eve. Another music composition, dedicated to the Poet Laureate, Alfred Tennyson, later Lord Tennyson.

St Francis of Assisi. Kenmare: Kenmare Series of the Lives of Irish Saints, n.d.

Life of St Clare. Kenmare: Kenmare Series of the Lives of Irish Saints, n.d.
Life of St Colette. Kenmare: Kenmare Series of the Lives of Irish Saints, n.d.
Life of St Gertrude. Kenmare: Kenmare Series of the Lives of Irish Saints, n.d.

D

DALTON, Mary
Between July 1929 and November 1929, five of Mary Dalton's poems were published in the *Irish Monthly*.

DARBY, Eleanor
Married name: Mrs Eleanor Darby

Bibliography:
The Sweet·South; or, a Month at Algiers, with a Few Short Lyrics. London: Hope and Co., 1854.
Lays of Love and Heroism, Legends, Lyrics, and Other Poems. London: Hope and Co., 1855.
Ruggiero Vivaldi, and Other Lays of Italy, with Ninfea, a Fairy Legend, and a Few Lyrics. London: Trubner and Co., 1865.
Legends of Many Lands, Sonnets, Songs, and Other Poems. London: William Freeman, 1870.

D'ARCY, Hal
Hal D'Arcy was the pseudonym of a woman whose identity has not been established.

Bibliography:
The O'Donoghue, and Other Poems. Dublin: Hodges, Figgis & Co.; and London: Simpkin, Marshall and Co., [1907].
A Handful of Days. London: John Long, 1913.
Poems. Dublin: Hodges, Figgis and Co., 1930.

DAVIS, Miss
Born: Dublin

Married name: Mrs Andre Messager
Pseudonym: Hope Temple

Miss Davis was the sister of Jim Davis, who wrote several musical plays. Miss Davis was a lyricist, and one operetta she composed was performed in London, in 1892.

DAWSON, Mrs Alfred
Bibliography:
The Sparrow's Oratorio. Dublin: Sealy, Bryers, and Walker, 1906.

DE PAOR, Eibhlín
The *Catholic Bulletin* published thirteen poems by Eibhlín de Paor, October 1923 to June 1929.

DERENZY, Margaret Graves
Bibliography:
Parnassian Geography; or, the Little Ideal Wanderer. Wellington: 1824.
A Whisper to a Newly-Married Pair, from a Widowed Wife. Wellington and Philadelphia: 1824. Other editions: 1825, 1828, 1833, 1866, and 1886.
Poems Appropriate for a Sick or a Melancholy Hour. [1824].
The Flowers of the Forest; Poems. 1828.
The Juvenile Wreath; Poems. 1828.
The Old Irish Knight; a Milesian Tale of the Fifth Century. 1828.

D'ESTERRE, Elsa
Born: circa 1860, in Dublin
Married name: Elsa Keeling

Elsa lived in Germany, and was educated there.

Bibliography:
The Songs of Mirza Schaffy; Translated from the German of F. M. Bodenstedy. Hamburg: 1880.
How the Queen of England was Wooed and Won; or William the Conquerer's First Conquest, a Play in Four Acts and in Verse. London: 1884.
The True Story of Catherine Parr; a Play in One Act and in Verse. London: 1884.
In Thought and in Dreamland; Prose and Verse. London: 1890.

DEVENPORT, Mary
Born: 3 August 1879, at Loughrea, Co. Galway
Died: 1967
Married name: Mary Devenport O'Neill

Mary Devenport was the daughter of a subconstable at Loughrea, and was convent educated before she attended the National College of Art, in Dublin. She married the poet, Joseph O'Neill, on 29 June 1908. The O'Neills lived in Rathgar, and Mary's Thursday salons were popular events. She became Yeats's consultant on *A Vision*, and his trusted friend. Following her husband's death in 1952, she lived in Dublin with relatives.

Her name, Devenport, is sometimes incorrectly spelled as Davenport. She wrote plays, in addition to her poetry, and was a frequent contributor to the *Irish Times*, *The Bell*, and *Dublin Magazine*. In the latter journal, four poems and two plays appeared between October 1938 and June 1949.

Bibliography:
The Kingdom-Maker. Lyrics by M. D. O'Neill, with Seosamh O'Neill. [1917].
Prometheus and Other Poems. London: Jonathon Cape, 1929.

DICKINSON, Eleanor
Eleanor Dickinson was an Irish Quaker woman who contributed to the *Dublin Penny Journal* during the period 1832 to 1836.

Bibliography:
The Pleasures of Piety, with Other Poems. London: Sherwood, Jones, and Co., 1824.
The Mamluck, a Poem. London: Effingham Wilson, 1830.

DOAK, Margaret
Born: Co. Down

Margaret was the sister of Marion Doak (see listing), with whom she co-authored several volumes. She is credited with contributing poetry to various Ulster papers. Her surname is occasionally given as Doake.

Bibliography:
Figaro, a Collection of Prose and Verse. With Marion Doak. Belfast: [c.1860].

Munro of Fort Munro. With Marion Doak Clarke. London: C. H. Clarke, 1873.

Not Transferable; or, Wooing, Winning and Wearing. With Marion Doak Clarke. London: C. H. Clarke, 1875.

May Darling. London: Library Production Committee, 1881.

Songs and Verses. London: Burns and Oates, 1913.

DOAK, Marion
Born: Dromara, Co. Down
Married name: Mrs Charles Marion Clarke
Pseudonym: Miriam Drake

Marion was the sister of Margaret Doak (see listing) and the wife of Charles Clarke, a popular novelist. Marion co-authored several volumes with her sister Margaret. Her maiden name is occasionally spelled Doake.

Bibliography:

Figaro, a Collection of Prose and Verse. With Margaret Doak. Belfast: [c.1860].

Oughts and Crosses; a Novel with a Moral. London: C. H. Clarke, [1872].

Munro of Fort Munro. With Margaret Doak. London: C. H. Clarke, 1873.

No Security; or, Rights and Wrongs. London: C. H. Clarke, 1873.

Not Transferable; or, Wooing, Winning, and Wearing. With Margaret Doak. London: C. H. Clarke, 1875.

Strong as Death. 3 vols. London: Tinsley Bros., 1875. Another edition: Aberdeen: Moran and Co., 1898.

Polly's Petition; or, Bread for a Stone. London: R. T. S. [1884].

The Slippery Ford; or, How Tom was Taught. London: R. T. S., [1885]. Another edition: [1903].

Out of Step; or, the Broken Crystal. London: S. W. Partridge and Co., [1886].

Anthony Ker; or, Living it Down. London: Sunday School Union, [1881].

Cousin Dorry; or, Three Measures of Meal. London: Sunday School Union, [1883].

Johnny's Search. London: Sunday School Union, [1884].

Con's Acre; a Tale of Gillcourt Farm. London: Sunday School Union, [1887].

Among Thorns. London: R. T. S., [1887].

More True than Truthful. London: Hodder and Stoughton, 1887.

DOBBIN, Elizabeth
Bibliography:
Lays of the Feelings; a Collection of Original Poetry. Belfast: n.p., 1839.

DOUGLAS, Bessie
Bessie Douglas is given generally as the proper name of this poet. There is one unsubstantiated suggestion that Bessie Douglas was a pseudonym.

Bibliography:
Excelsior, an Ethical Poetasm. Dublin: n.p., 1857.

DOWLING, Penelope
Bibliography:
Wild Flowers Gathered by a Wandering Pilgrim. London: n.p., 1862.

DOWNEY, Kathleen
A single poem, written by Kathleen, in collaboration with Alan Downey, was published in the *Green & Gold* September/November 1924 issue.

DOWNING, Ellen Mary
Born: 19 March 1828, in Cork
Died: 27 January 1869, at the Mercy Hospital, Cork
Name in Religion: Sister Mary Alphonsus
Pseudonyms: Mary, Ellen, E. M. P. D., and Kate

Ellen Mary Downing was the daughter of the resident medical officer at the Cork Fever Hospital. Her parents, especially her mother, gifted their child with a love of literature. She was born on the Feast of St Joseph, but made her First Communion on Low Sunday, 1839, in St Patrick's Church, Cork. Thereafter Ellen felt St Patrick to be her special patron, and she added Patrick to her name; Ellen Mary Patrick Downing, or E. M. P. D. She was an especially delicate child, plagued by shyness, and an intensely nervous temperament. 'She told her sister that to hear of the violent pain of anyone almost always caused her to feel a precisely similar pain' (Russell 461).

Ellen began to compose her poetry, orally, as a young child. Only on special occasions, or as a great favour, did she allow her sister to write down her verses. In her mid-teens she became an avid reader of *The Nation*, with a particular fondness for the ballads and lyrics contained therein. Thomas Davis and Denis Florence MacCarthy were among her favourite writers. Her first poem appeared on 10 May 1845, in *The Nation's* 'Answers to Correspondents' section, under the pseudonym of Kate when Ellen was approximately seventeen years old. Her sister write the following physical description of Ellen at about that same age:

> . . . she was in my eyes, and I think others would agree with me, singularly pretty and attractive. A brunette in complexion, with a brilliant though varying colour, her beautiful dark eyes dreamy, according to her mood. Her manner was perfectly unaffected, with a mingling of shyness and frankness; and she had a most affectionate disposition, with a vivid enthusiasm for everything good and noble (Russell 463).

There are two conflicting views regarding the early romance of Ellen Downing. Both agree that she was involved, to an undetermined extent, with one of the *Young Ireland* writers. The evidence seems to point to an informal, spoken engagement between the young couple while they were still in their teens. Downing's family indicated to Father Matthew Russell that the young man in question was Joseph Brennan. A. M. Sullivan states in *New Ireland* that her beau was transported for his politics, and forgot his youthful vow during his exile. As a result, according to Sullivan, Ellen was so heartbroken that she stopped writing and died shortly thereafter. The problem with Sullivan's theory is that Downing continued to live, and write, for some twenty years after he reported her death. A more likely explanation comes from Father Russell, who believed the couple had drifted apart before Brennan was transported. Ellen's growing sense of a religious vocation is Russell's theory for the split.

Ellen Downing decided to stop writing for *The Nation* around 1847. The departure of Mitchel and Reilly from the Irish Confederation, due to the policies of Gavan Duffy and Smith O'Brien being too moderate, is cited as the cause of her decision to leave *The Nation*. Her final contribution appeared in the New Year's Day, 1848 edition. Thereafter her work appeared in the *United Irishman*, and assumed a more radical tone. The subsequent political upheavals, and the arrest of Mitchel, created such a strain that Ellen's health was broken. She did not begin to recover until the Spring of 1849. During this period, she visited a relative at the North Presentation Convent, Cork.

July 1849 finds her writing to a cousin of the peace she has found in the convent, and her desire for a nun's life. The letter is signed 'Mary Alphonsus', in recognition of her decision to enter the convent. Her novitiate as a Presentation nun began on 14 October 1849. The formal beginning of a two-year novitiate, receiving her white veil, came on

29 May 1850. Before she had completed her first year of training a mysterious illness, which would eventually result in her death, caused the doctors to declare her 'unfit for the duties of a nun's life' (Russell 577). Ellen's illness was characterized by bouts of paralysis lasting for weeks, during which she would be helpless and bedridden. Then a sudden recovery would occur, completely restoring her ability to walk and move. Her mind was not affected by the paralysis, and she apparently had an amazing tolerance for pain. The doctors pronounced her only hope of recovery was to leave the convent, which she did in the Spring of 1851. She continued to use her religious name from the time she left the North Presentation Convent, and throughout her later life as a member of the Third Order of St Dominic. Ellen lived apart from the community in her own house: 'She lived faithfully to the end as a strictly observant Dominican Tertiary' (Russell 621). Father Russell also calls her a saint, 'sanctified chiefly by suffering — by the cheerful endurance of long years of suffering' (622).

Her mother died in 1860, after a year-long illness. Ellen was free of paralysis at that time, so she attempted to assume her mother's post as matron of the Fever Hospital, but the respite did not last long. The paralysis returned and she gave up the job. During periods of reasonable health she was much in demand as a religious instructor for both converts and children. Ellen was particularly noted for the hours she spent in prayer, regardless of the state of her health. By December 1868, she had entered the Mercy Hospital and the paralysis had become permanent. She had virtually no tolerance for either light or sound at this point:

'Things which usually relieve suffering served but to sharpen hers. There mere sound of a voice speaking to her, a bright ray of light in her room, would often cause her the most excruciating torture' (Russell 665).

An untitled poem, beginning 'Deep in the shadow of my room', records her physical and mental state shortly before her death, which occurred on 27 January 1869.

Anthologized in: *Birthday*, Brooke/Rolleston, Duffy, Hayes, Lover, MacDermott, and Sullivan.

Biographical References:
Anton, Brigitte. 'Women of the *Nation*.' *History Ireland* 1.3 (Autumn 1993): 34-7.

Cumming, G. F. 'Mary of the *Nation.*' *Irish Rosary* 28 (1924): 649-55.
Ghall, Sean (pseudonym). 'An Irish Woman-Poet'. *United Irishmen* 15
    March 1902: 7; 22 March 1902: 6-7; 29 March 1902: 7; 5 April 1902:
    6-7; and 12 April 1902: 6-7.
Markham, Thomas. *Ellen Mary Downing: 'Mary of The Nation'.*
    Dublin: Catholic Truth Society of Ireland, 1913.
O'Delany, M. Barry. "The Centenary of 'Mary of The Nation'". *Irish
    Rosary* 32 (1928): 175-82.
Russell, Matthew. "Ellen Downing: 'Mary' of The Nation." *Irish
    Monthly* 6 (Aug.-Oct. 1878): 459-65, 506-12, 573-80, 621-30, 661-67.
Russell, Matthew. "More about 'Mary' of The Nation." *Irish Monthly* 36
    (Feb. 1908): 69-82.
Russell, Matthew. 'Unpublished Relics of Ellen Downing'. *Irish
    Monthly* 12 (1884): 315-20, 425-32, 534-40.

Bibliography:
Voices of the Heart. Most Reverend J. P. Leahy, Bishop of Dromore, ed.
    Dublin: n.p., 1868. Another revised and enlarged edition: Dr
    Leahy, ed., 1880.
Novenas and Meditations. Dr Leahy, ed. Dublin: n.p., 1879.
Poems for Children. Dublin: n.p., 1881.

DRUMMOND, Mary Anne
Born: 1862
Died: 1953
Married name: Mary Anne Hutton

Mary Anne Hutton spent her early years in England, and was
educated at University College, London. She became the Margaret
Stokes Memorial Lecturer at The Queen's University, Belfast, in 1909.
A noted mediaevalist, in February 1911 she lectured to the Irish Literary Society on 'Irish Medieval Translations from the Classics'. Her
translation of *The Táin* took ten years to complete. *Dublin Magazine's*
obituary of Mary Anne Hutton states that she was 'a scholar [and] a
patriotic Irishwoman'.

Biographical Reference:
Obituary of Mrs Mary Anne Hutton. *Dublin Magazine* 28 ns 4
    (October-December 1953): 45.

Bibliography:
The Táin, an Irish Epic told in English Verse. Dublin: Maunsel and
    Co., 1907. Reprinted: 1908. Second, illustrated edition: Dublin:

Talbot, [1924].

DUDLEY, M. E.
A lengthy list of subscribers preceeds her second volume, and suggests she was the daughter of a Mr S. S. Dudley, of Mount Dudley, Roscrea. Her poem to Ireland, 'To My Country', celebrates her Irish nationality. Miss Mary Dudley, of Peckham, ordered twelve copies of the volume, and may have been the author herself, or a close relative. Her poem, 'Emmet, the Irish Patriot', is fifty-nine pages in length with a four-page introductory poem, and a twenty-five page preface of historical notes. M. E. Dudley was living at 58 Millbank Street, Westminster, in 1836.

Bibliography:
Juvenile Researches in Prose . . . Interspersed with Various Pieces of Poetry by a Sister (The prose portions were written by her brother). London: privately printed, 1835.
Emmet, the Irish Patriot, and Other Poems. London: Printed for the Author by J. Masters, 1836.

DUFFIN, Celia
Born: 27 September, 1887, in Belfast
Died: 28 January, 1983, in Newcastle, Co. Down, and buried in St Colman's Cemetery.
Married name: Celia Randall

Celia was the daughter of Adam Duffin, stockbroker, L.L.D., and J.P. for Co. Down and his wife Maria Drennan Duffin. The family residence was 22 University Square, Belfast, at the time of Celia's birth. Copies of their books, which belonged to the authors, list Strandtown as their residence. The first two poetry collections combined Celia's work with her sister's, Ruth Duffin (see listing). A third sister, Emma, illustrated her sisters' poetry books. Emma went on to write four prose volumes of children's tales. Celia married Mr H. C. Randall and published *The Leaping Flame* containing only her work, under her married name.

Celia Randall's poetry appeared in the following journals: *Ulster Parade*, 1945 issue; the *Irish Bookman*, August 1946; and three poems were in *Rann*, Spring 1952 to June 1953.

Anthologized in: Graves.

Bibliography:
The Secret Hill. With Ruth Duffin. Dublin and London: Maunsel, 1913.
Escape. With Ruth Duffin. London and Toronto: J. M. Dent and Sons, 1929.
The Leaping Flame. Manchester: The Poetry Lovers' Fellowship. 1949.

DUFFIN, Ruth
Born: 22 February, 1877
Died: 1 June, 1968 and buried in St Colman's Cemetery, Newcastle, Co Down.

Ruth was a daughter of Adam Duffin, and sister to Celia Duffin (see listing). Ruth published two volumes of poems in collaboration with Celia, which were illustrated by a third sister, Emma. Ruth's work also appeared in the *Irish Review*.

Anthologized in: Graves.

Bibliography:
The Secret Hill. With Celia Duffin. Dublin and London: Maunsel and Co., 1913.
Escape. With Celia Duffin. London and Toronto: J. M. Dent and Sons, 1929.
The Fairy Cup. Dublin: Browne and Nolan, 1958.

DUFFY, Mary E.
The September 1915 and April 1917 issues of the *Irish Monthly* contain poems by Mary Duffy. She may have been an emigrant to America, or possibly a first-generation American. The League of Self-Supporting Women published a volume containing her speeches, *Two Speeches of Industrial Women* (Mary Duffy and Clara Silver), in New York, circa 1907.

DUNN, Isabel
Married name: Isabel Irwin

Isabel Dunn was probably born in Dublin. She was the sister of Mary Catherine Dunn. Isabel emigrated to America as a child and published in America, except for the single volume listed below.

Bibliography:
The English Abroad. London: T. Fisher Unwin, 1894.

DUNN, Mary
Married name: Mary Benn
Pseudonym: Wilhelm

Mary was the daughter of Reverend William Dunn, Rector of Charleville, Co. Cork. After her marriage to Reverend William Benn she lived mainly in the South of Ireland. Her son, A. W. Benn, was a scholar and writer noted for writing on Greek topics. Mary Dunn was 'fervently Irish, and distinguished for her Latin poems' (O'Donoghue 25).

Bibliography:
The Solitary; or, a Lay from the West, and Other Poems in Latin and English.
    London: Joseph Masters; and Dublin: James McGlashan, 1853.
Lays of the Hebrews, and Other Poems. London: Joseph Masters, 1854.

E

ECCLES, Charlotte O'Conor
Born: circa 1860, in Ballingard House, Co. Roscommon
Died: 1911
Pseudonym: Hal Godfrey, H. B., A Modern Maid

Charlotte was the fourth and oldest surviving daughter of Alexander O'Conor Eccles, J.P., and founder of the *Roscommon Messenger*. She was educated at Upton Hall, Birkenhead, then in Paris and Germany. She was a prose writer, translator, and journalist of excellent reputation. Charlotte O'Conor Eccles also published essays on women's education and women's rights. Two poems are found in the *Irish Monthly*, July 1887 and March 1905 issues.

Biographical Reference:
Obituary. *Irish Book Lover* 2.12 (July 1911): 193.

Bibliography:
The Rejuvenation of Miss Semaphone; a Farcical Novel. London: Jarrold
    and Sons, 1897.
Aliens of the West. London: Cassell, 1904.

The Matrimonial Lottery. London: Eveleigh Nash, 1906.

ELGEE, Jane Francesca
Born: circa 1821
Died: 3 February 1896, in London
Married name: Lady Wilde
Pseudonym: Speranza

Jane Elgee claimed her date of birth was 1826, but the majority of her biographers suggest a date between 1820 and 1824 would be more accurate. Terence de Vere White attempts to precisely calculate a date of birth in his biography, and ultimately establishes that 1826 could not possibly have been the correct date. Joy Melville states that 'Jane's most likely birthdate is 29 December 1821, which she gave in 1888 when applying for a grant to the Royal Literary Fund' (6). As birth records were not required at the time, and Jane considered such enquiries unseemly, an exact date becomes impossible to ascertain. Both Dublin and Wexford have been suggested as the place of her birth, again inconclusively. The Elgee family was living at No. 6 Leeson Street, Dublin, from 1817 to 1822, the most probable period for Jane's birth. Other sources suggesting a Wexford birthplace are based upon the variations in birthdate and the Elgee family connections to Wexford.

Jane was the daughter of a Dublin solicitor, Charles Elgee, and his wife, Sara Kingsbury Elgee. Charles was the eldest son of John Elgee, Archdeacon of Wexford. Sara was the daughter of Thomas Kingsbury, Commissioner of Bankruptcy. The Kingsbury home was Lisle House, 'one of the finest mansions in Dublin' (Melville 4). Sara and her two sisters were considered leading beauties of their time. By all accounts the Kingsbury and Elgee families were both strongly Protestant and Unionist.

Jane's father died in August 1825, in Bangalore, India. The reason as to why he had travelled so far from home has not been discovered, but Jane was reared by her mother in Dublin, and educated by private tutors. She displayed a flair for languages, attaining competency in ten European languages by the age of eighteen. She later became a notable translator. During the period from 1822 to 1842, Sara Elgee's name does not appear in the Dublin street directory. In 1843, 34 Leeson Street is listed as Sara's residence, and Jane was still a member of her mother's household.

Jane did not begin her writing career until *The Nation* published her first poem on 21 February 1846, a verse translation from the German, 'The Holy War'. The poem was published under the pseudonym of Speranza, the Italian word for Hope, but Jane signed her correspondence with *The Nation* under a male pseudonym, John Fanshawe Ellis. Jane's poetry for *The Nation* appeared primarily between 1846 and 1848. Her famous piece, 'Jacta Alea Est' ('The Die is Cast') was published in the 19 July 1848 issue, and was instrumental in the government's closure of the paper. *The Nation* began publishing again on 1 September 1849, with one of Jane's poems prominently displayed.

Her mother died in 1851, and Jane accepted a marriage proposal from William Wilde, a medical doctor known for his skill in ophthalmology. They married in St Peter's Church on the 12th November 1851, with Jane's uncle, Reverend John Elgee, performing the ceremony. After the marriage Janew and William Wilde lived at 21 Westland Row, in Dublin. Their first son, William Charles Kingsbury Wills Wilde, or Willie, was born on 26 September 1852, slightly more than ten months after the marriage ceremony. This small calculation belies the rumour that Jane was pregnant at the time of the wedding. Jane's husband, however, had a reputation as a womanizer, having already fathered three illegitimate children prior to his marriage to Jane. Henry, Emily and Mary Wilde, the children born illegitimately, did not reside with Jane and William.

Oscar Fingal O'Flahertie Wills Wilde was born on 16 October 1854, the second son of Jane and William. A third child, Isola Francesca Emily Wilde, was born on 2 April 1857. Jane was reported to be extremely close to all her children.

Among Jane's closest friends in this period was Lotte von Kraemer, daughter of Baron Robert von Kraemer, governor of Uppsala in Sweden. Lotte introduced Jane to Rosalie Olivecrona, editor of a Swedish women's journal, an early feminist publication. Both Lotte and Rosalie influenced Jane's growing feminist beliefs, according to Joy Melville.

William Wilde was knighted in 1846, and Jane thereafter preferred to use her formal title, Lady Wilde. The Wildes were considered an integral part of the Dublin social scene at this point, living at No. 1 Merrion Square; and Lady Wilde's 'at home' salons were legendary. They built a second home, Moytura House, in Connemara, which became the family's retreat from Dublin.

In 1864, Mary Josephine Travers brought suit against Lady Wilde for libel, the result of a letter Jane had written to Mary's father concerning his daughter's behaviour towards William. Mary was later to allege that William Wilde had raped her. The jury found in favour of Mary regarding the libel suit, but set the damages at one farthing. Neither Mary nor the Wildes were fully vindicated by the decision.

Isola Wilde died of a fever in 1867, at age ten, and Lady Wilde was shattered by the loss of her only daughter. Further tragedy was visited upon William and Jane in 1871, when William's two illegitimate daughters died from burns suffered in an accident. William Wilde died five years later, on 19 April 1876, leaving his wife in emotional and financial despair. She was left an annuity of £200, linked to Moytura House. As the Moytura property was heavily mortgaged it was unable to provide her with the yearly pension. Her financial situation was to remain strained throughout the rest of her life.

Lady Wilde moved to London in May 1879, to be closer to her sons, and to allow Willie to sell the Merrion Square house which was his inheritance. She settled with Willie at No. 1 Ovington Square, in Chelsea. Her literary efforts at this time were directed to generating income rather than her previous ideological aims.

By 1822, Lady Wilde and Willie had moved to 116 Park Street, near Grosvenor Square. She remained at Park Street until 1888, when she and Willie again returned to the Chelsea area, at 146 Oakley Street.

Lady Wilde was granted a civil list pension of £70 per year in May 1890. The annuity lessened but did not alleviate her continuing financial crisis. Willie's marriage in October 1891, to the former Mrs Frank Leslie, an American newspaper publisher, brought Lady Wilde a gift of £100 per year from the wealthy bride. When Willie's marriage ended, in June 1893, Mrs Leslie's contributions ended shortly thereafter, by 1894.

After Oscar Wilde was sentenced to prison for homosexuality in May 1895, his mother became a recluse who never left her bedroom. She died of respiratory complications following a case of bronchitis on 3 February 1896. She was buried in plot 127 at Kensal Green Cemetery, in London. No headstone was purchased by her family, nor was the payment made for the plot, so her remains were exhumed seven years later and reinterred in an unidentified location.

Lady Wilde was a founder member of the Irish Literary Society. She wrote poetry, prose essays, translations, journalistic pieces and recorded folklore. She also published translations from French and German.

Anthologized in: *Birthday*, *Cabinet* III, MacIlwaine, Mrs Sharp, Sparling, and Varian.

Biographical References:
Anton, Brigitte. 'Women of *The Nation*'. *History Ireland* 1.3 (Autumn

1993): 34-7. (Her name is incorrectly given as Anne Francesca Elgee).

Byrne, Patrick. *The Wilde's of Merrion Square*. London and New York: Staples Press, 1953.

de Bremont, Anna. *Oscar Wilde and His Mother: A Memoir*. London: Everett, 1911.

Hamilton, C. J. *Notable Irishwomen*. Dublin: Sealy, Bryers and Walker, n.d.

Hoey, John C. and Frances C. Hoey. 'Recent Irish Poetry'. *Dublin Review* ns 4 (1865): 315-20.

'Lady Wilde'. *Anthenaeum* (15 February 1896): 220.

Lambert, Eric. *Mad with Much Heart: A Life of the Parents of Oscar Wilde*. London: Muller, 1967.

'Living Irish Literary Celebrities, No. 2: Lady Wilde'. *Nation* (10 November 1888): 4-5.

Melville, Joy. *Mother of Oscar*. London: John Murray, 1994.

White, Terence de Vere. *The Parents of Oscar Wilde: Sir William and Lady Wilde*. London: Hodder and Stoughton, 1967.

Wyndham, Horace. "'Speranza' and her First Editor". *English* 6 (1946): 73-7.

Wyndham, Horace. *Speranza: A Biography of Lady Wilde*. London and New York: Boardman, 1951.

Bibliography:

Sidonia the Sorceress. Translated from the German of W. Meinhold. 2 vols. The Parlour Library, vol. 29 and 30, 1847. Another edition: London: Simms and McIntyre, 1849. Another edition: 1 vol. Kelmscott Press, 1893. Third edition: Reeves and Turner, 1894. Another edition: 1926.

Pictures of the First French Revolution; being Episodes from the History of the Girondists. Translated from the French of Alphonse de Lamartine. (1847). Another edition: London: Simms and McIntyre, 1850. Another edition: The Parlour Library, vol. 45, 1850. Another edition: The Parlour Library, vol. 55, 1851.

The Wanderer and His Home. Translated from the French of Lamartine. London: Simms and McIntyre, 1851.

The Glacier Land. Translated from the French of A. Dumas. London: Simms and McIntyre, 1852.

Ugo Bassi: A Tale of the Italian Revolution. London: 1857.

The First Temptation; or, Eritis Sicut Deus. 3 vols. Translated from the German of W. Canz. London: Newby, 1863.

Poems by Speranza. Dublin: James Duffy, 1864. Another edition: Glasgow and London: Cameron and Ferguson, [1871]. Another

edition: Dublin: Gill and Son, [1907].
Memoir of Gabriel Beranger. 1880. (Lady Wilde wrote only the introductory portion of this work by her husband.)
Driftwood from Scandinavia. London: R. Bentley, 1884.
Ancient Legends, Mystic Charms, and Superstitions of Ireland. With William Robert Wilde. 2 vols. London: Ward and Downey, 1887. Another edition: 1888. Another edition: London: Chatto and Windus, 1919. Another edition: 1 vol. Galway: O'Gorman, 1971.
Ancient Cures, Charms and Usages of Ireland. London: Ward and Downey, 1887. Another edition: 1890.
Notes on Men, Women, and Books. London: Ward and Downey, 1891.
Social Studies. London: Ward and Downey, 1893.
Her status as author of this work is disputed.

ELLIOTT, Anne
Bibliography:
The Heart's Ease, Poems. Armagh: privately printed, 1837. Another edition: Exeter: 1841.
Serious Thoughts in Prose and Poetry. London and Exeter: privately printed, 1841.

ELLIS, Janet
The *Irish Monthly* published eleven poems by Janet Ellis, between May 1880 and October 1881.

EMERY, Helen Gladys
Helen Gladys Emery had four poems published in the *Irish Monthly*, July 1903 to June 1907.

ENGLISH, Katharyn
The *Catholic Bulletin* printed six poems by Katharyn English, April 1926 to June 1927.

ENRIGHT, Mary Josephine
Twelve poems by Mary Josephine Enright appeared in the *Irish Monthly*, November 1893 to February 1902.

ESMONDE, Eily
Married name: Mrs John Esmonde

Eily Esmonde was the wife of Dr John Esmonde, M.P. for Tipperary North in 1910. She published a total of eight poems in the *Irish Monthly*, September 1914 to November 1932. Eily's poems also appeared in the *Freeman's Journal* and the *Westminster Gazette*.

EVANS, Margaret
Married name: Mrs George Evans

Margaret became the wife of George Evans, M.P., and lived at Portrane, Co. Dublin.

Bibliography:
Poems. Paris: privately printed by Davies and Robertson, 1834.

EVATT, Anne
Bibliography:
An Address from Ireland to England; a Poem on the Lamented Death of H.R.H. the Princess Charlotte. Dublin: privately printed, 1818.

F

FAGAN, Mary Frances
One poem by Mary Frances Fagan was published in the June 1884 issue of the *Irish Monthly*.

FALLON, Susan Ann
Bibliography:
The May Wreath, a Selection of Hymns to the Virgin. London: Burns and Lambert, [1865].

FALLON, Mrs Garnett
Pseudonym: E. L. L.

The initials under which Mrs Fallon published were probably those of her maiden name. She is reported to have lived at Rosbercan, New Ross, Co. Wexford.

Bibliography:
Wild Flowers from the Glens. London, Dublin and Belfast: n.p., 1840. Fourth edition: 1866.

FERRAR, Mary Elizabeth

Born: Belfast
Died: circa 1890
Married name: Mary Elizabeth Patterson

Mary was the daughter of a Belfast magistrate, W. H. Ferrar. She married Robert Patterson, a Fellow of the Royal Society, and a noted zoologist. One of their eleven children was W. H. Patterson, the eminent antiquarian.

Bibliography:
Verses. With Robert Patterson. Belfast: Alexander Mayne and Bond, 1886. Printed for private circulation.

FFRENCH, Eleanor
Eleanor Ffrench (sometimes French) was the author of a single volume of poetry. The preface to her collection, dated April 1863, was written by an unidentified friend in Dublin, and states: 'This little book contains all the poems of the late Eleanor French, of Prospect Hill, Galway, which could be collected at a period of two years after her death'. One interesting poem, 'The Rival Lights', commemorates the installation of Galway's gas lighting on the 20th of November 1837. A number of the poems pertain to medical topics, doctors and an infirmary, suggesting that she was connected with a medical facility in the Prospect Hill or Bohermore areas.

Bibliography:
Poems. Dublin: privately printed, 1863.

FIELDING, Anna Maria
Born: 6 January 1800, in Dublin
Died: 30 January 1881, at Devon Lodge, East Moulsey, and buried in
    Addlestrong Churchyard
Married name: Mrs S. C. Hall

Anna Maria Fielding was born in Anne Street, Dublin. When she was about one month old, her mother and Anna went to live in Graige, near Bannow, Co. Wexford. They lived with George Carr, Esq., the step-father of Anna's mother, until Anna was a young woman. George Carr adored Anna, considering her his adopted daughter and the heiress of his estate. When Anna was about fifteen, the trio of George Carr, Anna's mother, and Anna, moved to London. Unfortunately Mr. Carr did not formalize his intentions regarding Anna's inheritance in a written will. Upon his death the estate went to a nephew, who is reported to have rapidly squandered the lot.

While in London, in 1823, Anna was introduced to Samuel Carter Hall, parliamentary reporter for the House of Lords. S. C. Hall had been born near Waterford, to English parents stationed at the Geneva Barracks. They married on the 20th of September 1824. Anna did not begin writing until 1825, when her story, 'Master Ben', appeared in *The Spirit and Manners of the Age*, a monthly journal edited by her husband. She was to become a friend to several of the leading women authors of the day, including Maria Edgeworth, and Caroline Sheridan (see listing).

The Halls made a living through their literary efforts. Anna and Samuel were frequent collaborators, and prolific novelists, amassing an estimated five-hundred books between them. Mr Hall stated that his wife was known to write her stories quickly, and did not revise her work. All editing, proof-reading and aspects of publishing were left to her husband. In 1868, Anna was granted a Civil List pension of £100, this amount eventually was increased to an annuity of £300. She was the originator of a fund to honour Florence Nightingale, and with her husband, contributed £45,000 to that fund. She was also financially supportive of the Hospital for Consumptives, the Home for Decayed Gentlewomen, the Governesses' Institute, and other philanthropic organisations. The Halls were firm advocates of temperance. For their fiftieth wedding anniversary, a subscription fund amounting to £1,500 was raised and presented to them, along with an album of five hundred testimonial letters from their friends.

Anthologized in: *Cabinet* III, and Lover.

Biographical References:
Hall, Samuel Carter. *A Book of Memories.* 1876.
Hall, Samuel Carter. *Retrospect of a Long Life.* New York: Appleton, 1883.
Hamilton, C. J. *Notable Irishwomen.* Dublin: Sealy, Bryers and Walker, n.d.
Maclise, Daniel. *A Gallery of Illustrious Characters.* London: Chatto and Windus, 1873.
Maginn, William. 'Gallery of Literary Characters, No. 73: Mrs S. C. Hall'. *Fraser's Magazine* 13 (1836): 718.
Mayo, Isabella Fyvie. 'A Recollection of Two Old Friends: Mr and Mrs S. C. Hall'. *Leisure Hour* 38 (1889): 303-7.
'Our Portrait Gallery, No. 10: Mrs S. C. Hall'. *Dublin University*

Magazine 16 (1840): 146-9.

Bibliography:
Mabel's Curse, A Musical Drama in Two Acts. London: Duncombe, [c.1825].
Sketches of Irish Character. London: F. Westley and A. H. Davis, 1829.
Chronicles of A School-Room. 1830.
Sketches of Irish Character; Second Series. London: F. Westley and A. H. Davis, 1831.
The Buccaneer; a Tale. 3 vols. London: R. Bentley, 1832.
The Outlaw. 1832. Another edition: London: R. Bentley, 1835.
Tales of Woman's Trials. London: Houlston, 1835.
Uncle Horace; a Novel. London: H. Colburn, 1837.
St Pierre the Refugee; a Burletta in Two Acts. London: J. Macrone, 1837. Another edition: revised and retitled *The French Refugee:* London: 1837.
The Groves of Blarney; a Drama in Three Acts. London: Chapman and Hall, 1838.
Lights and Shadows of Irish Life. London: H. Colburn, 1838.
The Book of Royalty: Characteristics of British Palaces. London: 1839.
Marian; or, a Young Maid's Fortune. London: H. Colburn, 1840.
The Hartopp Jubilee. With S. C. Hall. 1840.
Tales of the Irish Peasantry. 1840.
Ireland, Its Scenery and Character. With S. C. Hall. 3 vols. London: How and Parsons, 1841.
A Week at Killarney. With S. C. Hall. London: J. How, 1843.
Characteristic Sketches of Ireland and the Irish. With W. Charleton, and S. Lover. Dublin: P. D. Hardy and Sons, 1845.
Juniper Jack; or, My Aunt's Hobby, a Burletta. Privately printed, [circa 1845].
The Whiteboy; a Story of Ireland in 1822. London: Chapman and Hall, 1845.
Stories and Studies from the Chronicles and History of England. 1847.
A Midsummer Eve; a Fairy Tale of Love. London: Longman, 1848.
The Swan's Egg; a Tale. 1850.
Stories of the Irish Peasantry. Edinburgh: W. and R. Chambers, 1850.
Pilgrimages to English Shrines. 1850.
Stories of the Governess. 1852.
Handbooks for Ireland. With S. C. Hall. London: Virtue, 1853.
The Well-Worn Thimble; a Story. 1853.
The Drunkard's Bible. 1854.
The Book of the Thames. With S. C. Hall. 1854.

The Two Friends. 1856.
A Woman's Story. 1857.
The Lucky Penny and Other Tales. 1857.
Finden's Gallery of Modern Art; with Tales by Mrs S. C. Hall. 1859.
The Boy's Birthday Book. 1859.
Daddy Dacre's School. 1859.
Tenby. With S. C. Hall. 1860.
The Book of South Wales. With S. C. Hall. 1861.
Can Wrong Be Right? A Tale. 1862.
The Village Garland; Tales and Sketches. 1863.
Nelly Nowlan and Other Stories. 1865.
The Playfellas and Other Stories. 1866.
The Way of the World and Other Stories. 1866.
The Prince of the Fairy Family. 1867.
Alice Stanley and Other Stories. 1868.
Animal Sagacity. 1868.
The Fight of Faith; a Story. London: Chapman and Hall, 1869.
Digging a Grave With a Wineglass. 1871.
Chronicles of a Cozy Nook. 1875.
Boons and Blessings; Stories of Temperance. 1875.
Annie Leslie and Other Stories. 1877.
A Companion to Killarney. With S. C. Hall. 1878.
Grandmother's Pockets. 1880.
Tales of Irish Life and Character. T. N. Foulis, 1909.

FITZGERALD, Patricia
The *Irish Monthly* published one poem, in July 1926, by Patricia Fitzgerald.

FORBES, Lady
Lady Forbes was the wife of Col. Forbes, R.M., of Co. Longford.

Bibliography:
The Newsboy's Last Appeal. Privately printed, [c.1890].

FORRESTER, Fanny
Born: 1852
Died: November 1889

Although Fanny Forrester was born in Manchester, she was a daughter of Ellen Forrester (see listing for Ellen Magennis), an Irishwoman who had moved to England. Fanny was the sister of Mary Magdalene Forrester (see listing). Fanny was a frequent contributor of poetry to

The Nation and the occasional author of short stories.

The *Irish Monthly*, in volume 13, makes the statement that Fanny Forrester is not 'the real name of this poet', although there is no further elaboration (108). Since convincing information exists regarding the identities of Fanny and her mother Ellen, it appears the *Irish Monthly* was in error. In volume eighteen of the *Irish Monthly*, a brief obituary of Fanny appears which confirms the family link with Ellen.

Anthologized in: *Emerald Gems*, and Sullivan.

Bibliography:
Songs of the Rising Nation, and Other Poems. With Ellen and Arthur M. Forrester. Glasgow and London: n.p., 1869.

FORRESTER, Mary Magdalene
Mary was another daughter of Ellen Magennis Forrester (see listing under Ellen Magennis) and a sister to Fanny (see listing). Mary is credited with contributing poems to various Irish newspapers.

FOSTER, Eleanor
Eleanor Foster was reported to be of a Queen's County family.

Bibliography:
With the Tide, and Other Poems. London: Gay and Bird, 1896.

FOX, Olive Agnes
Born: 9 September, 1883
Died: 8 May 1972, in Dublin
Married name: Mrs Claud de Cheavassa
Pseudonym: Móirín ní Shionnaigh, Móirín Fox, Móirín Cheavasse, Móirín Cheavasa and Móirín Chavasse

Olive Agnes Fox was the daughter of Arthur Fox and the former Miss Knox, of Pinner, Middlesex. Her mother's family had aristocratic connections through the Earl of Ranfually, and it is said Mrs Fox 'looked down on her husband' (Aebhgréine Chavasse, letter, 26 Julys 1994). Agnes Fox was educated at home, by her mother and by governesses who were French and German, so Agnes was fluent in these languages almost from birth. She had one brother and two sisters, who were her elders. Agnes's elder sister died at an early age. Agnes' elder sister had been a clever girl, urged on at her studies by Mrs Fox, who later came to believe an excess of studying had contributed to her daughter's death. Consequently Mrs Fox was afraid to press Agnes's education. Mr Fox intervened, and Agnes was sent to a boarding school for several years. Her daughter, Aebhgréine Chavasse, reports her mother had a wild and passionate nature, which caused her to become 'emotionally attached to a Cypriot girl' while at school (letter 26 July 1994). Miss Fox's early literary influences were Tennyson and Malony. She appears to have taken an interest in writing at an early age. Agnes was musically talented, attaining more than common proficiency as a pianist, but was timid about playing for the public.

Agnes was reared in a strictly religious household, and was reluctantly forced to attend her parents' church. She found the family's religious adherence excessive, and Agnes believed the clergymen were hypocritical.

About 1901, when Agnes was eighteen years of age, she suffered a nervous breakdown. Her father provided her with a small pension and Agnes moved to Ireland. Always interested in the Celtic heritage, she studied the Irish language and assumed the Irish translation of her name, so Agnes Fox became Móirín ní Shionnaigh.

Móirín ní Shionnaigh shared a house in Dublin with Ella Young, the poet, mystic, and eventual IRA gun-runner. Ella Young introduced her to people in Dublin, while Móirín paid the expenses for the house where they lived. Through Young, Móirín met Thomas MacDonagh and other political and literary figures. Yeats praised her efforts, but she thought him aloof. She also met her future husband Claud de Cheavassa. A Scotsman by birth, Claud de Cheavassa was passionately interested in the Irish language and culture. He is still remembered in the Galway area for his love of the Irish language and his fondness for wearing Celtic attire, particularly kilts. After their marriage in 1917, Claud and Móirín maintained an Irish-speaking household, rearing their only child, Aebhgréine, in a home dedicated to the Irish language and culture. Although she spoke Irish fluently, Móirín reportedly lacked the confidence to publish in the Irish language, but she was an accomplished translator, particularly of poetry. Móirín was widely read, and her interests ranged from philosophy, where she had a special fondness for Platinus, to Irish history, particularly antiquarian Ireland. Her philosophical readings led her back to Christian theology, and thus to an examination of Catholic theology. She was received into the Catholic church in 1935, following a lengthy philosophical correspondence with a Jesuit priest.

After their marriage the couple moved to Connemara. They lived in Ross House, the former home of Violet Martin, who was better known as 'Martin Ross', half of the Somerville and Ross writing team. Ross House is located between Moycullen and Oughterard, outside

Galway City, on the shore of Ross Lake.

They later moved to Aebhgréine's home in the Kingston area of Galway, where their daughter cared for them as long as possible. Claud died on 1 August 1971, and Móirín died ten months later, in a Dublin nursing home.

Móirín's work appeared in the *Irish Review* and the *Dublin Magazine*.

Anthologized in: Fitzhenry, and Graves.

Bibliography:
Liadáin and Curithir. Adventurers All Series, no. 15. Oxford: Blackwell, 1916.
Midhir and Etain; a Poem. Dublin and London: Talbot Press Booklets, 1920.
The Fire-Bringers; a Play in One Act. Dublin: Talbot Press, 1920.
The One Unfaithfulness of Naoise; a Poem. Dublin: Talbot Press, 1930.
The Fall of the Year; Collected Poems. Dublin: Gayfield Press, 1940.
Terence MacSwiney. Dublin: Clonmore and Reynolds, 1961.

FURLONG, Alice
Born: circa 1875 at Knocklaiguin Lodge, near Pelia, Co. Dublin
Died: 1948, in Tallaght

Alice was a daughter of James Walter, originally a Wexford man, who became the sporting editor of a Dublin newspaper. She had three sisters: Katherine, Mary and Margaret. Kate and Mary were both published poets (see listings). Margaret married the poet and translator, Patrick Joseph (P. J.) McCall. Alice's childhood was spent at Fernvale, in Bohernabreena, on the River Dodder. Later the family moved to Old Bawn, near Tallaght. Their home was close to Whitehall, Katharine Tynan's family home.

Alice began publishing her poetry at about the age of sixteen, in the *Irish Monthly*. The editor of the *Irish Monthly*, Father Mathew Russell, took a keen interest in her poetic development, and was instrumental in obtaining a publisher for *Roses and Rue*. She was living at 5 Lebass Terrace, Leinster Road, Rathmines, in 1908. Alice was a regular contributor, and considered a prominent poet until the 1916 Rising. She considerably lessened her publishing activities after 1916, and assumed a semi-retired life in Tallaght.

There is a romanticised version of her later life, which suggests that she was so depressed after the executions following the 1916 Rising that she withdrew into seclusion in Tallaght, and never spoke or wrote in English again. This romantic ending to Alice Furlong's life is completely belied by her publishing record which continued for twenty-four years. Although she died in Tallaght, and is reported to have been buried in St Maelruan's Cemetery, they have no record of Alice Furlong being buried there.

Her poems appeared frequently in the *United Ireland, Sinn Féin* and *Weekly Independent*. Over fifty poems appeared, in both the English and Irish languages, in the *Irish Monthly*, August 1891 through June 1930.

Anthologized in: Graves, Cooke, Brooke/Rolleston, Browne, Gregory, and Rhys.

Biographical Reference:
Little, Arthur. 'Lest We Forget Alice Furlong'. *Irish Monthly* 75 (April 1947): 137-40.
O'Brennan, Kate. 'Alice Furlong: Some Memories'. *Irish Book Lover* 30 (May 1948): 105-8.

Bibliography:
Roses and Rue. London: Elkin Mathews, 1899.
*Tales of Fairy Folks, Queens and Heroes.*Dublin: Browne and Nolan, [1907].

FURLONG, Katherine
Born: 1872
Died: 27 July 1894, and buried in St Maelruan's Cemetery, Tallaght

Katherine was a daughter of John Furlong, and sister to Alice, Mary and Margaret (see listings for Alice and Mary). She was called Kate by her family and she used that diminutive name when her lone published poem, 'Foreshadowing', appeared in the January 1895 issue of the *Irish Monthly*.

Kate died of a fever at the age of twenty-two. In Glasnevin Cemetery there is a memorial marker for Kate, although St Maelruan's in Tallaght lists her as buried in their cemetery.

FURLONG, Mary
Born: 26 November 1866, in Dublin
Died: 22 September 1898, in Roscommon, and buried in
       St Maelruan's Cemetery, Tallaght

Mary Furlong was the eldest sister of Alice, Margaret and Kate Furlong (see listings for Alice and Katherine). Their father was John

Furlong, sporting editor of a Dublin newspaper, and the family moved to Tallaght shortly after Mary was born. She later assumed the care of her younger sisters when their parents died.

At age twenty-three she began her training as a nurse at the Old Hospital of Madame Steevens, in Dublin. Following her training, she worked at Madame Steevens as a nurse, until leaving to assume private nursing duties. While working at Madame Steevens Hospital, her father was admitted to her ward, the victim of an accident. He had attempted to stop a runaway horse at a local racecourse, was severely injured by the animal, and died a few days later. His wife survived him by only a few months. Mary later volunteered as a nurse during an outbreak of typhus in Connacht and she was the only nurse in her group of volunteers to die of the disease during the epidemic. Although she is buried in St Maelruan's Cemetery, in Tallaght, there is a memorial marker for her in Glasnevin Cemetery.

In *The Cabinet of Irish Literature*, Katharine Tynan states: 'From the age of fourteen Mary scribbled determinedly in spite of much good and unpalatable advice from editors' (Vol. 4; 241). Matthew Russell, editor of the *Irish Monthly*, must not have shared the opinion Tynan later expressed as Mary Furlong became a frequent contributor to his periodical. A total of sixteen poems by Mary Furlong appeared between November 1889 and February 1898 in *The Irish Monthly*. The *Irish Monthly* also published Mary Furlong's first poem approximately two years prior to Alice Furlong's first verse in the same journal.

Anthologized in: *Cabinet* IV.

G

GALLAGHER, Fanny
Pseudonym: Sydney Starr

Her name is sometimes spelled as Fannie Gallagher. She was the daughter of John Blake Gallagher, editor of the *Freeman's Journal* for twenty-six years. Fanny was a secretary to the Duchess of Bedford, Bedford Park, London, for more than thirty years.

Sydney Starr published poems in the December 1879 and September 1888 issues of the *Irish Monthly*.

Bibliography:
Kaity the Flash; a Mould of Dublin Mind. Third edition: Gill and Son, 1880.
A Son of Man; a Story in Three Chapters. Dublin: Gill and Son, 1880.
Thy Name is Truth. 3 vols. London: Maxwell, 1884.
The Dawn of Day. 3 vols. [1885].

GARLAND, Amelia
Born: Freshford, Co. Kilkenny
Married name: Amelia Mears

Amelia was the daughter of John Garland, a poet and schoolmaster who moved his family to England while Amelia was a child. She married a West Hartlepool merchant in 1864.

Bibliography:
Idylls, Legends and Lyrics. London: 1890.
The Story of a Trust; and Other Tales. London: 1893.
Sketches of Life: Tales of West Hartlepool. London: n.d.

GARNET, Viola
A single poem by Viola Garnet is in the *Irish Monthly*, December 1879 issue.

GARVEY, Maura
Pseudonym: Maureen

Maura Garvey's poetry suggests that she was a resident of the Galway area, near to Lough Corrib.

Bibliography:
A Handful of Irish Bog Lilies. Dublin: Sealy, Bryers, and Walker, [1910].

GEOGHEGAN, Mary
Born: Ennis, Co. Clare

Starting in 1886, Mary Geoghegan published in *Cornhill, Macmillan's Magazine, The Woman's World, Time,* and *Chambers' Journal*. There are a total of eleven poems by Mary Geoghegan, including some translations from the Irish language, in the *Irish Monthly*, October 1917 to August 1925.

GIBBONS, Margaret
Born: July 1884
Died: January 1969, in Dublin, and is buried at Fore,
     Co. Westmeath
Pseudonyms: Eithne, and Meda

Margaret's father was a member of the Royal Irish Constabulary and was transferred to Collinstown while Margaret was a child. Margaret was born either in Co. Cavan or Co. Westmeath. She was one of four children and her only brother, Edward, became a priest in the Diocese of Meath. Her sister, Kitty, became Mrs O'Doherty, while Maria (see listing) became Mother Columba, of the Loreto Convent, Navan.

Margaret was educated at the Fore National School in Collinstown, and at St Mary's College, Belfast, where she qualified as a teacher. She taught in Scotland, and at Cannistown, near Navan. She helped Lady Maloney to found the Sisters who were to accompany the St Columban priests on the Maynooth Mission to China, but her own desire to join the Maynooth Mission as a lay minister was not approved. Mrgaret 'then tried her own vocation to the pilgrim's life but did not persevere', recalls S. M. Ignatius Cooless (Letter; December 1993).

Margaret Gibbons was an avid reader, completing Dickens by the age of nine, and the entire works of Shakespeare by age eleven. Her first poem was written at the age of ten. She is noted for having prepared a book of hymns to unify the pilgrims' singing at Lough Derg. She travelled to India for two years when she was seventy-three years old, researching the life of Mar Ivanios, who had converted to the Catholic faith at the Eucharistic Congress of 1932, and later became Archbishop of Trivandrum.

Primarily known as a biographer and prose writer, only one poem by Margaret Gibbons is found in the *Catholic Bulletin*, July 1912.

Biographical Reference:
Letter from S. M. Ignatius Cooless, Loreto Convent, St Michael's, Navan. December 1993.

Bibliography:
The Good-Night Stories. London: Year Book Press, 1912.
The Rose of Glenconnel. London: Herbert Jenkins, 1917. Another edition: Red Letter Novels, No. 36. London: D. C. Thomson and Co., [1921].
An Anzac's Bride. London: Herbert Jenkins, 1918.
Whom Love Hath Chosen. London: Herbert Jenkins, 1920.
Hidden Fires. London: Herbert Jenkins, 1921.

Each Hour a Peril. Red Letter Novels, No. 20. London: D. C. Thomson and Co., [1921].

The Highest Bidder. Red Letter Novels, No. 25. London: D. C. Thomson and Co., [1921].

The Bartered Bride. London: Herbert Jenkins, 1921.

The Flame of Life. London: Herbert Jenkins, 1922. Another, abridged edition: London: Mellifont Press, [1942].

Shifting Sands. London: Herbert Jenkins, 1922.

His Dupe. Red Letter Novels, No. 45. London: D. C. Thomson, 1922.

Molly of the Lone Pine. Red Letter Novels, No. 51. London: D. C. Thomson and Co., [1923].

A Lover on Loan. Red Letter Novels, No. 66. London: D. C. Thomson and Co., [1923].

Her Undying Past. London: Herbert Jenkins, 1924.

Lone and Carol. London: Herbert Jenkins, 1925.

Love's Defiance. Red Letter Novels, No. 145. London: D. C. Thomson and Co., 1926.

Her Dancing Partner. London: Herbert Jenkins, 1926.

My Pretty Maid: Talks with Girls by Eithne. With a preface by His Grace the Most Reverend T. P. Gilmartin, D.D., Archbishop of Tuam. London: Sands, 1927

The Ukelele Girl. London: Herbert Jenkins, 1927. Another edition: Red Letter Novels, No. 184. London: D. C. Thomson and Co., 1927.

The Life of Margaret Aylward: Foundress of the Sisters of the Holy Faith. London: Sands, 1928.

Love, Courtship and Marriage. London: Sands, [1928].

Little Nellie of Holy God. London: Sands, [1929].

Dancers in the Dark. Herbert Jenkins, 1929. Another edition: Ivy Stories, No. 201. London: J. Long and Co., 1930.

Painted Butterflies. London: Herbert Jenkins, 1931.

Glimpses of Catholic Ireland in the 18th Century: Restoration of the Daughters of St Brigid, by Most Rev. Dr Delany. Dublin: Browne and Nolan, 1932.

Guide to St Patrick's Purgatory, Lough Derg. Dublin: Talbot Press, 1932.

Hollywood Madness. London: Herbert Jenkins, 1936.

Loreto, Navan: One Hundred Years of Catholic Progress, 1833-1933. Navan: The Meath Chronicle, 1937.

The Ownership of Station Island, Lough Derg. Dublin: Duffy, 1937.

Station Island, Lough Derg: with Historic Sketch of the Pilgrimage and Chronology. Dublin: 1950.

Mar Ivanios, 1882-1953: Archbishop of Trivandrum. Dublin: Clonmore and Reynolds, 1962.

GIBBONS, Maria
Born: 2 August 1874, in Bailieborough, Co. Cavan
Died: 1961, and buried at the Community Cemetery, Navan
Name in Religion: Mother Columba

Maria was one of four children. Her brother, Edward, became a priest in the Diocese of Meath. She had two sisters, Margaret (see listing), and Kitty. The Gibbons family lived in Collinstown.

Maria was educated at the Fore National School in Collinstown, and then trained as a primary school teacher at St Mary's College, Belfast. When she qualified Maria became principal teacher at Fanghalstown National School, in Castlepollan, where she remained until 1903. At that time there were two houses of the Loreto Convent in Navan. The earlier house, St Anne's, was founded in 1833, and served as the primary school, while the secondary school was St Michael's. Maria Gibbons became Sister Columba (Suir Colm), when she entered St Anne's Loreto Convent, Navan. Sister Columba assumed complete charge of the primary school after she was professed. She was a firm advocate of Irish culture, specifically of the language and dancing, both of which were emphasized in the convent, educational curriculum. Sister Columba later became Mother Columba.

Mother Columba was a close friend of Eamon de Valera who was an occasional visitor to the convent, and 'always the honoured guest' at convent functions such as the blessing of the school (Cooless, letter). Kitty Gibbons O'Doherty had earlier been one of Eamon de Valera's secret messengers.

Mother Columba is the author of a single piece, the ballad, 'Who Fears to Speak of Easter Week?' The piece was quite popular but apparently published only as a broadsheet. It is reported to have appeared in various anthologies and journals, but specific citations have not been uncovered.

Biographical Reference:
Letter from S. M. Ignatius Cooless, St Michael's, Loreto Convent, Navan. December 1993.

GIBLIN, Mary Josephine
Seven poems by Mary Giblin are in the *Irish Monthly*, January 1909 to October 1911.

Bibliography:
Stories of Nazareth House. London: Sands and Co., [1927].

Winds from the West; verses. Dublin: Duffy, 1938.

GIBSON, Charlotte
Born: 1827
Died: April 1889
Married name: Charlotte Gubbins

Charlotte Gibson began writing poetry at an early age, as a footnote to her collection states 'The Beacon' was written when Charlotte was twelve years of age. She married Blakeney Gough Gubbins, an Inspector of the Revenue Police in Sligo. The family lived in Sligo from the 1840s until the early 1870s, and their home was at Fort Louis, Rathbroughan, on the old Bundoran Road. Charlotte contributed poems to *Chamber's Journal* in the 1840s, and was a regular contributor to the Sligo *Chronicle* during her residence in the area. Her poem 'Farewell to Rathbroughan', published in September 1870 *Chronicle*, and announced the Gubbins family's departure from Sligo. In 1871 a subsequent piece in the same newspaper gives Rathmines as Charlotte's new address. The family returned to Sligo by 1880, again living at Rathbroughan, where they stayed until Charlotte's death in April 1889. She is buried in Sligo with her son who died in infancy. Her poem 'Composed During the Night of the 16th November, 1860', commemorates the death of her son, Louis John, at one year and nine months of age. Two of Charlotte's surviving children, a son and a daughter, later emigrated to New Zealand.

Biographical Reference:
Co. Sligo Library, local authors special collection.

Bibliography:
One Day's Journal, a Story of the Revenue Police, and Other Poems.
    Sligo: privately printed at the *Chronicle* Office, 1862.

GIFFORD, Grace
Married name: Mrs Joseph Mary Plunkett

Grace Gifford was born into a staunchly Protestant and Unionist family, yet Grace and four of her sisters became active in the Irish nationalist movement: Nellie Gifford Donnelly fought in the 1916 Rising, Muriel Gifford MacDonagh was married to Thomas MacDonagh (executed for his part in the Rising), Mrs Gifford Wilson served a gaol sentence for her 1916 participation and Sidney Gifford was an active nationalist writer, under the pseudonym of John

Brennan. Evidently all the Gifford sisters were attracted to nationalism at early ages, and the influence of their grand-uncle, Arthur Vandeleur of Co. Clare may have been critical in their decisions. Arthur Vandeleur had been a founder of the co-operative colony at Ralahine. Grace was better known as an artist than a poet, as she studied at the Slade School of Art, and two of the books she published contained caricatures related to the Abbey Theatre. One of her pieces, a religious banner, is reported to be in the Franciscan Church, Galway.

Joseph Mary Plunkett and Grace Gifford announced their engagement on 11 February 1916. Their banns were posted at the Rathmines Chapel, and the marriage was scheduled for 23 April 1916, but an error on the part of a messenger led to the wedding being delayed. The necessity for Plunkett to have a minor operation further delayed the ceremony. On Monday they were still unmarried when Plunkett left to participate in the 1916 Easter Rising. Following his arrest, Grace Gifford married Joseph Plunkett in Kilmainham Prison Chapel, around midnight on 4 May 1916. The newlyweds were allowed a ten-minute visit, in a room crowded with guards, prior to Plunkett's execution. Her wedding and her subsequent conversion to Catholicism completely alienated Grace from her parents, and she was refused admission to their home.

After her husband's execution Grace Plunkett remained active in nationalistic causes, becoming a member of the Provisional Republican Government of 1917, and publicly protesting against the British recruiting practices. Her article 'White Flags of 1916', in the March 1922 issue of *The Republic* presents a strong opposition to the London Treaty. In 1926 both Grace and one of her sisters were arrested and detained for three months.

The *Catholic Bulletin* published three of her poems during the period from December 1921 to December 1928.

Biographical Reference:
Fox, R. M. *Rebel Irishwomen*. Dublin: Talbot Press, 1935.

GILL, Alice
Six poems by Alice Gill appeared in the *Irish Monthly*, June 1912 to August 1922. She also published a short story in the same journal.

GILMORE, Mary Sarsfield
The December 1908 issue of the *Irish Monthly* contains one poem by Mary Sarsfield Gilmore.

GILTINAN, Nora S.
Nora S. Giltinan has a poem in the *Irish Monthly*, May 1909.

GLASGOW, Harriet
Married name: Harriet Acheson

Harriet was a daughter of Reverend Professor James Glasgow, D.D., a missionary in Gujarat, India. She was educated first at Walthamstow, and subsequently at Victoria College, Belfast. Her first poem appeared in *M'Comb's Almanack* for 1867, while she was still a student. Harriet was a staunch advocate of temperance, which features heavily in her work. She married John Acheson, Esq. and J. P., of Portadown, in 1879. Her poems appeared regularly in the Armagh papers, the *Presbyterian Churchman*, *Daybreak* and *Witness*.

Anthologized in: Paul.

Bibliography:
Willie's Quest. Religious Tract Society, [c.1894].

GODFREY, Mary S.
Married name: Mrs Henry Godfrey

Bibliography:
Sketches from the Bible, a Metrical Outline of the Holy Scriptures for the Use of Young Persons. Dublin: Ponsonby, 1852.
Melodies and Poems; Morn, Noon, and Eve. Second edition: Dublin: Ponsonby, 1854.
Darkness and Light, The Fallen Empire, and Other Poems. Dublin: Ponsonby, 1874.
Lyrics. Dublin: Ponsonby, 1876.

GOFF, Harriet Mary
Born: 1830
Married name: Harriet Mary Chester
Pseudonym: H.M.C.

Harriet Mary Goff married a Mr Chester in 1856, and was widowed twelve years later. Harriet was known as a translator of hymns from the German and Latin languages. Her work is found in *Hymnary* (1872).

GOODFELLOW, Kathleen
Born: 1891
Pseudonym: Michael Scot

The surname of Kathleen Goodfellow's pseudonym is infrequently spelled as Scott. Kathleen published reviews, essays and translations as Michael Scot, in addition to being a constant contributor to the *Dublin Magazine*, where over 35 of her poems appeared between August 1923 and June 1954.

GORE-BOOTH, Constance Georgina
Born: 4 February 1868, in London
Died: 15 July 1927, in Dublin, and buried at Glasnevin
Married name: Countess Constance Markievicz,
                sometimes Constance de Markievicz

Several full-length biographical studies of Constance Gore-Booth, later Countess Markievicz, are available and are listed in the biographical reference.

Constance Gore-Booth was the eldest child of Henry Gore-Booth, a wealthy, Protestant, Anglo-Irish landlord of Co. Sligo. Her mother was Georgina Hill Gore-Booth, originally from Tickhill Castle, Yorkshire, the daughter of Lord Scarborough. Although Constance was born at 7 Buckingham Gate, London, the family moved when she was an infant to Lissadell House in Co. Sligo. Constance had two brothers and two sisters. Her sister, Eva (see listing), was the one with whom Constance would form the closest bonds.

Constance was a noted beauty with an independent nature. She defied social conventions to study art in Paris where she met and later married Count Casimir Markievicz from Poland. Their only child, Maeve, was born a year after their marriage. Constance was heavily involved in nationalistic politics and the cause of women's rights, becoming a prominent figure in the development of the Republican Army and in organising the 1916 Rising. Constance was tried and sentenced to death for her part in the 1916 Rising, but her sentence was later commuted on the basis of her gender.

Constance was repeatedly imprisoned and, during the periods of her incarceration, she participated in hunger strikes. She was the first woman elected as M.P. to the British parliament, but was not allowed to take her seat as she was in prison at the time. When the independent parliament was established, the Dáil Éireann of 1919, she was the first Minister for Labour. Constance died of peritonitis in the public ward of a Dublin hospital in 1927. Her funeral procession attracted over 300,000 mourners, and Eamon de Valera delivered the eulogy over her grave in Glasnevin Cemetery.

Constance's skill as an artist is demonstrated by the illustrations she produced for her sister to decorate the pages of *The Death of Fionavar*, published by Eva in 1916.

The *Catholic Bulletin* has two poems, in the September 1921 and June 1922 issues. *The Capuchin Annual*, 1968, published one poem and a self-portrait.

Anthologized in: Fitzhenry.

Biographical References:
Coxhead, Elizabeth. *Daughters of Erin*. London: Secker and Warburg, 1965.
Fox, R. M. *Rebel Irishwomen*. Dublin: Talbot Press, 1935.
Haverty, Anne. *Constance Markievicz; Irish Revolutionary*. London: Pandora, 1988.
Marreco, Anne. *The Rebel Countess*. London: Wiedenfeld and Nicholson, 1967.
O'Faoláin, Sean. *Constance Markievicz or the Average Revolutionary*. London: Jonathan Cape, 1934.
Roper, Esther, ed. *Prison Letters of Countess Markievicz*. London: Longmans, Green and Co., 1934.
Van Voris, Jacqueline. *Constance Markievicz in the Cause of Ireland*. U.S.A.: University of Massachusetts Press, 1967.

Bibliography:
The Death of Fionavar. Text by Eva Selina Gore-Booth. Decorated by Constance Gore-Booth. London: Erskine MacDonald, 1916.
What Irish Republicans Stand For. Reprint from *Forward*. Glasgow: Civic Press, [1922].
Prison Letters of Countess Markievicz' — *Constance Gore-Booth*. London: Longmans, 1934.

GORE-BOOTH, Eva Selena
Born: 22 May 1879 at Lissadell House, Co. Sligo
Died: 30 June 1926 in Manchester

Eva Gore-Booth was a sister of Constance (see listing). As with Constance, a full-length biography of Eva is available, and is given in the biographical reference section of this listing.

Eva was a daughter of Sir Henry Gore-Booth, a wealthy Protestant, Anglo-Irish landlord, and she was raised at Lissadell House in Co.

Sligo. In 1894 she accompanied her father to the West Indies and America. The following year Eva accompanied her mother to Italy, and fell ill to what the doctors suspected was consumption. Eva was instructed to spend the winter in the warm, Mediterranean climate. She was following the advice of the doctors, staying at the Italian villa of George MacDonald the novelist, when she met Esther Roper in 1896. Esther was a suffrage union organiser from Manchester and had been ordered by her doctors to rest, with consumption as the tentative diagnosis. These two women formed a partnership and became life-long companions.

Eva moved to Manchester in 1897 and joined Esther in working for women's rights. Both women were advocates of women's rights, supporters of trades unions, and suffragettes. Eva continued to write poetry and developed an interest in writing about spiritual matters. Her exploration of mysticism included studying theosophy and Buddhism. Eventually she undertook a translation of the New Testament from fourth and fifth century Greek manuscripts in the British Museum. Eva died from cancer of the bowel in 1926.

Poems by Eva Gore-Booth were published in the *New Ireland Review*, *Irish Monthly*, *Catholic Bulletin*, and *Poetry Ireland*.

Anthologized in: AE, Cooke, Fitzhenry, Graves, Gregory, Hoagland, Kyle, Morton, Rhys, Tynan, and Walters.

Biographical References:
Booth, Constance G. *Prison Letters of Countess Markievicz. Also poems and articles relating to Easter Week by E. Gore-Booth*, 1934.
Lewis, Gifford. *Eva Gore-Booth and Esther Roper*. London: Pandora Press, 1988.
Roper, Esther. Biographical Sketch. *Collected Poems of Eva Gore-Booth*. London: Longmans, 1929.

Bibliography:
Poems. London: Longmans, 1898.
New Songs. London: Longmans, 1904.
Unseen Kings, a Play in Verse. London: Longmans, 1904.
The One and the Many. London: Longmans, 1904.
The Three Resurrections and the Triumph of Maeve; Poems and a Drama in Verse. London: Longmans, 1905.
The Egyptian Pillar and Other Poems. Tower Press Booklets, series 2, No. 3. Dublin: Maunsel and Co., 1907.
The Sorrowful Princess; a Drama in Verse. London: Longmans, 1907.
The Agate Lamp. London: Longmans, 1912.

The Perilous Light. Twentieth Century Poetry Series. London: Erskine MacDonald, 1915.

The Death of Fionavar; from The Triumph of Maeve. London: Erskine Macdonald, 1916.

Broken Glory. Dublin: Maunsel and Co., [1918].

The Sword of Justice. London: Headley Bros., 1918.

A Psychological and Poetic Approach to the Study of Christ in the Fourth Gospel. London: Longmans, 1923.

The Shepherd of Eternity. London: Longmans, 1925.

The House of Three Windows. London: Longmans, Green and Co., 1926.

The Inner Kingdom. London: Longmans, Green and Co., 1926.

The World's Pilgrim. London: Longmans, Green and Co., 1927.

Collected Poems of Eva Gore Booth. Esther Roper, ed. London: Longmans, 1929.

The Buried Life of Deirdre. London: Longmans, 1930.

Selected Poems of Eva Gore-Booth. Esther Roper, ed. London: Longmans, 1933.

GORMAN, Katharine Elizabeth
Born: 1899
Died: 1972
Married name: Mrs Wills

Anthologized in: *Birthday*, and MacIlwaine.

GOUK, Isabella J.
Born: Cork
Pseudonym: Isa Gouk

Isa Gouk began publishing circa 1884, in the *Christian Treasury*.

Anthologized in: Paul.

GRAHAM, Maud
Born: 13 March 1871, at Beechhill, Londonderry

Maud Graham's family moved to Paisley, Scotland, when she was about four years of age. She was educated in Scotland, and settled there, apparently opening a business in Paisley. Her poems appeared in a local anthology, Robert Brown's *Paisley Poets*.

Bibliography:
A Bitter Harvest. True Love Series. London: William Stevens, [1935].
Anybody's Darling; a Long Novel. True Love Series. London: William Stevens, [1936].
Dancing Mad. True Love Series. London: William Stevens, [1936].
She Wanted to be a Lady. True Love Series. London: William Stevens, [1936].
The Test of Love. True Love Series. London: William Stevens, [1936].

GRAHAM, Muriel Elsie
The February 1917 and April 1918 issues of the *Irish Monthly* contain poetry by Muriel Elsie Graham.

Bibliography:
A Mere Song. Vigo Cabinet Series, No. 94. 1900.
Vibrations. London: Erskine MacDonald, 1918.
Collected Poems. London: Williams and Norgate, 1930.

GRAVES, Clara
Born: 1808, in Dublin
Died: 1871
Married name: Clara Von Ranke

Clara was a sister to the Bishop of Limerick and married the German historian, Leopold Von Ranke. She is anthologized in Main's *Treasury of English Sonnets* (1880), and in Thomas Solly's, *Coronal of English Verse* (1880).

GRAVES, Clotilde Inez Augusta Mary
Born: 3 June 1864, in Buttevant, Co. Cork
Died: 1932
Pseudonym: Richard Dehan

Clotilde Graves was the daughter of an Irish clergyman. She studied art in Bloomsbury early in her life, and later worked as a journalist in London. She was a successful playwright, with about sixteen plays produced in New York and London. Clotilde was a frequent contributor to *Judy* and other London comic papers.

Bibliography:
The Belle of Rock Harbour; a Tale. London: *Judy* Office, [1887].
The Pirate's Hand; a Romance of Heredity. London: *Judy* Office, [1889].
Nitocris, a Play in Verse. 1887. Performed at Drury Lane in 1887.

Dragon's Teeth. London: Dalziel Bros., 1891. Another edition: London: Holden and Hardingham, [1916].

Maids in a Market Garden. London: W. H. Allen and Co., 1894. Another edition: Holden and Hardingham, [1914].

Seven Xmas Eves; Being the Romance of a Social Evolution. London: Hutchinson and Co., [1894]. Clotilde is one of seven contributors.

A Well-Meaning Woman. London: Hutchinson and Co., 1896.

The Lovers Battle; a Heroical Comedy in Rhyme; Founded upon Alexander Pope's 'Rape of the Lock'. London: Grant Richards, 1902.

A Mother of Three; an Original Farce in Three Acts. T. H. Lacy's Acting Edition of Plays, [1909].

The Dop Doctor. London: William Heinemann, 1911. Another edition: 1913.

Between Two Thieves. London: William Heinemann, 1912.

The Headquarter Recruit. London: William Heinemann, 1913.

The Cost of Wings. London: William Heinemann, 1914.

The Man of Iron. London: William Heinemann, 1915. Another edition: Paris: Thomas Nelson and Sons, [1916].

Off Sandy Hook. London: William Heinemann, 1915.

Earth to Earth. London: William Heinemann, 1916.

Gilded Vanity. London: William Heinemann, 1916.

Under the Hermes. London: William Heinemann, 1917.

That Which Hath Wings. London: William Heinemann, 1918.

A Sailor's Home. London: William Heinemann, 1919.

The Eve of Pasqua. London: William Heinemann, 1920.

The Villa of the Peacock. London: Heinemann, 1921.

The Just Steward. London: William Heinemann, 1922.

The Pipers of the Market-Place. London: Thornton, Butterworth, 1924.

The General's Past. London: The Stage Play Publishing Bureau, 1925.

The Sower of the Wind. London: Thornton, Butterworth, 1927.

The Lovers of the Market-Place. London: Thornton, Butterworth, 1928.

Shallow Seas. London: Thornton, Butterworth, 1930.

The Man with the Mask. London: Thornton, Butterworth, 1931.

Dead Pearls. London: John Long, 1932.

The Third Graft. London: John Long, 1933.

The Lovers' Battle. London: Richards, n.d.

GREEN, Miss
Born: Belfast

Miss Green was one of *The Nation* poets and lived in Dundee.

GREER, Sarah D.
Married name: Mrs John Greer

Sarah was a Quaker woman who became the wife of John R. Greer.

Bibliography:
The Chained Bible, and Other Poems. Dublin: privately printed, 1857.

GRUBB, Dorothea
Bibliography:
Gerald Fitzgerald, a Tale of the 17th Century, in Four Cantos. Waterford:
  privately printed, 1845.

GUINNESS, Mrs J. G.
Bibliography:
Sacred Portraiture and Illustration, and Other Poems. Dublin: privately
  printed, 1834.

GUINNESS, Jane Lucretia
Bibliography:
*Sketches of Nature; Comprising Views of Zoology, Botany, and Geology,
  Illustrated by Original Poetry.* London: privately printed, 1843.

GYLES, Althea
Born: Born: 1868, in Kilmurry, Co. Waterford
Died: January 1949, in London
Pseudonym: John Meade

Althea Gyles was the daughter of George Gyles and Alithea Emma
Grey, a distinguished Anglo-Irish family of Co. Waterford. Her
mother was the daughter of Reverend Edward Grey, Bishop of
Hereford, and related to the English aristocracy through the Greys of
Northumberland. Althea's paternal ancestors had settled in the
Youghal area of Co. Waterford in the mid-seventeenth century,
having originally come from Minehead, Somerset. In *Autobiographies*,
William Butler Yeats states that Althea was 'born into a country
family, who were so haughty that their neighbours called them the
Royal Family' (237). Yeats asserts that Althea had left home after a
quarrel with 'a mad father', to study art. Yeat's assertion belies the
fact that when Althea was twenty-one years old the Gyles family
accompanied her to Dublin as she began her studies at an art school
near Stephen's Green.
  Yeats was correct in his assessment of her career ambitions, for

Althea wanted to be an artist and poet who would be independent of family assistance. Yeats recalled one incident that illustrates Althea's adjustment from privileged daughter to struggling art student: 'For some weeks she had paid half-a-crown a week to some poor woman to see her to the art schools, for she considered it wrong for a woman to show herself in public places unattended; but of late she had been unable to afford the school fees'. (*Autobiographies* 237).

Althea had associated with the Theosophists and later became a member of the Golden Dawn. She was considered a disciple of AE [George William Russell] during the early stages of her artistic and poetic development. Althea had moved to London by early 1892, resuming her studies first at Pedders and then at the Slade School. She became a favoured book designer for William Butler Yeats and the list of her artistic contributions to his poetry volumes is substantial. Althea also provided book designs for Oscar Wilde and Matthew Russell.

A brief, one-year affair with Leonard Smithers, 1899 to 1900, contributed to the end of Althea's affiliation with Yeats. Ian Fletcher describes Smithers as a 'publisher of erotica and collector of first editions of women' (62). Yeats certainly did not consider him to be a socially acceptable gentleman and banned Smithers from his house. The end of Althea's romance was followed by a short period of inspired work, then her health failed and she began a gradual slide into poverty and illness. She was living in the Hampstead Road area in 1900.

In 1904, Arthur Symons reported her to be living in deplorable conditions. Symons was then acting somewhat as a literary agent for Althea, and other friernds who tried to assist Althea during this period included: Lady Colin Campbell, Clifford Bax, Eleanor Farjeon, and Cecil French. It was Cecil French who is reported to have said of Althea, 'a noble difficult being who invariably became the despair of those who had helped her' (Fletcher 77). Althea seems to have possessed an excess of artistic talent, hampered by a lack of focus.

About 1910 she was at Folkestone, and living in a small cottage near the harbour. She then moved on to Cornwall, where she left unfinished a church fresco. She may have briefly returned to Ireland, living with an aunt, before removing back to London. Despite repeated attempts by her family to provide assistance, she lived independently and in poverty. Her income in the later part of her life appears to have come from casting horoscopes. Althea died in a nursing home near the Crystal Palace in 1949.

The character Ariadne Berden, in Faith Compton Mackenzie's novel, *Tatting* (London: 1957) is based on Althea Gyles.

Althea Gyles contributed to a variety of journals: *Pall Mall Magazine, Saturday Review, Candid Friend, Kensington, Venture, Academy, Orpheus,* and *Vineyard.*

Anthologized in: Brooke/Rolleston (with an introduction to her work written by William Butler Yeats).

Biographical Reference:
Fletcher, Ian. 'W. B. Yeats and Althea Gyles'. *Yeats Studies* 1 (Bealtaine 1971): 42-79.

Bibliography:
Dew-Time. Privately printed, 1894.
Six Carols. Privately printed for the Order of the Holy Mount, c.1910.

H

HALVEY, Margaret
Born: 20 March 1859, at Kilaffan, Queen's County

Margaret edmigrated to New York in 1876, at age seventeen. She had begun writing at age seven and did publish some of her early verses in the *Carlow Poast* prior to leaving for America.

HAMILTON, Ann
Bibliography:
Descriptive Views of the Rose of Sharon. Dublin: 1837.
Ezra, a Little Narrative of Jewish Faith and Trial. Dublin: 1840.

HAMILTON, Anna Elizabeth
Born: 25 November 1843, in Dublin
Died: 26December 1875, Castle Hamilton, Killeshandra, Co. Cavan
Pseudonym: A. E. H.

Anthologized in: MacIlwaine.

Bibliography:
Ecce Agnus Dei — Emblems and Thoughts of Christ. London: 1872.

Dies Panis — Thoughts on the Sunday Lessons of the Year. Dublin: 1874.
He Giveth Songs . . . Religious Lyrics, by A. E. H., and Others. 1885.
   Published posthumously.

HAMILTON, Catherine Jane
Born: circa 1840
Died: 1935

According to the *Irish Book Lover*, Miss C. J. Hamilton had 'published a volume of verse recently', but further references to this volume have proven elusive and it may not have existed (Vol. 23; 83). Catherine Hamilton was a women's biographer and early feminist literary critic.

Bibliography:
Marriage Bonds; or, Christian Hazell's Married Life. London: Ward, Lock, [1878].
The Flynns of Flynnville. London: Ward, Lock, 1879.
True to the Core; a Romance of '98. 2 vols. London: F. V. White, 1884.
Dr Belton's Daughters. London: Ward, Lock, 1890.
Women Writers; Their Works and Ways. London: Ward, Lock, [1892].
Notable Irishwomen. Dublin: Sealy, Bryers and Walker, [1904].
The Luck of the Kavanaghs. London: Sealy, Bryers, 1910.
A Flash of Youth.

HAMILTON, Elizabeth Mary
Born: 4 April 1807, in Dublin
Died: 14 May 1851
Pseudonym: E. M. H., and Eliza Mary Hamilton

Eliza was a sister of Sir William Rowan Hamilton, the multi-talented scholar. O'Donoghue writes that 'she was highly esteemed by Wordsworth' (181). She was a constant contributor to *Dublin University Magazine*, with over seventeen poems published between November 1833 and December 1846. Additional poems by Elizabeth Hamilton appeared posthumously in *Dublin University Magazine*, June 1851.

Bibliography:
Poems. Dublin: Hodges and Smith, 1838.

HAMILTON, Mary Charlotte
Pseudonym: Etumos

Bibliography:
Poems, National and Other. Dublin: M'Glashan and Gill: 1874.

HANRAHAN, Nora
Her first name is sometimes spelled as Norah.

The *Catholic Bulletin* published seven of her poems, December 1930 to December 1939.

HARKNESS, Florence Law
One poem by Florence Law Harkness was published in the *Dublin University Review*, June 1887 issue.

HARLEY, Margaret
The *Catholic Bulletin* published eight of Margaret Harley's poems, July 1912 to December 1919.

HARNETT, Penelope Mary
Pseudonym: P. M. H., P. M. and D. L.

Penelope Hartnett lived at Newcastle West, Co. Limerick, for most of her life. She was a frequent contributor to *The Nation* and *Weekly News*. Her poems appear in the January 1874 and September 1874 issues of the *Irish Monthly*.

Anthologized in: *Emerald Gems*.

HARVEY, Hannah L.
Born: 1854, near Waterford

Hannah Harvey was a Quaker who later resigned her membership of the Society of Friends to pursue her strong nationalist political beliefs.

Anthologized in: Armitage.

HEALY, Monica
Born: Dublin
Died: 3 October 1876, and buried in Glasnevin Cemetery

Monica was the sister of Reverend James Healy, a man of great wit whose grave she shares in Glasnevin.

Bibliography:
Legends of the Saints; in Verse. Dublin: James Duffy, 1869. Published
    anonymously.

HERBERT, Jane Emily
Died: circa 1886

Jane was the sister of George Herbert, a Dublin publisher.

Anthologized in: Lover.

Bibliography:
Poetical Recollections of Irish History. Dublin: 1842.
*The Bride of Imael, or Irish Love and Saxon Beauty, a Poem of the Time of
    Richard II*. Dublin: 1847. Another edition: 1853.
Iona's Dream, and Other Poems. London: Pickering, 1853.
A Short History of Ireland. 1886.

HICKEY, Emily Henrietta
Born: 12 April 1845, at Macmine Castle, near Enniscorthy,
        Co. Wexford
Died: 19 September 1924

Emily was the daughter of Reverend J. S. Hickey, of Goresbridge, Co.
Carlow. Her mother, Miss Stewart of Stewart Lodge in Co. Carlow
was a descendant of the Stuart royal family. Her grandfather was
Reverend William Hickey, a noted writer of 'popular agricultural
works', under the pseudonym of Martin Doyle. Emily grew up in the
village of Goresbridge, Co. Carlow, where her father was rector. Her
mother planned a visit at Macmine to ensure that Emily's birth occurred in the ancestral castle of her maternal family. According to Enid
Dinnis, being born at Macmine was 'a fact which never failed to cause
her [Emily] satisfaction, and which fits in with the sequence of lordly
events in the life of one who, if she exaggerated the importance of a
noble lineage, in a corresponding degree, exaggerated, if such could
be, the importance of being noble' (2). Emily's mother apparently
passed on to her daughter an extreme sense of social class-conscious-
ness and excessive pride in the family genealogy. The Hickey family
was Protestant.

When Emily was thirteen she went to boarding school where her
aptitude for writing poetry began to be developed. Lord Alfred
Tennyson and Elizabeth Barret Browning were her early influences.
She memorized Sir Walter Scott but was not allowed to read Shakes-

peare, whose work was 'marred by Elizabethan coarseness' in her
father's opinion (Dinnin 17). Her first poem, 'Told in the Firelight',
appeared in *Cornhill Magazine* before she was twenty-one years old.
The Irish Book Lover reported in 1912 that she had taken First Class
Honours at Cambridge (*IBL* 4:214). Emily Hickey lived the majority of
her life in England, where she was a lecturer in English literature at
the London Collegiate School.

At one point in her life a physical breakdown demanded rest and
she travelled in France, Germany and Switzerland while regaining
her health. She later returned to England where she was received into
the Catholic Church on 22 July 1901, and her conversion to Catholicism heavily influenced her later poetry. Katharine Tynan, in *The
Cabinet of Irish Literature*, states that Emily regretted three of her early
poetry collections 'for a conscientious reason', and notes that
Hickey's later poetry involves 'a great advance on those earlier pieces,
which were full of the religion of humanity' (Vol. IV: 216). Although
her family did not understand her conversion, they graciously
accepted her decision. With Dr Furnivall, Emily Hickey founded the
Browning Society in 1881.

Anthologized in: *Cabinet* IV, Cooke, Graves' *Songs*, Gregory,
Hoagland, Mrs Sharp, and Walsh.

Biographical References:
Dinnis, Enid. *Emily Hickey; Poet, Essayist, Pilgrim — A Memoir.*
London: Harding and More, 1927.
Furlong, Alice. 'Emily Hickey'. *Irish Monthly* 53 (January 1925): 16-20.
Obituary. *Irish Book Lover* 14 (Nov.-Dc. 1924): 138.

Bibliography:
A Sculptor, and Other Poems. London: Kegan Paul and Co., 1881.
Browning's Strafford: Edited and Annotated. London: G. Bell, 1884.
Verse-Translations, and Other Poems. London: 1891.
Michael Villiers, Idealist, and Other Poems. London: Smith, Elder,
1891.
Poems. London: E. Mathews, 1896.
Ancilla Domini, Thoughts in Verse on the Life of The Blessed Virgin Mary.
London: Printed by the author, [1898].
Verse-Tales, Lyrics and Translations. Liverpool: W. and J. Arnold, 1899.
St Patrick's Breastplate; a Metrical Translation. [1901].
Our Lady of May. London: Catholic Truth Society, 1902.
Havelock the Dane. London: Catholic Truth Society, 1902.
Thoughts for Creedless Women. London: Catholic Truth Society, [1906].

A Parable of a Pilgrim: Selections from Walter Hylton. 1907.

Lois. London: Burns, Oates and Washbourne, 1908.

Our Catholic Heritage in English Literature. London: Sands and Co., 1910.

Later Poems. London: Grant Richards, 1913.

The Bishop and the Three Poor Men. London: Catholic Truth Society, 1922.

Devotional Poems. London: Elliot Stock, 1922.

Jesukin, and Other Christmastide Poems. London: Burns, Oates and Co., 1924.

* These volumes were later retracted by Hickey, following her religious conversion to Catholicism.

HIGGINSON, Agnes Nesta Shakespeare
Born: 1863
Died: 1955
Married name: Mrs Skrine
Pseudonym: Moira O'Neill

Agnes Higginson was married to Walter Clermont Skrine and she lived for some years in Canada, before returning to Rockport, Cushendall, Co. Antrim. She was the mother of Mary Nesta Skrine, later Mrs Robert Keane, who wrote under the pseudonym of M. J. Farrell. Moira O'Neill contributed to *Blackwood's Magazine*.

Anthologized in: Brooke/Rolleston, Brown, Cooke, Graves, Gregory, Hoagland, Lynd, Rhys, Robinson, Tynan, Walters and Welsh.

Bibliography:
An Easter Vacation. London: Lawrence and Bullen, 1893. Another edition: New York: E. P. Dutton, 1894.

The Elf-Errant. London: Lawrence and Bullen, 1893. Another edition: New York: E. P. Dutton, 1894. Another, illustrated edition: London: Lawrence and Bullen, 1895. Another edition: London: A. H. Bullen, 1902.

Songs of the Glens of Antrim. Edinburgh and London: W. Blackwood and Sons, 1900. Another edition: 1901.

More Songs of the Glens of Antrim. Edinburgh and London: W. Blackwood and Sons, 1921.

Songs and More Songs of the Glens of Antrim. (Combined edition). New York: Macmillan, 1922.

From Two Points of View. Edinburgh and London: W. Blackwood and Sons, 1924.

Collected Poems of Moira O'Neill. Edinburgh and London: W.
Blackwood and Sons, 1933. Another edition: Edinburgh:
Blackwood, 1934.

HILDEBRAND, Anna Louisa
Born: 5 August 1842, in Clifden, Co. Galway

MacIlwaine lists her as being from Castlerea in Co. Galway, but
Clifden is probably correct. She was a frequent contributor to *The
Lamp*, *Irish Fireside*, *North and South*, and to local papers in the west of
Ireland, particularly the *Mayo Examiner*.

Anthologized in: MacIlwaine.

Bibliography:
Western Lyrics. Dublin: McGlashan and Gill; London: Simpkin,
Marshall and Co.; Edinburgh: J. Menzies and Co., 1872.
Lays from the Land of the Gael. Belfast: M'Caw, Stevenson and Orr;
Linenhall Works, n.d. [1879].

HINE, Gertrude Elizabeth Heron

Born: 1877, in Belfast
Died: 1951
Pseudonym: Elizabeth Shane

Gertrude Elizabeth Heron Hine's surname is given as Hind occasionally. She was a resident of Carrickfergus, Co. Antrim and first
violinist for the Belfast Philharmonic Orchestra.

Bibliography:
Piper's Tunes. London: Selwyn & Blount, [c.1920]. Another edition:
[1927].
Tales of the Donegal Coast and Islands. London: Selwyn and Blount,
1921.
By Bog and Sea in Donegal. London: Selwyn and Blount, 1923. Other
editions: 1925 and 1929.
*Collected Poems I: Tales of the Donegal Coast and Islands, and By Bog and
Sea in Donegal.* Dundalk: W. Tempest; Dundalgan Press, 1945.
Collected Poems II: Piper's Tunes and Later Poems. Dundalk: W.
Tempest; Dundalgan Press, 1945.
Later Poems.

HOLMES, Mrs Dalkeith
Died: circa 1862

She was the wife of Capt. Dalkeith Holmes and became the mother of Mademoiselle Augusta Holmes, a noted composer. Mrs Holmes contributed a prose piece to the *Dublin University Magazine* in 1843.

Bibliography:
The Law of Rouen, a Dramatic Tale in Three Acts and in Verse. Dublin: privately printed, 1837.
A Ride on Horseback to Florence; by a Lady. 1842.

HOLMES, Elizabeth Emmet Lenox
Born: 1800
Married name: Elizabeth Emmet Lenox Conyngham

She was the daughter of Robert Holmes, a lawyer and orator. His wife, Mary Anne Emmet, was the sister of Robert and Thomas Addis Emmet of United Irishmen notoriety. Elizabeth married George Lenox Conyngham, who was employed by the War Office.

Bibliography:
Hella, and Other Poems. London: Edward Churton, 1836.
Horae Poeticae, Lyrical and Other Poems. London: Longman, Brown, Green, Longmans and Roberts, 1859.
Eiler and Helvig, a Danish Legend, in Verse. London: Chapman and Hall, 1863.
The Dream, and Other Poems. London: Edward Moxon, 1883.

HOPE, Constance
Constance Hope published several short stories and eleven poems in the *Irish Monthly*, September 1891 to June 1898.

HOPPER, Nora
Born: 2 January 1871
Died: 14 April 1906
Married name: Mrs W. H. Chesson

Nora Hopper was the daughter of an Irish army officer, and her mother was the former Miss Francis. Nora was born while her father was stationed in Exeter. She was educated at home by governesses, one of whom is reported to have been dismayed to find Nora's copy books were filled with poems and stories instead of the assigned lessons. Her first published poem appeared in the *Family Herald* in 1887. In 1901 she married W. H. Chesson, a noted writer. Nora wrote poetry, songs, stories, and one opera.

Nora Hopper was a cause of much concern for William Butler Yeats and Katharine Tynan, regarding their belief that she plagiarized from their work. Yeats appears to have been more generous about the similarities than Tynan, as evidenced by his letter to Katharine Tynan Hinkson dated 20 January [1895]: "You are certainly very badly plagiarized in 'The Lay Brother' which amazes me . . . I feel less inclined to be severe than you, for she seems to have great artistic fealing [sic], & very considerable imagination. Besides she has paid us 'the sincerest form of flattery'." (*Letters*, I, 425). In the same letter Yeats adds: "However there is no getting over the fact that she is an artist of very considerable distinction & artists are few in Irish literature . . . she can write & that, in a writer, is the main matter" (426).

Two of her poems are found in the *New Ireland Review*, the October 1897 and January 1898 issues. Another poem appeared in *The Celt*, September 1903 issue. She also wrote the lyrics, in English, for an Irish opera, 'Muirgheis; in three acts'. The Irish translation of 'Muirgheis' was done by Tadgh O'Donoghue, and the music by O'Brien Butler. 'Muirgheis' was published in *New Ireland Review*, September 1910. The March 1913 issue of the *Irish Book Lover*, in the gossip section, reported that Nora had written the lyrics for 'On Wicklow Hills', with the music composed by Isobel Quin.

Anthologized in: Brooke/Rolleston, *Cabinet* IV, Cooke, Graves, Rhys, Robinson, Sharp/Matthay, Tynan, Walters, and Yeats.

Bibliography:
Ballads in Prose. London: John Lane, 1894.
Under Quicken Boughs. London: John Lane, 1896.
Songs of the Morning. London: Grant Richards, 1900.
Aquamarines. London: Grant Richards, 1902.
Mildred and Her Mills, and Other Poems. London: Raphael Tuck and Sons, [1903].
Old Fairy Legends in New Colours; by T. E. Donnison, with Verses by N. Chesson. London: Raphael Tuck, 1903.
With Louis Wain to Fairyland. London: Raphael Tuck, 1904.
The Bell and the Arrow: An English Love Story. London: T. Werner Laurie, 1905.
Dirge for Aoine and Other Poems. London: Alston Rivers, 1906.
A Dead Girl to Her Lover and Other Poems. London: Alston Rivers, 1906.

Jack O'Lanthorn and Other Poems. London: Alston Rivers, 1906.
The Happy Maid and Other Poems. London: Alston Rivers, 1906.
The Waiting Widow and Other Poems. London: Alston Rivers, 1906.
Poems; Selected. 1908.
Father Felix's Chronicles. W. H. Chesson, ed. London: Unwin, 1907.
Children's Stories from Tennyson. [1914].

HOWARD, Catherine
Born: 23 August 1831
Died: 27 December 1882
Married name: Lady Catherine Petre
Pseudonym: C. P.

The *Irish Monthly* wrongly gives 1830 as the year of Catherine Howard's birth.

Lady Catherine Howard was a daughter of the fourth Earl of Wicklow. She married the Hon. Arthur Petre in July 1855. She was, by her own definition, "a convert from Anglicanism to Christianity" (O'Donoghue 205). Her collection, *Hymns and Verses*, reflects her religious change, and the first section of the volume was "written before conversion", while the second section was "written after conversion".

Catherine was a frequent contributor to Catholic magazines, especially *The Month*.

Bibliography:
The Chapel Bell and Other Poems. Dublin: 1854.
Sacred Verses. London: 1864.
Hymns and Verses. London: Burns and Oates, [1884].

HUDSON, Mary
O'Donoghue states that Mary Hudson was "a young Irish lady", when her volume was published (206).

Bibliography:
Churchyard Flowers. London: n.p., 1892.

HUGHES, Mary Jane Patricia
Born: 1834
Died: 12 October 1870, at Loreto Abbey, Rathfarnham, Dublin.
Name in Religion: Sister Mary Jane Patricia
Pseudonym: M. J. P. H.

Mary Jane Patricia Hughes was from Dublin, according to the Loreto Abbey records. She entered the Order on the 21st November 1855, and died there at age thirty-six.

Biographical References:
Blake, Sister Mary. Personal letter. 15 January 1994.

Bibliography:
Poems. Dublin: Browne and Nolan, 1871.

HULL, Eleanor Henrietta
Born: 1860
Died: 1935

Eleanor was born in Manchester to Professor Edward Hull from Co. Down. Professor Hull served as Director of the Geological Survey of Ireland from 1870 to 1890. Eleanor's grandfather was Reverend J. D. Hull, a poet of minor repute. The Hull family claimed the ability to trace their descent and their continuous residence in Co. Down, from the early part of the seventeenth century. The Hull family returned from England, where Eleanor was born, and took up residence in Dublin. Eleanor Hull lived in Dublin until she was about twenty years old. She was educated at Alexandra College, and became a Gaelic scholar, historian, and translator. Eleanor Hull was "always charming and looked more like a dainty piece of Dresden china than the learned editor of ancient Irish texts" (*Capuchin Annual* 1952: 478).

Kuno Meyer and Standish O'Grady were two of Eleanor's Irish Studies supervisors. The *Irish Book Lover*, in the July/August 1935 issue further calls Eleanor Hull "the intimate friend and favourite pupil of Standish Hayes O'Grady." Her article, 'A Personal Reminiscence', provides testimony to the impact of O'Grady on her life and career, as does her analytical article on O'Grady's work for *Studies*. Hull was the founder of the Irish Texts Society in 1899, and its secretary for almost thirty years. Eleanor received a D.Litt degree, and edited the *Irish Home Reading Magazine*, with Lionel Johnson, in 1894. Eleanor Hull died on the eve of her seventy-fifth birthday. She was a regular contributor to the *Irish Book Lover, Celtic Review, Literary World, Folk Lore Journal*, and *Studies*.

Anthologized in: *Cabinet* IV, Graves, Gregory, Hoagland, MacIlwaine, Morton, Rhys, Robinson, and Sharp/Matthay.

Biographical References:
Biographical Sketch, in 'Queries'. *Irish Book Lover* 2.12 (July 1911):
    194.
Obituary. *Irish Book Lover* 23.4 (July/August 1935): 82.

Bibliography:
The Cuchullin Saga. London: Alfred Nutt, 1889. Another edition:
    Grimms Library, 1898.
Pagan Ireland. Vol. 1 of the Epochs of Irish History. 1904.
Early Christian Ireland. Vol. 2 of the Epochs of Irish History, 1904.
A Text Book of Irish Literature. 2 vols. Dublin: M. H. Gill; and London:
    David Nutt, 1906. Another edition: 1908.
Cuchulainn: the Hound of Ulster. London: Harrap, 1909. Another
    edition: 1930.
The Poem Book of the Gael. London: Chatto and Windus, 1912.
The Northmen in Britain. London: G. G. Harrap and Co., 1913.
A History of Ireland and Her People to the Close of the Tudor Period.
    London: G. G. Harrap and Co., 1926.
Folklore of the British Isles. London: Methuen and Co., 1928.

HUME, Isobel
Married Name: Isobel Fisher

Her poems also appeared in the *Westminster Gazette.*

Anthologized in: Walters.

Bibliography:
The Pursuit and Other Poems. Dublin and London: Maunsel and Co.,
    1913.

HUMPHREYS, Cecil Frances
Born: 1818, Milltown House, Co. Tyrone
Died: 1895, in Derry.
Married name: Cecil Frances Alexander
Pseudonym: C.F.A. and X

Her name, Cecil, is sometimes misrepresented as Cecilia, although
she was generally called Fanny. She was the daughter of Major John
Humphreys, originally of Norfolk, who became a landowner in Co.
Tyrone and Co. Wicklow after serving in the Royal Marines. Her
mother was the former Elizabeth Reed. From his home, Miltown
House near Strabane. Major Humphreys was land-agent for exten-

sive holdings in Northern Ireland. Fanny developed a friendship during her childhood with Lady Harriet Howard, daughter of the Earl of Wicklow, when the Humphreys family was residing at Ballykean in Co. Wicklow. Their friendship led to a collaboration on a series of tracts, with Lady Howard being responsible for the prose sections, and Fanny writing the poetry. The tracts show that both women were influenced by the Oxford movement. Although the tracts were originally published separately, they were eventually compiled into a single volume in 1848. Their writing partnership ended when Lady Harriet died of consumption.

During a visit to her sister, Annie Humphreys Maguire, who was then living at Leamington, Fanny met Miss Hook and her brother. Dr Hook was vicar of Leeds when he met Fanny, but was later the Dean of Chichester. He edited Fanny's volume, *Verses for Holy Seasons*, and provided a 'sane and masculine influence', according to her husband's memoir (vii) She later developed her talents as a hymnist, and her hymns for children were especially popular.

In October 1850 she married Reverend William Alexander in the Strabane Church. Reverend Alexander was the rector of Termonamongan, diocese of Derry. He later became the Archbishop of Armagh and ultimately was elevated to Primate of Ireland. Cecil is described by her husband at the time of their marriage, as follows:

> . . . it is not an exaggeration of affection which says that she was a singularly attractive person. Her frame was lithe and active. Her face had no pretension whatever to regular beauty; but it possesed the sensitive susceptibility, the magic quickness of transition, the sacred indignation, the flash of humour, the pathetic sweetness, with which genius endows its chosen children (vii-ix).

It is noteworthy that most biographical accounts of Cecil either omit her birthdate, or erroneously report it as 1825. Her daughter reveals that Cecil was six years older than her husband, a source of great concern to herself and her husband's family. Out of deference to her feelings, and perhaps to avoid malicious gossip by interested parties, her birthdate was usually reported to be seven years later than it actually occurred.

After their marriage, the Alexanders lived at Derg Lodge in Termonamongan for five years and Cecil wrote many poems and hymns during this period. The family moved in 1855 to Upper Fahan, on Lough Swilly, where they remained for five years. From 1860 to 1867 they were in Strabane, with several extended trips to Archachon and Bagneres-de-Bigorre to improve the health of their two sons. In 1867 William was named Archbishop of Derry and Raphoe, and Fanny became acquainted during this period with Dean Stanley, Mr Lecky, and Matthew Arnold. She was a patron of the Derry Home for Fallen Women, and the District Nurses.

Anthologized in: *Birthday*, Brooke/Rolleston, Drury, MacIlwaine, Paul, and Taylor.

Biographical References:
Alexander, Eleanor. *Primate Alexander; Archbishop of Armagh.* London: Edward Arnold, 1914.
Alexander, William. Memoir. *Poems by Cecil Frances Alexander.* London: Macmillan, 1896.
Quotations from 'British Weekly'. *Irish Book Lover* 3 (December 1911): 85.
'Some Irish Centenaries: Cecil Frances Alexander'. *Irish Book Lover* 10 (Oct.-Dec. 1918): 35-6.
Wallace, Valerie. *Mrs. Alexander.* Dublin: Lilliput, 1995.

Bibliography:
Verses for Holy Seasons. 1846. Another edition: London: Bell and Daldy, 1858.
Hymns for Little Children. 1848. Fourth edition: 1850. Fifth edition: 1852. Further editions: 1857, 1862, 1864, 1867, 1878. (546,000 copies were printed by 1878). Sixty-second edition: 1884. Pictorial edition: London: Christian Knowledge Society, 1903.
The Lord of the Forest and His Vassals; an Allegory. 1848.
Moral Songs. 1849. Second edition: [c.1850]. Another edition: 1855. Another, illustrated by L. Masters: 1880. (Fourteen editions in total were estimated to have been published.)
Narrative Hymns for Village Schools. 1854.
Poems of Subjects in the Old Testament. 1854.
Hymns, Descriptive and Devotional. 1858. Another edition: J. Masters and Co., 1880.
The Legend of the Golden Prayers, and Other Poems. London: Bell and Daldy, 1859.
Easy Questions on the Life of Our Lord. London: Griffith and Farran, 1891.
Hymns for Children. London: Marcus Ward and Co., [1894].
Poems by Cecil Frances Alexander (C.F.A.) Edited with a preface and portrait, by William Alexander. London: Macmillan & Co., 1896.
Selected Poems from William and Cecil Frances Alexander. A. P. Graves,

ed. London: Society for Promoting Christian Knowledge, 1930.

HUNT, Emma Maria
Died: 21 September 1851, in Dublin
Married name: Emma Maria De Burgh

Emma married Major De Burgh of the 93rd Regiment. She was living at Newbridge, Co. Kildare, when her son was born in 1845. That son, Hubert John De Burgh, also became a writer. Her sister edited Emma's posthumously published volume.

Bibliography:
The Voice of Many Waters, a Selection from the Compositions, in Prose and Verse, of the Late Emma Maria De Burgh. Caroline Hunt, ed. London: privately printed, 1858.

I

IRWIN, Emma Margaret
Born: 4 July 1856, at Manor Cunningham, Co. Donegal
Died: 1904
Married name: Emma Margaret Samuels

Emma was a daughter of Reverend James Irwin. She married A. W. Samuels, Q.C., in 1881. She was educated at Alexandra College. Emma was a frequent contributor to *Fortnightly Review*.

IRWIN, Mary Jane
Born: 27 January 1845, in Clonakilty, Co. Cork
Died: 17 August 1916 in New York
Married name: Mrs Jeremiah O'Donovan Rossa
Pseudonyms: M. J. I., Cliodhna, and Cliathna

Mary Jane Irwin was reared in Co. Cork, and was convent educated. She became the third wife of Jeremiah O'Donovan Rossa, meeting her future husband when she was barely eighteen and when O'Donovan Rossa was thirty-four years of age. They married despite the difficulties involved in obtaining approval from the Church authorities, due to O'Donovan Rossa's refusal to give up his Fenian activities. Mary Jane immediately assumed responsibility for the six children from her husband's previous two marriages, and twelve more children resulted from their union. O'Donovan Rossa was imprisoned six months after their wedding, and their first child was born while he was still serving a gaol sentence.

Following his release, the entire family emigrated to America where they lived until O'Donovan Rossa's death in 1915. His body was returned to Ireland for burial, and Mary Jane also returned to Ireland to attend the funeral, before returning to New York. She died in New York the following year.

Mary Jane Irwin contributed to several American newspapers following the family's emigration. In Ireland, the October 1916 issue of the *Catholic Bulletin* contains her poetry. Her only volume of poems, *Irish Lyrical Poems*, was published in New York in 1868.

Anthologized in: Sparling.

Biographical Reference:
O'Kelly, Seamus G. *Sweethearts of the Irish Rebels*. Dublin: A1 Books, 1968.

J

JAMES, Sophie A. M.
Sophie was living at Rockmount House, Dundrum, Co. Dublin when both her volumes were written.

Bibliography:
Holly Berries; Poems. Dublin: Robert C. Gerrard, 1879.
God's Answer and Other Poems. Dublin: Robert C. Gerrard, (1879).

JOHNSTON, Anna Isabel
Born: 1866 in Ballymena, Co. Antrim
Died: 2 April 1902, and buried at Frosses, Co. Donegal
Married name: Mrs Seumas MacManus

Pseudonyms: Ethna Carbery, and Ethna

Her name is incorrectly listed once in the *Irish Monthly* as Anna T. Johnston. Anna was one of two daughters born to Robert Johnston, a Belfast Fenian. Her mother was originally from Donegal. Anna, her brother, and a sister named Maggie lived with her parents in the Donegall Park area of Belfast. Anna was a cousin of the poet Joseph Campbell, and a close friend of Katharine Tynan (see listing). Anna freqeuently stayed with the Tynan family during her visits to the Dublin area.

In collaboration with another close friend, Alice Milligan (see listing), Anna edited *The Northern Patriot* from 1894 to 1895. Anna and Alice next founded, edited, and wrote *The Shan Van Vocht*, a Belfast periodical, from 1896 to 1899. In 1901 she married Seumus MacManus, a schoolmaster from the Donegal mountains who had been a frequent contributor to *The Shan Van Vocht*. After their marriage the couple moved to Revelinn, a home on the Lough Eske estuary in Donegal. The marriage was happy but extremely brief, as Anna lived only about one year after the wedding. Following her death Alice Milligan wrote the poem 'The House of the Apple Trees', to commemorate both the poet and her home.

Anna Johnston was a contributor to *United Irishmen*, and a variety of American journals.

Anthologized in: Brown, Cooke, Graves, Hoagland, Rhys, Walsh, and Welsh.

Biographical Reference:
MacManus, Seumas. Memoir. *The Four Winds of Éirinn*. 1918 edition.

Bibliography:
The Four Winds of Éirinn. Dublin: 1902. Other editions: Dublin: M. H. Gill and Son, 1902 (seventh edition, with preface by Seumas MacManus, and portrait). Dublin: M. H. Gill and Son, 1905 (enlarged edition). Dublin: M. H. Gill and Son; Jas. Duffy and Co., 1906. (Ten thousand, new enlarged edition, with portrait and preface by Seumas MacManus). New edition, with memoir and additional poems: 1918. Another edition: 1927. Dublin: M. H. Gill and Son, 1934. Illustrated edition, with the preface from the first edition and a memoir written for the 1918 edition by Seumas MacManus. Dublin: M. H. Gill, n.d. Another edition, entitled: *Songs from The Four Winds of Éirinn*. Music by Charlotte Milligan Fox and pictures by Seaghan Mac Cathmhaoil.

The Passionate Hearts. Dublin: M. H. Gill and Son; and London: Isbister and Co., 1903.

In the Celtic Past. Dublin: M. H. Gill and Son, 1904. Another edition: Dublin and Cork: Educational Co. of Ireland, [1928]. Reissued: Dublin and Cork: Talbot Press, [1929].

We Sang for Ireland; Poems of Ethna Carbery, Seumas MacManus, Alice Milligan. Dublin: Gill, 1950.

JOHNSTONE, Wilhelmina E.
Born: Dalkey, Co. Dublin

Wilhelmina was the only daughter of Eustace M. Johnstone, B.L. She was educated at home, where her reading schedule was systematic: "Having read the works of an author her parents were in the habit of testing her knowledge of what she had gone over, marking out the imperfectly studied portions to be read over again" (Paul 112). In addition to the rigorous home education, Wilhelmina attended Alexandra College, Dublin. Her favourite poets were Shelley, Keats, and Shakespeare. Her poetry appeared in the *Weekly Irish Times*, *The Muses*, and *Poetry and Prose*.

Anthologized in: Paul.

K

KAVANAGH, Ethna
The *British Museum General Catalogue of Books Before 1956*, lists Ethna Kavanagh as a pseudonym of Sara Spain. It is the only reference to Ethna Kavanagh being a pseudonym.

Ethna Kavanagh was as frequent contributor to the *Irish Monthly*, with eleven poems published between December 1918 and January 1927. The September 1918 and June 1919 issues of *Studies* also contain her poetry.

Bibliography:
The Priest of Isis, and Other Poems. London: John Long, 1920.
The Sonnets of the Lady in the Garden. London: Heath Cranton, [1920].

The Fool's Paradise, and Other Poems. London: A. H. Stockwell, [1924].

KAVANAGH, Rose
Born: 24 June 1859, at Killadroy, Co. Tyrone
Died: 26 February 1891, in Co. Tyrone
Pseudonyms: Rose, Ruby and Uncle Remus

Rose Kavanagh was born on the Clougher side of the Avonban River, in Killadroy, Co. Tyrone. When she was eleven the family moved to the other side of the river, near Augher, beside the Blackwater. She was educated initially at home, then sent to the Loreto Convent, Omagh, before deciding to pursue a career as an artist. At the age of twenty she went to study at the Metropolitan School of Art in Dublin. Rose began writing verses about this time, and eventually decided to forsake art for poetry. Rose Kavanagh was a staunch friend of the author and rebel, Charles Kickham, tending him through physical decline, the loss of his hearing and sight, and through the mental depression which ended with his death. It has been suggested that Kickham fell in love with Rose, who did not reciprocate his feelings beyond friendship. Her poem in memorial to Kickham supports the view that Rose's feelings did not extend beyond a strong friendship.

She was considered one of the most promising young women poets of her generation, but this promise was cut short when she died of consumption at the age of thirty-two. Until shortly before her death, she wrote a children's section for *The Irish Fireside,* and subsequently for the Dublin *Weekly Freeman,* under the pseudonym of Uncle Remus.

Rose was a close friend of Katharine Tynan, Dora Sigerson, Anna Johnston and Alice Milligan (see listings). Her death was the occasion of commemorative poetry by these women and others. Ellen O'Leary (see listing) was among the poets who allude to Rose in their poetry. Rose seems to have epitomised the tragedy of a promising talent, cut short by an early death. William Butler Yeats wrote an obituary of Rose which was published in the *Boston Pilot* of 11 April, 1891.

Her single volume of work was published posthumously, and edited by Reverend Matthew Russell of the *Irish Monthly.* Rose was a frequent contributor to several publications: *Irish Monthly, Dublin University Review, Nation, Shamrock, Young Ireland,* and various publications in America.

Anthologized in: Brooke/Rolleston, Cooke, Graves, Sparling, and
    Yeats.

Biographical References:
Russell, Matthew. 'Herself'. Preface. *Rose Kavanagh and Her Verses.*
  Dublin and Waterford: M. H. Gill, 1909.
Russell, Matthew. 'Rose Kavanagh; Some Scraps from Her Life and
  Letters'. *Irish Monthly* 19 (October to November 1891): 512-21, and
  601-7.

Bibliography:
Rose Kavanagh and Her Verses. Reverend Matthew Russell, ed. Dublin
  and Waterford: M. H. Gill, 1909.

KEARY, Annie
Born: 3 March 1825
Died: 3 March 1879, in England

Annie Keary was the daughter of William Keary, the only son of an Irish family from the Tuam area of Co. Galway. Her mother was Lucy Plumer, the fifth daughter of Hall Plumer, Esq., of Bilton Hall near Wetherby in Yorkshire, and Annie was born at Bilton Hall. Annie was the sister of Maud and Elizabeth Keary (see listing for Elizabeth). Her brother, Charles F. Keary, also became a writer. A total of six children were born to the Kearys, with Annie being the youngest child. The Kearys were Irish Protestants, although Father Matthew Russell says Annie later developed 'Catholic tendencies' (201).

Annie's parents were married in England where her father was in the army. He lost his property in Ireland shortly thereafter, so he left the Army to become a clergyman, and later became curate of Sculcoats, a part of Hull. Annie remained in England for the rest of her life, dying on her fifty-fourth birthday as she was trying to finish her novel, *A Doubting Heart.*

Annie Keary was predominantly a novelist, although she wrote one story for children, *A York and Lancaster Rose.* In a lecture given in Cork, John O'Leary rated her novel, *Castle Daly,* as one of the best of the 'so-called Irish novels' of the time. The volume of poems she wrote was co-authored with her two sisters, Elizabeth and Maud, and contains verses suitable for children. *Enchanted Tulips* was published by her sisters following Annie's death.

Biographical References:
Keary, Elizabeth. Preface. *Letters of Annie Keary.* London: Christian
  Knowledge Society, [1883].
Keary, Elizabeth. *Memoir of Annie Keary.* London: Macmillan and Co.,
  1882.

Russell, Matthew. 'Nutshell Biograms, No. 12; Annie Keary'. *Irish Monthly* 14 (1886): 201.

Bibliography:
Mia and Charlie. 1856.
The Heroes of Asgard. With E. Keary. 1857. Another edition, entitled *Christmas Week and Its Stories; or, the Heroes of Asgard:* [1860]. Another edition, illustrated: London: 1871. Another edition, adapted for use of schools, with new introduction and glossaries: 1905. Another edition, adapted and arranged by Herbert Hayens: John Drinkwater Series for Schools. London and Glasgow: [1924]. Another edition, new illustrations: London: Macmillan and Co., 1930.
The Rival Kings; or, Overbearing. 1857.
Sidney Grey; A Tale of School Life. 1857. Another edition, entitled *Sidney Grey; or, a Year from Home:* London: Warne and Co., [1883].
Through the Shadows. 1859.
Blind Man's Holiday; or, Short Tales for the Nursery. [1859]. Other editions: 1860, and [1883].
Early Egyptian History for the Young. With E. Keary. 1861.
Janet's Home. 1863.
Little Wanderling and Other Fairy Tales. Books for the Young Series. London: 1865.
Clemency Franklyn. 1866.
Oldbury. 3 vols. London: 1869. Another edition: London: Macmillan and Co., 1891.
The Nations Around (Palestine). Sunday Library for Household Reading Series. London: 1870.
Castle Daly; the Story of an Irish Home Thirty Years Ago. London: R. Clay, Sons, and Taylor, [1875]. Reprint: London: Macmillan, 1899. Philadelphia: Porter, 1889. Another, French edition: Paris, 1889.
A York and Lancaster Rose. London: 1876.
A Doubting Heart. 3 vols. London: Macmillan, 1879.
Letters of A. K. Selected, with a preface, by E. Keary. London: Christian Knowledge Society, [1883].
Enchanted Tulips; and Other Verses for Children. With E. and M. Keary. 1914. Published posthumously.

KEARY, Elizabeth
Pseudonym: E. K.

Elizabeth Keary was probably born in England, in Bilton Hall, her mother's family home. She was the elder sister of Annie Keary (see listing) and of Charles F. Keary, also an author of note. Elizabeth was one of six children born to William Keary and his wife, Lucy. William was the only son of an Irish family from Co. Galway, and Lucy, her mother, was the daughter of Hall Plumer, Esq., of Bilton Hall, near Wetherby, in Yorkshire. Elizabeth's father was an army officer who lost his property in Ireland. He decided to take holy orders after leaving the army, and following his marriage. William Keary eventually became the curate of Sculcoats, part of Hull, where Elizabeth was reared. Another sister, Maud, contributed to some volumes jointly authored by the three sisters.

Elizabeth wrote Annie Keary's biography, and edited a collection of her sister's correspondence. She was called Eliza, and is frequently listed under that diminutive.

Bibliography:
The Heroes of Asgard. With Annie Keary. 1857. Another edition, entitled: *Christmas Week and Its Stories; or, the Heroes of Asgard*. [1860].
Early Egyptian History for the Young. With Annie Keary. 1861.
Little Seal-Skin, and Other Poems. London: 1874.
The Magic Valley, or Patient Antoine. London: 1877.
Memoir of Annie Keary. 1882. Another edition: 1883.
Letters of Annie Keary. Edited. [1883].
Rays of Light; Bible Selections. [1884].
The River of God; Bible Selections. [1884].
A Casket of Pearls; Bible Selections. [1884].
At Home Again; Verses. London: Marcus Ward and Co., [1886].
Pets and Playmates; Verses by E. K. London: Marcus Ward and Co., 1887.
The Francis Letters (Sir Philip Francis). Edited by Beata Francis and Eliza Keary. [1901].
Enchanted Tulips; and Other Verses for Children. With A. and M. Keary. 1914.

KEENAN, Louisiana
Born: Dublin
Married name: Louisiana Murphy

Louisiana was the daughter of Hugh Keenan, an Ulsterman who emigrated to America and became a lawyer. Hugh Keenan later returned to Ireland as the American Consul for Dublin and Cork. Louisiana accompanied her family back to Ireland and later married an officer of Excise. The couple settled in Dublin. Her play, 'Myra; or

Filial Devotion', was 'occasionally performed at schools', but no record exists of its publication (O'Donoghue 329).

Anthologized in: O'Reilly.

Bibliography:
Dunmore, or the Days of the Land League, an Irish Dramatic Episode of Our Own Time. Dublin: 1888.
Centenary Ode — Father Mathew, October 10, 1890. Dublin: 1890.
Poems of Old and New Ireland. Dublin: The Talbot Press, and London: Simpkin, Marshall, Hamilton, Kent and Co., 1925.
The Epic of Lourdes.

KEILLY, Anne
Born: circa 1850

Anne Keilly's name is sometimes given as Keily. She was the daughter of an under-agent of Annaghs, on the estate of Walter Sweetman of New Ross, Co. Wexford.

Anne Keilly was the subject of a literary controversy, regarding whether or not she was the author of an anonymously published poem entitled 'Beautiful Snow'. The debate appears to have been quite heated, and one scholar, a Dr Madden, expended a noteworthy amount of time and effort in collecting evidence to indicate that Anne was indeed the author.

Anne Keilly emigrated to America about 1875 or 1876 and was a frequent contributor to American papers thereafter. The work she published in Ireland appeared in the 1870s, prior to her emigration, in the *Munster Express, Waterford Daily Mail, Kilkenny Moderator, Wexford Express*, and *Waterford Express*.

KELLY, Eleanor Frances
Eleanor Kelly published a single poem in the *Irish Monthly*, January 1905, with a short story following in the March 1929 issue of the same journal.

Bibliography:
Shamrock Sprays. Galway: Connaught Tribune Office, 1911.
Blind Maureen and Other Stories. London: R. and T. Washbourne, 1913.
Our Lady Intercedes. London: R. and T. Washbourne, 1913.
The Three Requests. Dublin: Duffy, 1914.

KELLY, Mary
Died: 15 December, 1911, in Kingstown.
Married name: Mary Gorges

There is great confusion about this woman's name, whether it was Mary or May, but the majority of references point to Mary as the proper name, with May as a familiar form.

Mary was the daughter of William Daniel Kelly of Castlepark, Turrock, Co. Roscommon. She married Major Gorges, who was an East India Company officer, and survived him by many years. She apparently lived an erxtremely long life and is described as "a broad-minded, gentle-hearted, Christian woman" (Obit, IBL: 171).

Mary published in *Chambers' Journal*, and five of her poems appeared in the *Irish Monhly*, between January 1892 and November 1894.

Biographical Reference:
Obituary of Mrs Mary Gorges. *irish Book Lover* 3 (May 1912): 171.

Bibliography:
A Twelfth Night King. London and Edinburgh: W. and R. Chambers, 1897.
Killarney. Beautiful Ireland series. London: A. and C. Black, 1912.
On Life's Journey: Poems and Ballads. London: W. G. Wheeler, 1916.

KELLY, Mary Eva
Born: circa 1825, in Headford, Co. Galway
Died: May 1910, in Brisbane, and buried in Toowong Cemetery,
        Brisbane, Australia
Married name: Mrs Kevin Izod O'Doherty
Pseudonym: Eva

P. J. Dillon states that Kelly was born at Killeen House, near Portumna, but Justin McCarthy's memoir prefacing Kelly's revised volume gives Headford as her correct birthplace. Several sources list her name as Mary Anne Kelly, while others, such as Katharine Tynan in the 1904 eddition of *The Cabinet of Irish Literature*, call her Eva Mary Kelly. The most reliable biographical source seems to be the memoir written by Justin McCarthy, for the revised and enlarged edition of her poetry collection published in 1909, the year prior to her death, and states the collection was 'prepared by the authoress', suggesting that Eva had seen the memoir portion prior to its publication. No date of birth is given for the poet, which would have been considered highly indelicate during her lifetime, and the memoir seems intent on correcting several popular misconceptions regarding incidents in the lives of Kelly and her husband, Kevin Izod O'Doherty, thus suggesting she had a part in the memoir's preparation.

McCarthy states that Mary Eva Kelly was born in her grandfather O'Flaherty's home at Headford, Co. Galway. The Kelly family were landed gentry with strong Unionist beliefs. Her uncle, Martin O'Flaherty, was a solicitor and the exception to the family's political views. He was noted for his defence of Daniel O'Connell in the State trials. Eva's patriotic instincts and nationalistic views developed during a lengthy visit to this uncle in 1849. According to P. J. Dillon she was obscurely related to John and Ellen O'Leary (see listing for Ellen O'Leary).

Eva was educated at home by a series of governesses, one of whom instilled in her the love of literature. Her early poems were translations, and included a version of Lamartine's 'Dying Christian'. She began writing patriotic verses for *The Nation*, and her first submission, 'The Banshee', was accepted for publication. She published under a variety of pseudonyms prior to settling on 'Eva', which was used exclusively, beginning with her poem 'Lament for Thomas Davis'. She also wrote prose pieces for *The Nation*.

Eva was already engaged to Kevin Izod O'Doherty when he was arrested for his connection with the 1848 armed rising, according to McCarthy. After two inconclusive trials, O'Doherty was privately offered a plea bargain, a pardon in return for his public statement of guilt. The authorities allowed O'Doherty to consult with family and friends before making a decision, and a meeting with Eva occurred. The popular view held that O'Doherty was at least indecisive, if not fully in favour of the guilty plea, until she told him to 'be a man and refuse to bargain'. McCarthy stresses that O'Doherty was himself against the plea bargain, and Eva bolstered his resolve by promising to wait for him indefinitely. Although the circumstances are disputed, the outcome is not, for O'Doherty did not bargain and was thus exiled to Van Diemen's Land. Eva did wait for O'Doherty, and married him in 1854, following his early release. One condition of his early release was that he reside outside Ireland, so the couple settled in Paris. When the O'Dohertys were given permission, they did return to Ireland, but emigrated to Brisbane, Australia, a short time later. In Brisbane, Kevin O'Doherty was elected to the Legislative Assembly of Queensland. They returned to Ireland in 1886, long enough for O'Doherty to be elected a representative for Co. Meath, but his failing health soon necessitated another move back to Australia. Kevin O'Doherty died in 1905, and Eva survived him by five years.

Anthologized in: Brooke/Rolleston, Brown, Cooke, Hayes, MacDermott, Sparling, Varian, and Welsh.

Biographical References:
Dillon, P. J. 'Eva of *The Nation'*. *Capuchin Annual* (1933): 261-6.
'Irish Literary Celebrities, No. 5: Mary Izod O'Doherty'. *Nation* 8 December, 1888: 3.
McCarthy, Justin. Biographical Sketch. *Poems by 'Eva' of 'The Nation'*. Dublin: Gill, 1909.
Obituary. *Irish Book Lover* 2.12 (July 1910): 163.

Bibliography:
Poems, by 'Eva' of 'The Nation'. San Francisco: 1877. Another edition, revised and enlarged with a preface by Seumas MacManus and memoir by Justin McCarthy: Dublin: M. H. Gill and Son, 1909.

KELLY, Maura
A single poem by Maura Kelly appears in the *Irish Monthly*, March 1925 issue.

KENNY, Annie M.
Born: Castlecomer, Co. Kilkenny
Pseudonym: Stormy Petrel

Annie Kenny was convent educated in Dublin. O'Donoghue states that she 'was married a few years ago, and recently left a widow' (233). She appears to have written mainly for newspapers: *Kilkenny Journal*, *The Cork Herald* and the *Boston Pilot*.

KEON, Grace
Married name: Mrs J. F. Donovan

All of Grace Keon's books were published in New York or Chicago, suggesting that she emigrated at an early age. She did publish in the *Irish Monthly*, but only in the November 1908 issue.

KIERMAN, Harriet
Pseudonym: H. K.

Harriet Kierman was a contributor to the *Transaction of the Royal Irish Academy* in 1816. She was apparently well-regarded as a hymnist.

Bibliography:
The Invalid's Hymn Book. Preface by H. White, and edited by H. K. Second edition: London: 1841.

KILGALLEN, Mary
Born: Skreen, Co. Sligo
Pseudonym: Merva

Mary Kilgallen was the only child of a large farmer, or grazier, in the parish of Skreen. She was educated at the Ursuline Convent in Sligo during the period when Reverend James Casey was the convent chaplain. Mary seems to have remained in Co. Sligo throughout her life. She was a frequent contributor to *The Nation, Weekly News, Young Ireland,* and *The Shamrock.*

Anthologized in: *Emerald Gems.*

KILNORTH, Nora
The *New Ireland Review*, March 1902 and April 1902 issues, published poems by Nora Kilnorth.

KING, Catherine
Married name: Catherine Pennefather
Pseudonym: C. P.

Catherine was the daughter of Admiral King, the brother of the Earl of Kingston. She married Reverend William Pennefather on 16 September 1847. Catherine was known primarily as a writer of hymns and of religious works.

Bibliography:
Gather Up the Fragments: Notes of Bible Classes. 2 vols. London: S. W. Partridge and Co., 1869.
'The Peace of God' and 'The God of Peace'. London: 1879.
Follow Thou Me; Discipleship. London: J. F. Shaw and Co., [1881].
Follow Thou Me; Service. London: J. F. Shaw and Co., [1881].
Am I Guided? London: John F. Shaw and Co., [1881].
Wonderful Words of Life; a Manual for Flower Missions. Preface by Mrs Pennefather. [1882].
Sowing and Reaping; a New Year's Address to Teachers. London: Sunday School Union, [1882].
Hints on Bible Reading; a Word to Young Workers. London: J. F. Shaw and Co., [1883].

The Blessed Hope. Reprinted from *Service for the King.* London: J. F. Shaw and Co., [1883].
Women's Wayside Ministry. London: J. F. Shaw and Co., [1883].
Songs of the Pilgrim Land. Edited by E. St. B. H., London: J. F. Shaw and Co., 1886.
Wait: Thoughts on Psalm lxxiii. London: J. F. Shaw and Co., [1886].
The Homeward Journey; Poems. London: J. E. Hawkins, 1888.
A New Commandment; John xiii, 34-35. London: J. F. Shaw and Co., [1888].
Rest in the Lord; with Verses by Mrs C. P. [1890].
That Nothing Be Lost; Selections from Addresses Given by Mrs Pennefather. London: Elliot Stock, 1892.

KINGSTON, Eileen
Five poems appeared in the *Irish Monthly*, March 1894 to October 1933, by Eileen Kingston.

KINSELLA, Margaret
The *Irish Monthly*, March 1897, contains verse by Margaret Kinsella.

KINSELLA, Mary
A single poem, in the *Irish Monthly*, December 1896 issue, is credited to Mary Kinsella.

KINSLEY, Miss
Bibliography:
The Emerald Isle, a Poem. Liverpool: Booker and Co., 1846. Second edition: Liverpool: 1846.

KIRCHHOFFER, Julia Georgiana Mary
Born: 1 June 1855, at Ballyvourney Glebe, Co. Cork
Died: 29 January 1878

Anthologized in: *Birthday*, and MacIlwaine.

Bibliography:
Poems and Essays. Paisley: J. and R. Parland, [1885].

KIRWAN, Charlotte T.
Charlotte Kirwan's poems are in the December 1875 and June 1884 issues of the *Irish Monthly*.

KIRWAN Rose
Born: Belfast
Pseudonym: Rose

Rose was a governess in the family of Lord Fermoy. Frances Maria Roche (see listing), the sister of Lord Fermoy, was 'De Rupe', who co-authored their volume of poetry.

Bibliography:
Poems, by Rose and De Rupe. London: Longman, Brown, Green and Longmans; and Dublin: James M'Glashan, 1856.

KNIGHT, Olivia
Born: circa 1830, in Co. Mayo
Married name: Mrs Hope Connolly
Pseudonym: Thomasine

Olivia was the daughter of Patrick Knight, an engineer who had written a book about County Mayo. Olivia was a schoolteacher at Gainstown near Mullingar, and married Mr Hope Connolly, who was later elected M.P. for Meath, about 1885. The Connollys eventually emigrated to Australia.

Olivia, under her pseudonym, was a constant contributor to *The Nation* during the 1850s, with her first poem appearing in that publication on 6 September 1851. She was a translator of French, and wrote short stories in addition to her poetry.

Anthologized in: MacDermott.

Biographical Reference:
Irish Monthly 11 (1883): 522.

Bibliography:
Wild Flowers from the Wayside. Introduction by Sir C. G. Duffy. Dublin: 1883.

KNOX, Kathleen
Pseudonym: Edward Kane

Kathleen was the daughter of Charles George Knox, Esq., L.L.D., Vicar-General of Down and Connor, and the younger brother of the Lord Primate, Dr Knox. Her first poems appeared in the *Belfast Weekly Whig* while she was still a young girl. In 1879 she was reported to be living in Howth, Dublin. Kathleen was a well-known author of literature for children.

Anthologized in: MacIlwaine, and Paul.

Bibliography:
Father Time's Story Book. London: 1873.
Fairy Gifts; or, a Wallet of Wonders. London: 1875.
Lily of the Valley; a Story for Little Boys. London: 1876.
Meadowleigh; a Holiday History. London: 1876.
Seven Birthdays; or, The Children of Fortune. London and Edinburgh: 1876. Another edition: New York: Pott, Young and Co., [c.1880].
Wildflower Win; The Journal of a Little Girl. London: 1876.
Queen Dora: The Life and Lessons of a Little Girl. London: 1879.
Cornerstown Chronicles: New Legends of Old Lore. London: 1880.
Poor Archie's Girls; a Novel. 3 vols. London: Smith, Elder and Co., 1882.
English Lessons for Schoolroom Use. London: Bell and Sons, 1882.
Captain Eva; The Story of a Naughty Girl. London: Society for Promoting Christian Knowledge, [1880].
The Islanders, a Poem. London: 1888.
The Organist's Baby; a Story. London: Blackie and Co., 1895. Another edition, retitled *Bab's Two Cousins:* London and Glasgow: Blackie and Son, [1927].

L

LAMBERT, Nannie
Born: Athenry, Co. Galway
Married name: Mrs Power O'Donoghue
Pseudonym: N. P. O'D.

Nannie was the youngest child of Charles Lambert of Athenry. She married William Power O'Donoghue, Mus. Doc., and became a highly respected journalist as well as an accomplished equestrian. One of her volumes, *Riding for Ladies*, was translated into five languages and over 94,000 copies were printed. Her novel, *A Beggar on Horseback*, sold over 23,000 copies. In her capacity as a journalist, Nannie contributed prose pieces to a varierty of newspapers.

Anthologized in: Sullivan, and Welsh.

Bibliography:
Spring Leaves. London: 1877.
Ladies on Horseback; Learning Park-riding and Hunting; With Hints upon Costume and Numerous Anecdotes. London: W. H. Allen and Co., 1881. Another, revised edition: 1891.
Unfairly Won. 3 vols. London: Chapman and Hall, 1882. Another edition: London: Mellifont Press, [1939]. Another edition: London: Griffith, Farren, n.d.
A Beggar on Horseback. 3 vols. London: Hurst and Blackett, 1884.
The Common Sense of Riding; Riding for Ladies, With Hints on the Stable. London: W. Thacker and Co., 1887. Another edition: 1904.
Rhymes for Readers and Reciters. Dublin: 1895.

LAMONT, Elish
Born: c. 1800, in Belfast
Died: 1870, in England
Pseudonym: Elish

Elish Lamont's surname occasionally appears as La Mont. She was the sister of Frances Lamont (see listing), with whom she co-authored a single volume of poetry. Both women were probably natives of Belfast and Eilish was a noted artist who exhibited regularly, between 1840 and 1860. Their volume was printed and published by their brother, and was dedicated to Lady Dufferin (see listing for Helen Selina Sheridan). The Lamont sisters were also acquainted with Charles Dickens.

Elish Lamont taught herself to be an artist and specialized in painting miniatures. She was so successful that her reputation as a painter eclipsed her reputation as a poet. Elish exhibited her work at the Royal Hibernian Academy, Dublin.

Bibliography:
Christmas Rhymes, or Three Nights' Revelry. Belfast: Lamont Bros.; Dublin: Curry; and London: Whittaker, 1846.
Love Versus Money: a Novel. London: 1855.

LAMONT, Frances
Pseudonym: Frances

Frances Lamont was probably born in Belfast. She co-authored a single volume of poetry with her sister, Elish (see listing). Both women were artists, although Frances seems to have been less successful than Elish. Their only book was printed and published by their brother, and dedicated to Lady Dufferin (see listing for Helen Selina Sheridan).

Bibliography:
Christmas Rhymes, or Three Nights' Revelry. Belfast: Lamont Bros.; Dublin: Curry; and London: Whittaker, 1846.

LANYON, Helen
Helen was the daughter of Elizabeth Helen Owens Lanyon and Sir Charles Lanyon, a well-known architect who was a mayor of Belfast, and M.P. Her brother, Sir William Owen Lanyon, was a colonel and a colonial administrator. The Lanyon family residence was The Abbey, Whiteabbey, Co. Antrim.

Ruth, Celia, and Emma Duffin were close friends of Helen Lanyon, and Emma illustrated one of Helen's books, *Fairy Led, and Other Verses.* A total of four poems by Helen were published in the *New Ireland Review* between October 1907 and July 1915.

Anthologized in: Graves, Gregory, and Robinson.

Bibliography:
Hill o' Dreams and Other Verses. Dublin: Sealy, Bryers and Walker, 1909.
Fairy Led, and Other Verses. Belfast: W. and G. Baird, 1915.
What the Kind Wind Said.

LARGE, Dorothy Mabel
Pseudonyms: M. L., and D. M. L.

Bibliography:
Songs of Slieve Bloom. Dublin and Cork: Talbot Press, 1926.
Cloonagh. London: Constable and Co., 1932.
Irish Airs. London: Constable and Co., 1932.
The Open Arms. London: Constable and Co., 1933.
An Irish Medley. Belfast: Quota Press, [1934].
The Cloney Carol, and Other Verses. Belfast: Quota Press, 1934.
The Kind Companion. Dublin and Cork: Talbot Press, 1936. Another edition: London: Lutterworth Press, 1936.
Talk in the Townlands. Dublin and Cork: Talbot Press, 1937.
The Glen of the Sheep. Dublin and Cork: Talbot Press, [1938].
Man of the House. Dublin: Browne and Nolan, 1939.

The Onlooker. London: Methuen and Co., 1940.
The Quiet Place. London: Methuen and Co., 1941.

LA TOUCHE, Maria
Married name: Mrs La Touche

Mrs La Touche was a resident of Harristown.

The *Irish Monthly* published eight of Maria La Touche's poems between May 1877 and June 1878.

Biographical Reference:
The Letters of a Noble Woman. Margaret Ferrier Young, ed. London: George Allen and Sons, 1908.

LAWLESS, Emily
Born: 1845, at Lyons House, Co. Kildare
Died: 1913, at Surrey

Emily Lawless's date of birth is alternately listed as 1843. Emily was the daughter of the third Lord Cloncurry, and his wife, the former Miss Kirwan from the Tuam area of Co. Galway. Emily was the fourth of nine children born to this prominent family. Her early childhood appears to have been deeply distressed, and the family began to disintegrate as Emily reached adulthood. Her father committed suicide in 1869 and two of her sisters later took their own lives. Her mother died suddenly in 1895, and another brother died in 1900, following a lengthy illness. One sister became a recluse and her remaining brothers were considered to be quite irresponsible. Emily was herself a noted eccentric, suffering with bouts of severe depression, and by all reports she led an unhappy adult life. Her later years were spent "in nearly complete seclusion while tormented by physical pain, mental instability, and an addiction to drugs" (Grubgeld 36).

Emily had a passion for exploring Ireland and travelled extensively throughout Connemara. She was, according to Padraic Fallon, "tough enough to live in the Aran Islands long before Synge was born, and to write of them" (7). Emily is described as "a thoroughly independent character", and as one "born a rebel" (Fallon 7-8). She was dedicated to the preservation of Irish culture, an expert on wildlife, and an accomplished equestrian.

Emily was a prolific writer of prose, in addition to poetry. She was awarded a D.Litt. degree from Trinity College, Dublin. In 1909 she had moved to England where she lived at Hazelhatch, Gomshall, Surrey.

Only two poems by Emily Lawless appeared in journals: the 1901-4 edition of the *Limerick Field Club Journal*, and the *Irish Review*, July 1911 issue.

Anthologized in: Browne, Cabinet IV, Cooke, Graves, Gregory, Hoagland, Robinson, and Tynan.

Biographical Reference:
Fallon, Padraic. Introduction. *The Poems of Emily Lawless.*
Grubgeld, Elizabeth. *Turn of the Century Women* 3.2 (1986): 35-42.
Obituary. *Irish Book Lover* 5 (December 1913): 84-5.

Bibliography:
A Chelsea Householder. 3 vols. London: Sampson Low, 1882.
Ireland: The Story of the Nations. With additions by Mrs A. Bronson. London: Unwin, 1885. Another edition revised and with two new chapters: 1912.
A Millionaire's Cousin. London: Macmillan, 1885.
Hurrish: A Study. 3 vols. Edinburgh: W. Blackwood and Sons, 1886. Another edition: London: Methuen, 1902. Another edition: Nelson's Library. London and Edinburgh: T. Nelson and Sons, [1913].
Major Lawrence, F.L.S. 3 vols. London: J. Murray, 1887. Another edition: 1888.
Plain Frances Mowbray and Other Tales. London: J. Murray, 1889.
With Essex in Ireland. London: Smith, Elder, 1890. Another edition: London: Methuen, 1902.
Grania: The Story of an Island. 2 vols. London: Smith, Elder, 1894.
Maelcho; a Sixteenth-Century Narrative. 2 vols. London: Smith, Elder, 1894. Another edition: 1895. Another edition: London: Methuen; and New York; Appleton, 1905.
Traits and Confidences. London: Methuen, 1898. Another edition: 1898.
A Garden Diary; September 1899-September 1900. London: Methuen and Co., 1901.
With the Wild Geese: Verses. Introduction by Stopford Brooke. London: Isbister, 1902.
Maria Edgeworth. London: Macmillan, 1904.
The Book of Gilly; Four Months Out of a Life. London: Smith, Elder, 1906.
The Race of Castlebar; Being a Narrative Addressed by Mr. John Bunbury to His Brother, Mr. Theodore Bunbury, Attached to His Britannic Majesty's Embassy at Florence, October 1798, and Now First Given to

the World. With Shan F. Bullock. London: John Murray, 1913.

A Point of View: Some Talks and Disputations. Suffolk: Privately printed, Richard Clay and Sons, 1909.

The Inalienable Heritage; and Other Poems. Suffolk: Privately printed, Richard Clay and Sons, 1914.

LEADBEATER, Lydia Jane
Born: 1800, in Ballitore, Co. Kildare
Died: 16 April 1884, at Stradbally, Co. Laois
Married name: Lydia Jane Fisher

Lydia was the daughter of Mary Leadbeater (née Shackleton), the eighteenth-century poetess. Charles Read claims Lydia as his niece, in the 1880 edition of the *Cabinet of Irish Literature.*

Lydia was known as a prose writer, yet she wrote a substantial body of poetry which was never collected. She edited *The Leadbeater Papers,* authored a memoir of the naturalist Dr W. H. Harvey, and anonymously published *Letters from the Kingdom of Kerry, in the Year 1845.*

Bibliography:
The Leadbeater Papers. Edited.
Letters from the Kingdom of Kerry, in the Year 1845.
Memoir of Dr W. H. Harvey.

LEAHY, Norah
One poem attributed to Norah Leahy is in the *Irish Monthly's* December 1921 issue.

LECKY, Elizabeth
Elizabeth Lecky was reported to be of an Irish family, and specialized in writing poetry and children's tales.

Bibliography:
The Little Traveller. Dean's Rose and Lily Series. London: Dean and Son, [1883].
The Story of Jack the Cat. Dean's Rose and Lily Series. London: Dean and Son, [1883].
The Story of the Good Dog, Rover. Dean's Rose and Lily Series. London: Dean and Son, [1883].
Fairy Folk; in Verse. London: Griffith, Farran and Co., 1886.
Here, There, and Everywhere, Rhymes. London: Raphael Tuck, 1890.

LECKY, Mary R.
Bibliography:
Old James, the Irish Pedlar. Dublin: n.d.

LEECH, Sarah
Pseudonym: S. L.

"A peasant girl of Donegal", says O'Donoghue (248). Sarah's only volume features a portrait of the author seated at a spinning wheel.

Bibliography:
Poems on Various Subjects. Dublin: n.p., 1828.
Poems: The Donegal Peasant. 1828.

LEESON, Jane Eliza
Born: 1807
Died: 1882
Pseudonym: J. E. L.

Jane Leeson was a hymnist and religious writer. Her work appears in the following collections of hymns: Roger's *Child's Hymnal*, Irvingite's *Hymns for the Use of the Church*, and *Paraphrases and Hymns for Congregational Worship*.

Bibliography:
The Lady Ella; or, The Story of Cinderella in Verse. 1847.
The Wreath of Lilies. 1847.
Hymns of Scenes of Childhood; or, a Sponsor's Gift. 1842. Second edition: 1848. Third edition: [1850].
The Christian Child's Book. 1848.
Songs of Christian Chivalry. 1848.
Chapters on Deacons. 1849.
The Orphan's Home. 1849.
The Child's Book of Ballads. 1849.
Margaret, An Olden Tale. 1850.
The Story of a Dream; or, a Mother's Version of an Olden Tale. 1850.
The Child's New Lesson Book; or, Stories for Little Readers. [1850].
The Seven Spiritual Works of Mercy. 1861.

LENIGAN, Henrietta Jane
Henrietta Lenigan's first collection is "a scrappy volume illustrated by the authoress, and containing pieces by herself and others" (O'Donoghue 250).

Bibliography:
Ornaments of the Mind, With a Promiscuous Collection of Modern Poetry.
    Paris: 1842.
Hymns. Edited by Rev. J. Leifchild. 1843.

LESLIE, Emma
Born: 9 August 1812, at Holywood, Belfast
Died: 1872
Married name: Emma Toke

Emma was the daughter of Dr John Leslie, Bishop of Kilmore, and she married Reverend Nicholas Toke, of Ashford, Kent, in 1837. Emma was a popular hymnist whose work was frequently anthologized. There are twenty-one of her hymns in Judd's, *Sunday School Liturgy* (1870).

Anthologized in: MacIlwaine

Bibliography:
Poems. London: Privately printed, 1866.

LESLIE, Mary Isabel
Born: 1899, in Dublin
Died: 1982
Pseudonyms: Temple Lane, and Jean Herbert

Mary Isabel Leslie was born in Dublin, but her childhood was spent in Co. Tipperary. She was educated in England, and later attended Trinity College, Dublin. Mary Leslie held a doctor of philosophy degree and was the recipient of the Large Gold Medal in 1922.

   Almost all of her poetry which appeared in magazines or journals was published after 1937. She also wrote critical pieces about the works of Teresa Deevy, Kathleen Nott, and Winifred Letts among others. Some of her work appeared in *Ireland Today, Poetry Ireland, Envoy, Dublin Magazine* and *Irish Writing.*

Biographical Reference:
'Self-Interview No. 3: Temple Lane'. *Poetry Ireland* 17 (July 1952): 3-9.

Bibliography:
Burnt Bridges. London: John Long, 1925. Popular edition: 1926.
No Just Cause. London: John Long, 1925. Popular edition: 1926.
Defiance. London: John Long, 1926.

LETTS

Second Sight. London: John Long, 1926.
Watch the Wall. London: John Long, 1927.
The Bands of Orion. London: Jarrolds, [1928].
The Little Wood. London: Jarrolds, [1930].
Blind Wedding. London: Jarrolds, [1931].
Sinner Anthony. London: Jarrolds, 1933.
The Trains Go South. London: Jarrolds, [1938].
Battle of the Warrior. London: Jarrolds, [1940].
Fisherman's Wake. Dublin and Cork: Talbot Press, n.d. Another
    edition: London: Longmans, [1940].
House of My Pilgrimage. Dublin: Talbot; and London: Frederick
    Muller, 1941.
Friday's Well. Dublin: Talbot, 1943.
Come Back! Dublin: Talbot, 1945.
Curlews. Dublin: Talbot Press, 1946.
My Bonny's Away. Dublin: Talbot, 1947.

LETTS, Winifred M.
Born: 1881, in Dublin
Died: 1972.
Married name: Mrs W. H. F. Verschoyle

Winifred Letts was educated at St Anne's Abbots, Bromley, and at
Alexandra College, Dublin. In later life she resided in Faversham,
Kent, and evidently trained as a masseuse. Letts wrote in a wide
variety of genres: poetry, novels, plays, children's stories, hagiog-
raphy, biography. Her plays were produced by the Gate Theatre and
the Abbey. Some of her work appeared in the *Irish Review*, the *Dublin
Magazine* and *Irish Writing*.

Anthologized in: Graves, Gregory, Hoagland, Morton, Rhys, Tynan,
    and Walters.

Bibliography:
The Story-Spinner. London: T. C. and E. C. Jack, 1907. Another
    edition: London: T. Nelson and Sons, [1920].
Waste Castle. London and Edinburgh: T. C. and E. C. Jack, 1907. Other
    editions: London: T. Nelson and Sons, [1916], [1918], and [1920].
Bridget of All Work. London: Hodder and Stoughton, 1909.
Diana Dethroned. London and New York: John Lane, 1909.
The Quest of the Blue Rose. London: Hodder and Stoughton, [1909].
    Another edition: 1910.
The Rough Way. London: Wells Gardner and Co., [1912].

143

Naughty Sophia. London: Grant Richards, 1912.

The Mighty Army. Lives of Saints Series. New York: F. A. Stokes; London: Wells Gardner and Co., 1912.

Songs from Leinster. London: Smith, Elder and Co., 1913. Reprinted: 1913 and 1914. London: John Murray, 1917. Reprinted: 1920, 1923 and 1928. Another edition: Dundalk: Dundalgan Press, 1947.

Helmet and Cowl; Stories of Monastic and Military Orders. London: Wells, Gardner and Co., 1913.

Christina's Son. London: Wells, Gardner and Co., 1916.

Hallow-e'en and Poems of the War. London: John Murray, 1916.

The Spires of Oxford and Other Poems. New York: E. P. Dutton; London: J. Murray, 1917.

Corporal's Corner. London: Wells, Gardner and Co., 1919.

What Happened Then? London: Wells, Gardner and Co., [1921].

More Songs from Leinster. London: J. Murray; New York: E. P. Dutton, 1926.

St Patrick the Travelling Man. London: J. Nicholson and Watson, 1932.

Knockmaroon. London: John Murray, 1933.

Pomona and Co. London: T. Nelson and Sons, [1935].

The Gentle Mountain. Dublin: Talbot Press, [1938]. Another edition: London: R. T. S., [1939].

LINDSAY, Fanny E.
Married name: Fanny E. Fisher

Fanny Lindsay was born in Northern Ireland. She married a Dr Fisher from Limerick and lived in London for a time. The preface to her 1864 volume was written from Limerick.

Bibliography:
Lonely Hours. Dublin: Hodges, Smith, 1864.
Ainsworth's Heir, and Other Poems. London: 1866.
Poems. London: 1889.
Poems and Notes, Descriptive of Killarney. London: 1890.
Poems, Collected Edition. London: 1891.

LITTLE, Elizabeth Mary
Born: 1864, in Co. Roscommon
Died: 5 May 1909, at Bray, Co. Wicklow
Pseudonyms: L. M. Little, and Lizzie M. Little

There is some confusion regarding the proper name of this author. O'Donoghue lists her as Elizabeth Mary, while other sources list her as Mary Elizabeth, and Lucy Mary. Almost all the sources agree that she was called Lizzie, which suggests that Elizabeth Mary may have been the correct formal name. Her volumes were published under her initials, L. M. Little.

Lizzie was one of three children of Joseph Bennett Little, who reportedly gambled away the family estate in Co. Roscommon shortly after receiving his inheritance. Her sisters were Grace and Isabella (see listing for Grace Little). Grace married the poet Ernest Rhys, and Isabella became Mrs Richardson. It was Isabella who wrote the introduction to Lizzie's posthumous collection, *Poems*.

Lizzie was a teacher at the South Hampstead High School for Girls in Maresfield Gardens. In 1889 she was listed as living at 5 Claremont House, Lithos Road, Hampstead.

Anthologized in: Cooke, and Graves.

Bibliography:
Persephone, and Other Poems. Dublin: Maunsel and Co., 1884.
Wild Myrtle, Poems. London: J. M. Dent and Co., 1897. Another edition: 1898.
Poems. Isabella Richardson, ed. Dublin: Maunsel and Co., 1894. Another edition: 1909.

LITTLE, Grace
Born: 12 July 1865, at Knockadoo, Boyle, Co. Roscommon
Died: 1929
Married name: Mrs Grace Rhys

Grace was the youngest of three daughters born to Joseph Bennett Little, a Co. Roscommon squire. Her father was an improvident man, who gambled away the family estate. Grace's two sisters were Elizabeth Mary Little (see listing) and Isabella, later Mrs Richardson. Grace married Ernest Rhys, the poet, in 1891. She was editor of the Banbury Cross Children's Series, a twelve-volume set, published by Dent.

Anthologized in: *Cabinet* IV, and Rhys.

Bibliography:
Cradle Songs and Nursery Rhymes. Edited with introduction. London: W. Scott, 1894.
The Banbury Cross Series. Edited. 12 vols. London: J. M. Dent, 1894-5.
Mary Dominic. London: Dent, 1898.

The Wooing of Sheila. London: Methuen, 1901. Another edition: New York: Holt, 1908.

The Diverted Village; a Holiday Book. London: Methuen, 1903.

Five Beads on a String. Priory Press Booklets. 1903.

The Prince of Lisnover. London: Methuen, 1904.

The Children's England. London: Cassell, 1908.

The Bride. London: Methuen, 1909.

Poems. Foreword by Isabella Richardson. Dublin: Maunsell, 1909.

Mother Goose's Book of Nursery Rhymes and Songs. Edited with Ernest Rhys. Everyman's Library, 1909.

The Charming of Estercel. London: Dent, 1913.

The Quest of the Ideal. Fellowship Books, 1913.

English Fairy Tales. With Ernest Rhys. 1913.

In Wheelabout and Cockalone. London: G. G. Harrap, 1918.

About Many Things; Essays. London: Methuen, 1920.

The Children's Garland of Verse. Edited. London and Toronto: Dent, 1921.

Eleanor in the Loft. London: J. Cape, 1923.

A Little Philosophy of Love. London: Chapman and Dodd, 1923.

Jacob. By J. Rainis [pseudonym of Janis Krisjunis Plieksans]. Translated by Grace Rhys. 1924. Another edition: 1965.

A Celtic Anthology. London: Harrap, 1927.

A Book of Grace; Essays and Poems. London and Toronto: Dent; and New York: Dutton, 1930.

The Magic Beyond the World. London: G. G. Harrap, 1931.

LLOYD, Harriet Ker
One poem by Harriet Ker Lloyd is found in the *Irish Monthly*, March 1905 issue.

LLOYD, Isabel Keith
The *Irish Monthly* published three poems between April and August 1905 by Isabel Keith Lloyd.

LOGUE, Emily
A frequent contributor to the *Irish Monthly*, twelve poems by Emily Logue appeared between July 1906 and July 1912. She also published several short stories.

LUBY, Catherine
Catherine Luby was a Tipperary native, and a relative of T. C. Luby, the Fenian.

Bibliography:
The Spirit of the Lakes, or Muckross Abbey; a Poem in Three Cantos with Notes. London: Longman, Hurst, Rees, Orme and Brown, 1822. Another edition: 1823.
Father Mathew, or Ireland As She Is; a National Poem. Dublin: S. J. Machen, 1845.

M

McARDLE, Maureen
Three poems published by Maureen McArdle are in the *Catholic Bulletin*, December 1920 to July 1922.

McCALL, Josephine
A single poem by Josephine McCall is in the *Irish Monthly*, January 1919 issue.

McCARTHY, Ely
Born: c. 1828, in Cork
Died: 1848, in Cork

Ely was the eldest of three children, and the only daughter, born to the clerk of the City Magistrates of Cork. One of her brothers was Justin McCarthy, a prominent journalist, biographer, historian, scholar and politician. Ely demonstrated both literary and linguistic talents, for she was fluent in French and Italian. She supplemented the family income by teaching these languages to young ladies in the Cork area. Ely died after a prolonged illness shortly after reaching her twentieth birthday.

Ely translated one of George Sand's novels, according to her brother, Justin, who claimed it was published by an unidentified magazine. Ely also translated poems by Petrarch and Alfieri which were published locally.

Justin McCarthy intended to compile and issue a collection of Ely's poetry, but never completed the task.

McCARTHY, Mary
Born: c. 1815, in Kilfadimore, near Kenmare, in Co. Kerry

MacCARTHY

Died: 1881
Married name: Mrs Mary Downing
Pseudonyms: Christabel, Myrrha, C**1, and M. F. D.

Mary was the eldest daughter of Daniel McCarthy, Esq. She married Mr Washington Downing, from the Cork area. Mary was a devoted Nationalist, who aided both James Stephens and Michael Doheny during their flight from Ireland. In 1871 the Downings lived in Hilldrop Crescent, Camden Town, London. Their previous address was reported to have been Cumming Street, Pentonville. Mary became a widow in 1877.

In James Stephens' memoir, *Reminiscences*, he mistakenly refers to Mary McCarthy as 'Claribel' instead of 'Christabel'.

Anthologized in: Cooke, Duffy, Hayes, and Varian.

Bibliography:
Scraps from the Mountains, and Other Poems. Dublin: William Curry, 1840. Another edition: London: 1841.

MacCARTHY, Mary Stanislaus
Born: 26 December 1849
Died: 11 August 1897, in Blackrock, Co. Dublin
Name in religion: Sister Mary Stanislaus
Pseudonym: S. M. S.

Mary Stanislaus MacCarthy was the daughter of Denis Florence MacCarthy, the poet who wrote pseudonymously as Desmond of *The Nation*. Mary became a student at St Catherine's Dominican Convent, Sion Hill, Blackrock, at the age of ten. She later joined the community and became Sister Mary Stanislaus of the Order of St Dominick. St Catherine's was her home for the remaining thirty-eight years of her life.

Sister Mary Stanislaus is credited with having edited *A Birthday Book of the Dead*, although that decidedly unique anthology was published anonymously. Her posthumously published *Songs of Sion* contains a brief sketch of her life and several memorial poems, two of which were written by her father.

The *Irish Monthly* published twenty of her poems, December 1873 to June 1895, and a further two poems appeared posthumously, in July 1898 and June 1903.

Anthologized in: MacIlwaine.

148

Biographical Reference:
Russell, Matthew. 'Denis Florence MacCarthy's Daughter: Sister
    Mary Stanislaus MacCarthy, O.S.D.' *Irish Monthly* 25 (Sept., Nov.,
    and Dec. 1897): 495-6, 561-74, and 617-23.

Bibliography:
A Birthday Book of the Dead. Edited. Dublin: M. H. Gill, 1886.
Songs of Sion. Dublin: Browne and Nolan, 1898.
*A Saint Among Sinners; Sketch of the Life of St Emmelia, Mother of St
    Basil the Great.* Second edition: Dublin: M. H. Gill, 1885.
Life of Blessed Emily Bicchieri, O.S.D. Dublin: M. H. Gill, 1902.

McDERMOTT, Mary
Pseudonym: M. McD.

Mary McDermott was living in Killyleagh, Co. Down, when her
volume was published in 1832. She occasionally composed music to
accompany her poetry. Her volume, *My Early Dreams*, was dedicated
to the Marchioness of Bristol, and the preface was written from
Killileagh Glebe, on 31st January 1832.

Bibliography:
My Early Dreams. Belfast: n.p., 1832.
Lays of Love. Dublin: M'Glashan and Gill, 1859.

McDONAGH, Mary
Born: 23 November 1849, in Ireland
Married name: Mary Pearle
Pseudonym: M. M. D.

Mary was the daughter of a Mr McDonagh, and the former Miss
McGreal. Mary was educated at Kildare Place Training College,
Dublin, and she was a frequent contributor to the *Church of Ireland
Parochial Magazine.* She married Mr Pearle, and they emigrated to
America with an infant daughter, in 1881. Thereafter, all her work was
published in American journals and newspapers.

McGINLEY, Bridget
Born: Breenagh, Glenswilly, Co. Donegal
Died: July 1894, at New Mills, Letterkenny
Married name: Bridget Gallagher

Bridget was the sister of P. T. McGinley, a poet who wrote in both the

Irish and English languages. She married Mr P. Gallagher, a merchant from Letterkenny, and moved to New Mills permanently. She was a frequent contributor to the *Derry Journal* and the *Donegal Vindicator*.

McGRATH, Mary Elizabeth
Born: 1 September 1849, in Clonmel, Co. Waterford
Died: 1907
Married name: Mary Elizabeth Blake

Mary Elizabeth McGrath's maiden name is sometimes given as Magrath. Her family emigrated to America in 1855 when she was six years of age. She wrote a large body of poetry and was a contributor to the *Irish Monthly*, where six poems appeared from March 1890 to May 1898.

Although she did not publish her poetry collections in Ireland, a travel book was published in Dublin and is listed below.

Biographical Reference:
Russell, Matthew. 'Our Poets, No. 15: Mary Elizabeth Blake'. *Irish Monthly* 13 (Dec. 1885): 663-6.

Bibliography:
A Summer Holiday in Europe. Dublin: Eason and Son, 1890.

M'KITTRICK, Anna Margaret
Born: 8 December 1860, Drumaness, near Ballynahinch, Co. Down
Died: 1939
First Married Name: Mrs Andrew Ross
Second Married Name: Mrs Thomas Rodgers
Pseudonym: Amanda M'Kittrick Ros

Amanda claimed that her mother named her after the female protagonist in Regina Maria Roche's novel, *Children of the Abbey*, and that her full name was Amanda Malvina Fitzalan Anna Margaret McLelland M'Kittrick. Another of her claims was to kinship with Danish royalty, based on Sitric, 'King of the Danes'. Such claims are indicative of her extravagant personality.

Anna's father, Edward Amland M'Kittrick, was the head teacher of Drumaness High School and Anna was his fourth child. She also trained as a teacher at Marlborough Training College in Dublin. While gaining practical teaching experience at Larne, she met Andrew Ross, the stationmaster. They were married on 30 August 1887, following Anna's obtaining a permanent teaching post in

Larne. Her husband was fifteen years older than Anna, and apparently an extremely tolerant man. For their tenth wedding anniversary present, her husband paid the cost of printing the first Amanda Ros novel, *Irene Iddesleigh*. The novel was a success, and the home they subsequently built in Larne was named Iddesleigh in its honour. Andrew Ross's health failed in 1915 and he died in 1917.

Amanda remarried a wealthy farmer named Thomas Rodgers on 12 June 1922, and her second husband died circa 1933. Six years later Anna died, leaving her last novel, *Helen Huddleson*, unfinished. The novel was published in 1969, edited and revised by Jack Loudan, who also wrote the final chapter of the uncompleted novel.

Anna frequently included in her work personal attacks against those she believed had wronged her, making revenge an important element in her writings. Her love of alliteration is evidenced by the titles of her works. It is said that Mark Twain added one of her novels to his library of 'hogwash literature'. Aldous Huxley considered her novels to be 'classics', although Amanda misunderstood his meaning and assumed Huxley meant her writings were to be taken seriously.

Biographical References:
'Amanda M'Kittrick Ros'. *Irish Book Lover* 12 (December 1920): 57-9.
Loudan, Jack. *O Rare Amanda!* London: Chatto and Windus, 1954.
Millar, Ruddick. 'Amazing Amanda'. *Irish Bookman* 1.5 (December 1946): 13-9.

Bibliography:
Irene Iddesleigh. Belfast: W. and G. Baird, 1897. Other editions: London: Nonesuch, 1926. New York: Boni and Liveright, 1927.
Delina Delaney. Belfast: R. Aickin, 1898. Another edition: London: Chatto and Windus, 1935.
Poems of Puncture. London: Arthur H. Stockwell, 1931.
Fumes of Formation. Belfast: R. Carswell, 1933.
Bayonets of Bastard Sheen. Privately printed, 1949.
Donald Dudley: The Bastard Critic. Thames Ditton, Surrey: Merle, 1954.
St Scandalbags. T. Stanley Mercer, ed. Thames Ditton, Surrey: Merle, 1954.
Helen Huddleson. Edited and with the final chapter by Jack Loudan. London: Chatto and Windus, 1969.

McNEILL, Violet
Born: 1864, in Co. Antrim
Died: 1902
Married name: Violet Hobhouse

Violet was the eldest daughter of Edmund McNeill, and her work reflects her family's strong Unionist views. She had an abiding interest in Irish culture, particularly folklore and mythology. Violet was fluent in the Irish language.

Bibliography:
An Unknown Quantity. London: Downey and Co., 1898.
Warp and Weft; a Story of the North of Ireland. London: Skeffington and Son, 1899.

MACARTNEY, Mary
Mary Macartney wrote devotional poetry.

Bibliography:
Poems. Newry: *The Reporter* Office, [c. 1855].

MACLEAN, Anna Jane
Bibliography:
Conviction, a Poem. Dublin: 1851.
Eman More, a Tale of Killarney in Verse. Dublin: 1852.

MACREADY, Catherine Frances Birch
Born: 1835
Died: 1869

O'Donoghue lists Catherine F. B. Macready as an Irish poet, without further detail.

Bibliography:
Leaves from the Olive Mount. London: 1860.
Cowl and Cap; or, The Rival Churches and Minor Poems. London: 1865.
Devotional Lays. London: 1868.

MADDEN, Mary Anne
Born: 31 December 1820, at Cootehill, Co. Cavan
Died: 5 April 1903, in Montreal, Canada
Married name: Mary Anne Sadlier
Pseudonym: M——— Cootehill

Mary Anne Madden emigrated to Canada in 1844, at the age of twenty-four, and married the American publisher D. J. Sadlier two years later. She published poetry, tales and plays, in addition to many translations of works from French. She continued to publish in

Ireland after her emigration to America, and her output was prolific on both continents.

Bibliography:
The Confederate Chieftains. Dublin: Gill, 1859.
The Red Hand of Ulster; or, The Fortunes of Hugh O'Neill. London and Dublin: [c. 1862].
The Hermit of the Rock. Dublin: Gill, 1863.
The Daughter of Tyrconnell: a Tale of the Reign of James I. Dublin: Duffy, 1863.
The Old House by the Boyne. Dublin: Gill, 1865. Other editions: London: 1888. New York: Benziger, 1904.
The Secret; a Drama. London: R. Washbourne, 1880.
The Knout; a Tale of Poland. Translated from French. Dublin: Gill and Son, 1884.
Alice Riordan; the Blind Man's Daughter. Dublin: Gill and Son, 1884.
The Old House by the Boyne. Dublin: Gill and Son, 1888.
Willy Burke. Dublin: Duffy, 1909.

MAGENNIS, Ellen
Born: c. 1828, at Clones, Co. Monaghan
Died: 6 January 1883, at Salford, England
Married name: Ellen Forrester

Ellen Magennis was the daughter of a schoolmaster. The family moved to Liverpool while she was still a young girl, then on to Manchester before settling at Salford. Ellen married Michael Forrester, a stone mason, and three of their five children also became poets: Arthur, Fanny and Mary Magdalene (see listings for Fanny Forrester and Mary Magdalene Forrester).

Ellen Magennis contributed poetry to *The Nation, Dundalk Democrat* and various periodicals in England.

Anthologized in: Graves, and Varian.

Bibliography:
Simple Strains. London: [c. 1860].
Songs of the Rising Nation, and Other Poems. With Arthur and Fanny Forrester. Glasgow and London: 1869.

MAGRATH, Anna Jane
Born: 1821

Anna Jane Magrath was age thirteen when her first volume was published. She later wrote a play that was based on Carleton's novel, *Fardarougha, the Miser*, but Carlton disliked her adaptation of his novel and some bitter correspondence ensued between the two authors.

Bibliography:
Blossoms of Genius, Poems on Various Subjects. Dublin: 1834.
A Changed Heart. Dublin: 1840.

MAGUIRE, Annie P.
Born: Dublin

Bibliography:
A Wreath. Dublin: [c. 1880s].

MAGUIRE, Mrs John Francis
Died: c. 1905

She was the wife of John Francis Maguire, M.P. for Cork.

Bibliography:
Beauty and the Beast, a Play in Three Acts and in Verse, with a New Version of Old Fables. Dublin: M. H. Gill, 1878.

MAGUIRE, Mary
Born: 13 June 1887, in Derryhollow, Co. Fermanagh
Died: 22 October 1957, in New York, America
Married name: Mrs Padraic Colum

Mary Maguire was the daughter of Charles Maguire and his wife, the former Mary Gunning. Mary was raised by elderly relatives who lived in the northwest of Ireland, until she was thirteen years of age, when she was sent to a convent boarding school at Vaals, Netherlands. Mary then attended the National University in Dublin. She married Padraic Colum in 1912 and they emigrated to America in 1914.

Mary was known predominantly as a literary critic and she published little poetry outside of America. Her work appeared in *Anthology of Irish Verse*, compiled by her husband, and also in the *Irish Review*.

Biographical References:
Life and the Dream. London: Macmillan, 1947. (Autobiography).

Bibliography:
From These Roots; The Ideas That Have Made Modern Literature.
London and New York: Charles Scribner's Sons, 1937. Other
editions: London: Jonathan Cape, 1938. New York: Columbia
University Press, 1944.
The Dirge of the Lone Woman. Dublin: Dolmen, 1958.

MAHON, Catherine Hartland
Born: 24 June 1815, at Roscommon
Married name: Catherine H. Inglis

Catherine Mahon married a Capt. Inglis in 1844.

Bibliography:
*Short Notes of a Tour Through the South and West of Ireland, with Some
Account of the Operations of The General Irish Reformation Society.*
Castle Douglas: 1850.
Songs in Sorrow and Songs of Joy. Second edition: Edinburgth: 1864.
Third edition, with miscellaneous poems: 1864.
One Hundred Songs in Sorrow and Joy. Edinburgh: 1880.

MAHONY, Agnes
Born: Dromore Castle, Co. Kerry
Died: c. 1840
Married name: Agnes Hickson

Agnes was the daughter of Col. John Mahony, an Irish Volunteer and
delegate to the Dungannon Convention of 1782. She married Conway
Hickson, of Formoyle, Co. Kerry, in 1831. Her brother was High Sheriff
of Kerry, and she was the aunt of Richard John Mahony, a poet.

Bibliography:
A Minstrel's Hours of Song. London: 1825.

MANNING, Mrs R.
Died: 1883

Mrs R. Manning was a resident of Clonmel.

Bibliography:
*In Memoriam. Very Rev. T. N. Burke, O.P., Died July 2, 1882. Dedicated
to His Brethren of the Order in Dublin.* Clonmel: *Chronicle* Office,
1883.

MARCUS, Lily
The foreword to *Lyrical Links* was written from 2 Westland Villas, Londonderry, in 1920. Her poetry indicates she was Unionist in her political stance. There is a reference to indicate Lily may have written another volume, entitled *War Poems*, but publishing information has not been found.

Bibliography:
Lyrical Links. Londonderry: Derry Standard Printing Works, 1920.

MARSHALL, Meta
Bibliography:
Poetical Fancies, By an Irish Girl. Dublin: 1910.

MARTIN, M. E.
Pseudonym: M. E. M.

M. E. Martin was a frequent contributor to *Dublin University Magazine* and the *Irish Metropolitan Magazine*. She was reported to have written a prose volume about Rathmore.

MAYNE, Isabella
The *Dublin University Review* published one of Isabella's poems in the October 1886 issue.

MAYO, Finnuola
Two poems by Finnuola Mayo appeared in the May 1919 *Irish Commonwealth*. The name is possibly a pseudonym.

METCALFE, Rose
The *Irish Monthly* published three poems, November 1897 to July 1903, by Rose Metcalfe.

MILLIGAN, Alice Letitia
Born: 14 September 1866, in Gortmore, near Omagh
Died: 13 April 1953, at Tyrcur, Omagh, Co. Tyrone and
      buried in Drumragh Cemetery
Pseudonym: Iris Olkyrn

Alice was a daughter of Seaton F. Milligan of Belfast, an Irish antiquarian of good reputation and a wealthy businessman. Her mother was Charlotte Burns Milligan, a native of Omagh. Her sister, Charlotte Milligan Fox, became an expert on Irish folk music, and her two brothers were Charles F. Milligan and W. H. Milligan. Alice was educated at a private school in Omagh, then at the Methodist College of Belfast, Magee College in Derry, and at King's College, London, where she studied history. Following her university education, she went to Dublin to concentrate on learning Irish. It was her great-uncle Armour Alcorn, a farmer, who spoke with his labourers in Irish, who introduced Alice to the language and cultivated her interest in Irish. Alice taught at a women's college in Derry, before moving to Belfast where she teamed with Anna Johnston (see listing) to edit the *Northern Patriot*, from 1894 to 1895. Alice later continued her partnership with Johnston as they founded and edited the *Shan Van Vocht* from January 1896 to April 1899. She became a member of the Gaelic League and was a driving force for that organization in Ulster. When the first modern stage production in Irish was staged at Letterkenny, in November 1898, Alice Milligan was one of the performers. Alice was a playwright and her sister composed the music for Alice's play, 'The Harp That Once'. She also travelled throughout Ireland lecturing on Irish history. Alice collaborated with her father in 1888, to produce *Glimpses of Erin*, a travel book.

Alice was one of the Anti-Partition League founders; both the civil war and the partitioning of Ireland were extremely difficult for her to accept. She was a foundation member of the Irish Academy of Letters, and received an honorary D.Litt. from the National University of Ireland in May 1941.

Alice Milligan was a frequent contributor to *Sinn Féin, United Irishman* and *United Ireland*. Her plays were produced by the Irish Literary Theatre, and the Abbey. Her poems can be found in the following journals and issues: *Belfast Naturalists' Field Club Report and Proceedings*, 1894; *Bealtaine*, February 1900; *Uladh*, February 1905; *Irish Review*, 25th November 1922. A prose tribute to George William Russell (AE), written by Alice Milligan, was published in *Dublin Magazine*, October 1935 issue.

Anthologized in: AE, Brown, Cooke, Fitzhenry, Graves, Hoagland, Lynd, Robinson, Tynan and Welsh.

Biographical References:
Johnston, Sheila Turner. *Alice: a Life of Alice Mulligan*. Omagh: Colourpoint Press, 1993.
MacDonagh, Thomas. 'The Best Living Irish Poet; Alice Milligan'. *Irish Review* 4 (Sept.-Nov. 1914): 287-93.
Obituary. *Dublin Magazine* 28 ns 4 (Oct.-Dec. 1953): 45.
Obituary. *Irish Book Lover* 32 (:March 1954): 63-4.

Bibliography:
Glimpses of Erin. With Seaton F. Milligan. London: Marcus Ward, (1890).
A Royal Democrat. London: Simpkin, Marshall, and Dublin: Gill, 1892.
The Life of Theobald Wolfe Tone. Belfast: J. W. Boyd, 1898.
The Last Feast of the Fianna. London: David Nutt, 1900. Another edition: Chicago: De Paul University, 1967.
The Daughter of Donagh: a Cromwellian Drama in Four Acts. Dublin: Lester, 1920.
Hero-Lays. Dublin: Maunsel and Co., 1908.
Sons of the Sea Kings. With W. H. Milligan. Dublin: Gill, 1914.
Two Poems. Dublin: At the Sign of the Three Candles, 1943.
We Sang for Ireland. With Seumas MacManus and Ethna Carbery (Anna Johnston). Dublin: Gill, 1950.
Poems. Henry Mangan, ed. Dublin: Gill, 1954.
The Dynamite Drummer. With Seaton F. Milligan.

MILLIGAN, Sophia
Sophia Milligan is listed as an Irish poet by D. J. O'Donoghue, without further substantiation.

Bibliography:
Original Poems, With Translations from the Scandinavian and Other Poets. London: 1856.

MITCHELL, Susan Langstaff
Born: 5 December 1866, at Carrick-on-Shannon, Co. Leitrim
Died: 4 March 1926, in Dublin

Susan was the eldest daughter of seven children born to Michael Mitchell and the former Kate Teresa Cullen. Her father was from Birr, and later managed the Carrick-on-Shannon Provincial Bank. In 1873, Michael Mitchell died and the family separated. Susan's mother and the four youngest children moved to Sligo, while another two children were sent to live in Sligo with a maternal aunt. Susan, age six, was sent to live with three paternal aunts in Dublin, where she attended a private school for girls on Morehampton Road, and received private tutoring in music, dance and art. Susan and her aunts later moved to Birr, where her father's brother was Crown Solicitor. The family was Protestant and Susan Mitchell never converted.

Susan Mitchell was a woman noted for her charm, intelligence and gaiety. In 1899 she developed an illness which severely affected her hearing. She sought medical assistance in London and lived with the John B. Yeats family for about one year while undergoing treatment. Her health remained fragile from this point throughout her life. She returned to Sligo from London and temporarily helped two of her younger sisters run a school.

Following a brief stay in Sligo she moved to Dublin in 1901, becoming assistant editor to AE [George Russell] on *The Irish Homestead*. During her assistant editorship, Mitchell wrote extensively for *The Irish Homestead*, and one estimate is that she contributed almost two hundred articles in the two-and-a-half-year period just before she died. She was especially noted for her skill as a satirist. The degree of intimacy between Susan Mitchell and AE has been cause for speculation, and was apparently gossiped about in their day.

One frequent target for the pointed end of Susan Mitchell's pen was George Moore. Her jabs at Moore, and his pretentions, are frequent and sometimes lengthy. It would not be unfair to call Moore an obsession in Mitchell's work, although she frequently targeted members of the Parliamentary Party in lieu of George Moore. Susan was an early and devoted member of Sinn Féin.

Anthologized in: AE, Cooke, Graves, Hoagland, Rhys, Robinson, and Welsh.

Biographical References:
AE [George William Russell]. Obituary. *Irish Statesman* 6.3 (13 March 1926).
Skelton, Robin. *Celtic Contraries*. Syracuse, U.S.A.: Syracuse UP, 1990.

Bibliography:
Aids to the Immortality of Certain Persons in Ireland, Charitably Administered by S. L. M. Dublin: The New Nation, 1908. Another edition: with portrait and additional poems: Dublin and London: Maunsel and Co., 1913.
The Living Chalice. Tower Press Booklets, Series 2, No. 6, 1906. Another edition: Dublin: Maunsel, 1908. Another edition, with poems added: Dublin and London: Maunsel and Co., 1913.
Frankincense and Myrrh. 1912.
George Moore. Dublin: Maunsel, 1916.
Secret Springs of Dublin Song. Dublin: Talbot, 1918.

MONCK, Mary C. F.
Born: c. 1835, at Banagher, King's County (Co. Offaly)

Died: 16 January 1892, at Holywood, Co. Down.
Married name: Mrs Alfred Münster
Pseudonym: Tiny

Mary was the eldest daughter of Richard Monck. She married Alfred M. Münster, the Danish Consul for Ireland, in 1858, and thereafter lived in Holywood, Co. Down. Her two poems commemorating Robert Burns's Centenary are in Finlay and Anderson's collection (Glasgow: 1859).

She was a regular contributor to *Dublin University Magazine*, *Bentley's Miscellany*, *Household Words*, and *Chambers' Journal*. Six of her poems appeared in the *Dublin University Magazine*, between May 1853 and August 1857.

Bibliography:
Waifs and Strays. London and Belfast: Marcus Ward and Co., 1879.
What the Wind Said in the Trees Above Burns' Grave On the 25th of January; In Verse. The Burns Centenary Poems, 1859.

MONGEY, Mary
The *Irish Monthly* published fourteen poems by Mary Mongey, October 1919 to April 1933.

MONTGOMERY, Mrs Alfred
Married name: Lady Montgomery

Lady Montgomery was from Co. Down, near Strangford and Mourne.

Bibliography:
The Rose and the Fire. London: 1908.
Angels and Symbols. Virgo Cabinet Series. London: Elkin Matthews, 1911.

MONTGOMERY, Eliza
The preface to Eliza Montgomery's lone volume was written from Ballymena, but her poetry refers frequently to the Enniskillen area.

Bibliography:
The Fallhead Trophy. Belfast: E. S. Mayne; and Ballymena: Wm. Erwin, 1874.

MORGAN, Alice M.
Between October 1897 and October 1898, five poems appeared in the

Irish Monthly by Alice M. Morgan.

MORNA, Gilla
In addition to her translations from the Italian, sixteen poems in English by Gilla Morna appeared in the *New Ireland Review*, between March 1909 and February 1911.

MORTIMER, Margaret
Born: c. 1871, in Wexford

When she was sixteen years of age, Margaret Mortimer attended the Kildare Place Training College in Dublin. Two years later, she became principal teacher at a school in Clonlara, near Limerick. Mortimer was a Fellow in the Brotherhood of Poets and published regularly in that society's paper, *The Muses*. Her work also appeared in the *Weekly Irish Times*.

Anthologized in: Paul

MORTON, Mary Elizabeth
Born: 1876, in Co. Limerick
Died: 1957
Pseudonym: May Morton

May Morton was raised in Co. Limerick before moving to Belfast in 1900, at the age of twenty-four. She later became the vice-principal of the Girls' Model School. May was a founding member of the Young Ulster Society and served as the secretary and later the chairperson of the Belfast P. E. N. May was associated with the Quota Press in Belfast.

May contributed to the following journals: *Rann*, where three poems were published from the Autumn 1948 issue to the June 1953 issue; *Lagan*, in the 1945 issue; and *Poetry Ireland*, in the January 1950 issue. *Rann's* Autumn 1948 issue calls her collection, *Masque in Maytime*, 'a ballet in words'.

Bibliography:
Day and Afterglow. Belfast: Quota Press, 1936.
Masque in Maytime. Lisburn: Lisnagarvey Press, 1948.
Spindle and Shuttle. Festival of Britain Committee for Northern Ireland, Prize Poems: 1951.
Sung to the Spinning Wheel. Belfast: Quota Press, 1952.

MULHOLLAND

MULHOLLAND, Rosa
Born: 1841, in Belfast
Died: 1921, at Villa Nuova, Blackrock, Co. Dublin
Married name: Lady Gilbert
Pseudonyms: Ruth Murray, Ruth Millais, and R. M.

Rosa was the second daughter of Dr Joseph S. Mulholland of Belfast, and sister to Lady Russell of Kilowen. Rosa was educated at home before leaving to study art in South Kensington. Originally she intended to be an artist, but her first comic pictures were rejected by *Punch*. Her next effort was a lengthy poem, 'Irene', and was accepted by *Cornhill* magazine. After its acceptance she decided to concentrate on writing. Following her father's death, she travelled in the remote areas of western Ireland for a time. She married John T. Gilbert, the historian, in 1891, and he was knighted in 1897. Rosa Mulholland became a widow the following year, on 23 May 1898. The Gilberts were credited with having had one of the largest private libraries in Ireland.

Rosa Mulholland was as close friend to Charles Dickens, who was very supportive of her work. It was Dickens who selected the title 'Hester's History' for her serial story in *All The Year Round*. Another of her stories, 'The Late Miss Hollingford', appeared with Dickens' 'No Thoroughfare', in a volume published as part of the Tauchnitz Collection.

Rosa Mulholland was as novelist, short story-writer and poet. She was a constant contributor of both prose and verse to the *Irish Monthly*, and a contributor to *Cornhill Magazine*, *The Lamp*, and *Duffy's Hibernian Magazine*.

Anthologized in: *Birthday*, Brooke/Rolleston, *Cabinet* III, Cooke, Furlong/Hyde, Gregory, Graves, Mrs Sharp, Sharp/Matthay, Sparling, Sullivan, and Walsh.

Biographical References:
Life of Sir John T. Gilbert. London: Longmans, 1905.
Obituary. *Irish Book Lover* 13 (Aug.-Sept. 1921): 21-2.

Bibliography:
Dunmara. London: Smith, Elder, 1864.
Hester's History. 2 vols. London: Chapman and Hall, 1869.
The Wicked Woods of Tobereevil. 2 vols. London: 1872. Another, retitled edition: *Wicked Woods*. London: Burns and Oates, [1897].
The Little Flower Seekers; Being Adventures of Trot and Daisy in a

Wonderful Garden by Moonlight. London and Belfast: 1873.

Eldergowan; or Twelve Months of My Life, and Other Tales. London and Belfast: 1874.

Five Little Farmers. London and Belfast: 1876.

Four Little Mischiefs. 1882. Another edition: London: Blackie, 1883. Another edition: [1925].

The Wild Birds of Killeevy. London: Burns and Oates, 1883.

Gems for the Young from Favourite Poets. Edited. Dublin: Gill, 1884.

Hetty Gray, or Nobody's Bairn. London: Blackie, 1884. Another edition: Blackie's Continuous Readers, 1899. Another edition: [1919].

The Walking Trees, and Other Tales. Dublin: Gill, 1885.

The Late Miss Hollingford. London: Blackie, [1886]. Another edition, No. 921 of the Seaside Library. New York: G. Munro, 1887.

The Life and Adventures of Robinson Crusoe. Edited. 1886.

Marcella Grace; an Irish Novel. London: Kegan Paul, 1886. Another edition, illustrated: [1896].

Vagrant Verses. London: Kegan Paul, 1885. Another edition: 1886. Another edition: London: Elkin Mathews, [1899].

A Fair Emigrant. London: Kegan Paul, 1888. Another edition: 1889.

Calendar of Ancient Records of Dublin. Edited. Dublin Corporation: 1889.

Gianetta; a Girl's Story of Herself. London: Blackie, 1889. Another edition: 1901. Reissued: 1925.

The Haunted Organist of Hurly Burly, and Other Stories. The Idle Hour Series. [1891]. Another edition: 1894.

The Mystery of Hall-in-the-Wood. London: Sunday School Union, [1893].

Fifty-Two Stories of Girl-Life at Home and Abroad. [1894].

Marigold and Other Stories. Dublin: Eason, 1894. Another, retitled edition: *The Marigold Series of Tales:* Dublin: Catholic Truth Society, [c.1911].

Banshee Castle. London: Blackie, 1895. Another edition, retitled *The Girls of Banshee Castle.* London: Blackie and Son, [1925].

Puck and Blossom; Our Own Story and Other Tales. London: Catholic Truth Society, 1896.

Nanno; a Daughter of the State. London: Grant Richards, 1899.

Onora. London: Grant Richards, 1900. Another retitled edition: *Norah of Waterford:* London and Edinburgh: Sands, 1915.

Terry; or, She Ought to Have Been a Boy. London: Blackie, [1900].

Cynthia's Bonnet Shop. London: Blackie, 1901.

The Squire's Grand-Daughters. London: Burns and Oates; and New York: Benziger, 1903.

The Tragedy of Chris. London and Edinburgh: Sands, 1903.

A Girl's Ideal. London: Blackie, 1905. Another edition: [1925].
Life of Sir John T. Gilbert. London: Longman's, 1905.
Our Boycotting: a Miniature Comedy. Dublin: Gill, 1907.
Our Sister Maisie. London: Blackie, 1907. Reissued: [1940].
The Story of Ellen. London: Burns and Oates, and New York: Benziger, 1907.
The Return of Mary O'Murrough. Edinburgh and London: Sands, 1908. Reissued: 1910.
Spirit and Dust; Poems. London: Elkin Mathews, 1908.
Cousin Sara; a Story of Arts and Crafts. London: Blackie, 1909.
Father Tim. London and Edinburgh: Sands, 1910.
The O'Shaughnessy Girls. London: Blackie, 1911. Reissued: [1933].
Fair Noreen; The Story of a Girl of Character. London: Blackie, 1912. Reissued: London and Glasgow, [1927]. Another edition: *The Omnibus Book for Girls.* [1940].
Twin Sisters; an Irish Tale. London: Blackie, 1913. Reissued: [1925].
Old School Friends. London: Blackie, 1914. Reissued: [1925] and [1940].
The Daughter in Possession; The Story of a Great Temptation. London: Blackie, 1915.
Dreams and Realities; Poems. London and Edinburgh: Sands, 1916.
Narcissa's Ring. London: Blackie, 1916. Reissued: [1926].
O'Loughlin of Clare. London and Edinburgh: Sands, 1916.
The Cranberry Claimants. London: Sands, [1932].
Price and Saviour; The Story of Jesus Simply Told for the Young. Dublin: Gill, n.d.

MULVANY, Eliza

Eliza Mulvany is listed in *The Poets of Ireland*, without further biographical substantiation.

Bibliography:
Thoughts in Verse. London: 1878.

MURPHY, Bessie

Born: 1857, at Birkenhead
Died: 17 December 1880
Married name: Bessie Mullen

Bessie Murphy was born in England of Irish parents from Tully-donnell. The family returned to Ireland in 1872, and she married Patrick Mullen in 1878. She contributed to *The Nation*, *Weekly News*, and other Dublin papers.

MURPHY, Eileen
Eileen Murphy was apparently from the Kilkenny area. The *Irish Monthly* published three of her poems, in issues from June 1924 to November 1924.

Bibliography:
Our Last Two Thousand Years; an Irishwoman's History of England.
  London: L. Dickson and Thompson, 1935.

MURPHY, Katharine Mary
Born: 1840, in Ballyhooley, Co. Cork
Died: 10 April 1885, in Cork, and buried in
        Killavullen Churchyard, Co. Cork
Pseudonyms: Brigid, and Elizabeth Townsbridge

There is an alternative birthdate of 1825 for Katharine Murphy, but 1840 seems the more likely date as she is reported to have been a relatively young woman at the time of her death.

Katharine Mary Murphy was the daughter of a coal merchant on Pope's Quay, Cork. Her mother was the former Miss Foley from Ballyhooley. Katharine spent her first two or three years in Ballyhooley before the family moved to Cork. She had one sister who died in infancy, and her only brother later became a doctor and emigrated to Australia. Mr Murphy's business failed shortly before his death and there arises a discrepancy regarding her mother's death. One account states that Katharine's mother predeceased her father, while another report says that Mr Murphy's death left his family destitute, and that Katharine's mother died shortly thereafter from the stress of the family's collapsed finances.

Following her mother's death, Katharine opened her own shop, but it failed, and she was barely able to support herself by writing for the Irish papers. Beginning in 1884 her health deteriorated, while she suffered with a progressively debilitating illness, probably cancer. Katharine entered the South Infirmary in Cork and died there at the age of forty-five. In the final seven or eight years of her life she wrote only prose pieces.

Katharine was as regular contributor to *The Nation, Cork Examiner, Young Ireland, Sharp's London Magazine,* and to some American publications. Her poem, 'Sentenced to Death' first appeared in *The Nation* and was frequently reprinted by that periodical.

Anthologized in: *Birthday*.

Biographical References:

Russell, Matthew. 'Our Poets, No. 14: Katharine Murphy (Brigid)'. *Irish Monthly* 13 (1885): 433-40.

Sherlock, Thomas. 'Kate Mary Murphy (Brigid)'. *Young Ireland* 11 (1885): 320-1.

MURPHY, Kathleen M.
Died: 22 March 1963, in Birr

Kathleen Murphy was born in Birr to a devout Catholic family. Her two step-brothers became priests in the Killaloe diocese. Kathleen was generally acknowledged to be the most widely travelled Irishwoman of her era, and she was well-qualified to write the travel articles she occasionally published in Catholic journals. Kathleen won first prize in the 1932 *Aonach Tailtean* Literary Competition, and received the Papal decoration *Pro Ecclesia et Pontifice* for her poetry. When she was not travelling, Kathleen regularly attended all Dublin's theatrical and musical events. She was a tall woman, and always wore a black mantilla without the high combs.

Kathleen Murphy sent an autobiographical letter to Father Senan, editor of *The Capuchin Annual* for the 1945/46 edition. This letter merits inclusion in its entirety.

Dear Father Senan,

. . . As to the autobiographical note: there is nothing whatever interesting about me except the fact that I have travelled more than anyone I ever met — indeed I believe I might justly claim to be Ireland's super-tramp! Intensely interested in ancient civilisations, I have visited nearly all the famous ruins of the world, including even those of the Khmers and the Incas. Not only have I climbed the Great Pyramid of Egypt and the Great Wall of China but — a far rarer achievement — I have stood on the pillar of St Simon Stylites in Syria. I have seen pageants of all kinds, ranging from the wonderful carnival of Rio to the weird, colourful cremation ceremony of Bali; have been in a Lapp camp and an opium den; dined with a sheik in Morocco, and accompanied a muezzin at sunset to the summit of a minaret when he chanted across the Sahara the impressive call to evening prayer. I succeeded in penetrating into the palace of the Shah of Persia to see the marvellous Peacock Throne; then, in a Peruvian port, had to submit to the humiliating experience of being treated as a mere piece of merchandise when I was hoisted by a crane on board a boat just like the cargo. Having lived alone in a stark simplicity of a jungle shack and in the tense atmosphere of a desert hut in Iraq while the tribes waged war against the Government, it seemed to me most luxurious to rest in peace when my sleeping apartment happened to be one of the rock tombs of Petra. Among memorable incidents I may mention finding myself locked inside the mausoleum of a Shogun in Japan; a narrow escape from being shot by a sentry in the fortress of Belgrade; and being nearly buried alive in Babylon. My volume of poems (published in 1932) won the First Prize in the *Tailteann* Literary Competition of that year, and I received the Papal decoration *Pro Ecclesia et Pontifice* for religious poetry. I hope you will be able to select eighty words from the above. I must ask you to excuse me for not sending photo. Very rarely in my life have I been photographed, and the only fair modern one I possess represents me mounted on what I believe was the tallest camel in Africa. I am sure you would consider this far too unconventional to be published in 'The Capuchin Annual' . . .

Sincerely yours, K. M. Murphy

In issues of *Studies*, March 1918 to June 1919, are four poems by Kathleen M. Murphy. Another two poems are in the *Capuchin Annual*, issues of 1950-51 and 1959.

Biographical Reference:
Mac Greevy, Thomas. 'The Lady of Birr; the late Miss K. M. Murphy'.
   Capuchin Annual (1963): 384.

Bibliography:
Poems. Dublin and Cork: Talbot Press, 1932.

MURPHY, Maureen
The *Catholic Bulletin* has three poems by Maureen Murphy in issues from July 1929 to September 1929.

MURRAY, Nora J.

Bibliography:
Wind Upon the Heath. Dublin: Munsel and Co., 1918.

N

NALLY, Lilian Mary
The *Catholic Bulletin* published twenty-seven poems by Lilian Mary Nally, during the period from July 1927 to March 1939.

Bibliography:
A Knapsack of Dreams. Dublin: Brian O'Higgins, [c.1935].

NEALE, A.
A Quaker woman, apparently from Coleraine, Co. Derry.

Bibliography:
Biblical Sketches and Hymns. London: 1854.

NEEDHAM, Mary P.
Born: Ballynure, Co. Wicklow
Died: 7 November 1907

Mary was the fourth daughter of Reverend George Needham of Ballynure, Co. Wicklow.

Bibliography:
Irish Legends, Poems and Verses. Dublin: 1904.

NETHERCOTT, Henrietta
Pseudonym: Henrietta

Bibliography:
Poetical Pieces of Religion and Nature. Dublin: John Robertson, 1856.
The Traveller's Dream, and Other Poems. Dublin: John Robertson, 1859.

NETHERCOTT, Maria
The *Irish Monthly* issue of October 1890, contains a poem by Maria Nethercott.

Bibliography:
The Story of Mary Aikenhead. London: Quarterly Series, vol. 96, 1872.

NEVILLE, Rosie
Rosie Neville published a single poem in the *Catholic Bulletin*, March 1918 issue.

NÍ CHATHÁIN, Nora

Catholic Bulletin published three poems in English by Nora Ní Chatháin between August 1928 and August 1938. A short story by this author appeared in the same journal.

NIC GHIOLLA CHRÍOST, Caitlín

Studies, December 1922 issue, has one poem in English by Caitlín Nic Ghiolla Chríost.

NOOTH, Charlotte

Charlotte Nooth may have been born in the eighteenth century, as her single volume of poetry was published in 1815. W. H. Patterson refers to Charlotte Nooth's poetry in the *Bibliography of the Dialect Society* (1873) because of her usage of Northern Irish dialects.

Bibliography:
Original Poems, Including Ballads, Written in the Dialect of the Northern Parts of Ireland, With a Play, entitled Clara; or, the Nuns of Charity, in Verse. London: 1815.
Eglantine; or the Family of Fortescue. 2 vols. London: 1816.

NUGENT, Ermengarda Greville
Title: Lady Nugent

Bibliography:
The Rueing of Gudrun, and Other Poems. London: D. Bogue, 1884.
A Land of Mosques and Marabouts; Algeria and Tunis. London: Chapman and Hall, 1894.

O

O'BRIEN, Charlotte Grace
Born: 23 November 1845, at Cahirmoyle, Co. Limerick
Died: 3 June 1909, and buried at Knockpatrick

Charlotte Grace was the daughter of William Smith O'Brien and his wife, the former Miss Gubbert of High Park, Co. Limerick. Charlotte was one of five sons and two daughters born to that union. Her family occupied a somewhat unique position, for they were both wealthy Protestant landlords and members of the native Irish aristocracy, claiming genealogical connections back to Brian Boru. Charlotte was three years old in 1848, when her father was convicted of high treason and exiled to Tasmania for his political activities. In 1854 he was allowed to return to Europe, so the family joined him in Brussels, where they lived until 1856. They were not allowed to return to Ireland until Charlotte was eleven years old.

William Smith O'Brien's home was Cahirmoyle, but the family lived with Sir Lucius O'Brien at Dromoland for a short time following the famine. Steven Gwynn, the nephew of Charlotte, wrote a memoir of his aunt and edited her posthumous collections. Gwynn reports that she always considered Cahirmoyle her true home for the first sixteen years of her life, until her mother died in 1861.

Following her mother's death, Smith-O'Brien took his daughters to live in Killiney, near Dublin. Charlotte returned to Cahirmoyle, which was then the home of her brother Edward, to finish her education under the instruction of Miss D'Arcy. Later Charlotte joined her father and another brother William, at Bangor, where her father had fallen ill while staying at a hotel. Smith-O'Brien died there, and Charlotte accompanied his body back to Dublin, before returning to live with her brother's family at Cahirmoyle. Charlotte and her brother's wife Mary were to become close friends.

Deafness appears to have been a hereditary trait for Smith-O'Brien's children, and Steven Gwynn recalls that all seven were afflicted with hearing problems to some degree. William, the second son, was entirely deaf and almost totally unable to speak. Charlotte's hearing problems began rapidly to descend upon her when she was about twenty-one years of age and she required someone to assist her with hearing by age thirty-five.

Mary O'Brien died in 1868, leaving the care of her husband and three children to Charlotte. The children were then ages four, three and two. For the next ten years Charlotte was fully occupied with caring for her nieces and nephews. Stephen Gwynn describes Charlotte during this period as:

> a big, large-boned woman, rough in her movements — could not enter a room without knocking things down, and as a girl had been the despair of those who wished her to tie her bootlaces . . . her broad square figure — which always had something of a peasant woman's dignity in its carriage — was loosely garbed in garments of her own making; and she never had the gift of delicate finish (37).

When Edwards' children left for boarding school, Charlotte's duties ended and she moved to a home of her own, Ardanóir, near Mount Trenchard. Prior to the age of thirty-five, her chief interest had been in archaeology, and she showed little interest in politics prior to 1880. It was the famine of 1879 to 1880 that redirected her attention towards the Land League, and to the question of Home Rule. She became a firm supporter of Charles Stewart Parnell, and of the 'organised revolution' concept, as she called it. Motivated by reading emigration statistics and by J. F. McGuire's book *The Irish in America*, she determined to make Irish emigration her primary concern. In particular she was interested in bettering shipboard conditions for female emigrants. She campaigned for a priest to be assigned to each of the emigrant ships, and the fact that this request was made by a Protestant lady received much publicity.

Charlotte then founded an emigrant home in Queenstown, where she provided lodging for one hundred and five emigrants at a time. She assumed the responsibility for emigrant welfare before they embarked, and she worked with Archbishop Ireland in America to provide post-emigration support. About three-thousand people annually stayed in Charlotte's boarding house. Through her efforts the shipboard conditions were greatly improved; horses were no longer stabled amid the steerage passengers, and sleeping berths were rearranged to separate married couples, unmarried men and unmarried women. Charlotte even travelled on the 'coffin ships' during Atlantic crossings to ascertain shipboard conditions. She kept the emigration home open until 1882, and was well-known during her life for her work on behalf of the emigrants. After closing the Queenstown emigration home Charlotte lived quietly at Ardanóir, caring for her group of pet dogs. In later life she converted to Catholicism.

In addition to her poetry, Charlotte Grace O'Brien wrote novels, a play and children's tales. She was a frequent contributor to *The Nation, United Ireland,* and the *Limerick Field Club Journal*. Six poems by Charlotte appeared in the *Irish Monthly*, March 1879 to May 1896 issues. *Dublin University Review* published one poem in the November 1885 issue.

Anthologized in: *Cabinet* IV, Cooke, Graves, Sparling, and Welsh.

Biographical References:
Coleman, James. 'From South and West'. *Irish Book Lover* 1 (September 1909): 21-2.
Gwynn, Stephen. Memoir. *Charlotte Grace O'Brien: Selections.*

Dublin: Maunsel and Co., 1909.

Keogh, M. C. 'Charlotte Grace O'Brien'. *Irish Monthly* 38 (May 1910): 241-5.

O'Kennedy, Richard. 'With the Emigrant'. *Irish Monthly* 38 (May 1910): 661-72.

Russell, Matthew. 'Our Poets, No. 20: Charlotte Grace O'Brien'. *Irish Monthly* 16 (December 1888): 728-33.

Bibliography:
Dominick's Trials: an Irish Story. Gall and Inglis, 1870.

Light and Shade. London: Kegan Paul, 1878.

A Tale of Venice, A Drama and Lyrics. Dublin: M. H. Gill, 1880. Another edition: London: 1881.

Lyrics. London: 1887.

Cahirmoyle, of the Old Home. Limerick: 1888.

Charlotte Grace O'Brien, Selections from her Writings and Correspondence, with Memoir by Stephen Gwynn. Dublin: Maunsel and Co., 1909.

Selections from the Writings and Correspondence of Charlotte Grace O'Brien. Stephen Gwynn, ed. Dublin: Maunsel, 1909.

O'BRIEN, Frances Marcella Attie
Born: 24 June 1840, at Peafield, near Ennis, Co. Clare
Died: 5 April 1883, in Dublin, and buried in the
        old churchyard, at Kildysart
Pseudonym: Attie O'Brien

Attie, as she was called, was the daughter of Marcella Burke Browne and William O'Brien. She was born at Peafield, a farm close to Ennis in Co. Clare. Marcella Burke Browne had been from Newgrove, near Tulla, and she died at the age of thirty, when Attie was four or five years old. William O'Brien was not successful as a farmer, so he emigrated to America in 1849, about four years after Attie's mother died. He took the older children with him, leaving Attie and her younger brother, Mahon, in Ireland with their maternal grandmother at Tulla. Attie was nine years old and Mahon was eight when their father emigrated. Shortly after their father's departure, Attie was sent to live with an aunt in Kildysart.

Attie was a delicate child who suffered with violent asthma attacks, a condition that lasted throughout her life. She never received formal schooling, but was encouraged to read from her aunt's domestic laibrary. Milton was her favourite author, and her fondness for the epic form is evidenced by Father Matthew Russell's description of her first submission to the *Irish Monthly* as, 'a cargo of blank verse which had to make two journeys from Kildysart' (*Irish Monthly* 15: 412).

Attie O'Brien was a devout woman who spent a great amount of time assisting the inmates of a workhouse located about a mile from her aunt's home. Her devotion and patience served her well, for 'any rude young lads whom the parish priest could make nothing of were entrusted to her to prepare for the Sacraments' (*Irish Monthly* 15: 414). She lived a quiet life, and her asthma worsened as she aged, leaving her physically drained for several days following an attack. She found the attacks mentally terrifying, and continued to feel that each would be the death of her, even after years of surviving the spasms. She died 'a calm and holy death' while on a brief trip to Dublin. Her body was returned to Kildysart for burial.

Attie's poems appeared in *The Nation, Weekly Freeman, Young Ireland, United Ireland, ZOZ,* and *Tinsley's Magazine.* Fifteen poems by Attie O'Brien appeared in the *Irish Monthly* during the period from February 1878 to September 1881. The *Irish Monthly* published one poem posthumously, in June 1886.

Anthologized in: *Birthday, Cabinet* IV, Sparling, and Sullivan.

Biographical References:
'Attie O'Brien: "A Hidden Life".' *Molua* (1943): 15-23.
Dawson, Charles. 'Attie O'Brien'. *Irish Monthly* 40 (Nov. 1912): 633-40.
Fairbairn, Margaret. 'Some Literary Remains of Attie O'Brien of Kildysart'. *Molua* (1944): 9-22.
O'Connell, Mrs Morgan John. *Glimpses of a Hidden Life: Memories of Attie O'Brien.* Dublin: Gill, 1887.
Russell, Matthew. 'Attie O'Brien; in Memoriam'. *Irish Monthly* 11 (May 1883): 279-81.
Russell, Matthew. 'Attie O'Briern'. *Irish Monthly* 15 (July 1887): 406-15.

Bibliography:
The Carradassan Family. New York: Sadlier, 1897. Originally serialised in the *Irish Monthly*, Vol. XVI, 1888.

O'BRYNE, Eva Bride
The June 1883 issue of *Hibernica* has a poem by Eva Bride O'Bryne.

O'CALLAGHAN, Miss
Born: Co. Meath
Died: c. 1840

Miss O'Callaghan was a resident of Drogheda, and her poetry appeared in the *Drogheda Argus*.

O'CALLAGHAN, Matilda Sophia
Matilda Sophia O'Callaghan published verse translations from the French language.

Bibliography:
The Glories of Jesus. Translated from the French of V. Huby. Dublin: privately printed, 1835.

O'CONNELL, E. M.
Married name: Mrs E. M. Ffrench

One poem in the *Irish Monthly*, July 1884 issue, is attributed to Mrs E. M. O'Connell Ffrench.

O'CONNELL, Ellen Bridget
Born: 12 November 1805, at Westland Row, Dublin
Died: 27 January 1883, in London and buried in Kensal Green Cemetery
Married name: Ellen Fitzsimon
Pseudonydm: L. N. F. and F. L. N.

Ellen O'Connell's married name is alternately spelled FitzSimon, or Fitz-Simon.

Ellen was the eldest daughter and the third child of Daniel O'Connell, the famous politician known as the Catholic Liberator. In 1825 she married Christopher Fitzsimon, a landowner and barrister who was twelve years her senior. Ellen's was an arranged marriage, with the dowry involved reported to be £5,000. Ellen's husband became M.P. for Co. Dublin from 1832 to 1837. He served as clerk of the crown and hanaper from 1837, until his death in 1856.

Ellen's poems were among the first published by the *Irish Monthly*, where four poems appeared between September 1873 and February 1879. She also contributed to *The Nation, Duffy's Fireside Magazine*, and to the *Dublin Review*.

Anthologized in: Cooke, Duffy, and Graves.

Bibliography:
Derrynane Abbey in 1832, and other Poems. Dublin: W. B. Kelly, 1863.

O'CONNOR, Ruth
The *Irish Monthly* published four poems, March 1882 to January 1884, by Ruth O'Connor.

O'CONNOR, Violet
Born: 1867
Died: 1946

Between May 1922 and July 1924, a total of four poems by Violet O'Connor appeared in the *Catholic Bulletin*.

Bibliography:
Sweet Scented Leaves and Other Stories. Ludlow: Mary's Meadow, 1913.

O'DOHERTY, Margaret T.
Born: 1865, near Belfast in Co. Antrim
Married name: Margaret T. Pender
Pseudonyms: M. T. P., Colleen, Marguerite, and M.

Margaret O'Doherty was the daughter of a farmer. She was educated at home, then at Ballyrobin National School, and at the Convent of Mercy, in Belfast. Margaret began writing poetry at an early age. She married a Mr Pender shortly after leaving the Convent of Mercy school. Her son, John Justin Pender, was as promising young poet who died at age thirty-five.

Margaret Pender won several of the *Weekly Freeman's* poetry competitions, and was placed second in the *United Ireland* poetry competition of 1884. She was a novelist and short story-writer, in addition to writing verse, and published in both the English and Irish languages.

Margaret was a frequent contributor to the *Belfast Morning News*, *The Nation*, *Shamrock*, and *United Ireland*, usually writing under one of her pseudonyms.

Bibliography:
The Green Cockade; a Tale of Ulster in 'Ninety-Eight'. Dublin: Sealy and Co., 1898. Another edition: Dublin: Martin Lester [1920].
The Outlaw. Dublin: Lester, 1925.
The Bog of Lilies. Dublin: Talbot, 1927. Another edition: 1929.
The Spearmen of the North. Dublin: Talbot, 1931.
The Last of the Irish Chiefs. Dublin: Talbot, n.d.

O'DONNELL, Dorothy
Dorothy O'Donnell published one poem in *Green and Gold's* September/November 1922 issue.

O'FARRELLY, Agnes Mary Winifride

Born: Raffenny House, Co. Cavan
Died: 1951

Agnes O'Farrelly was educated at University College, Dublin. She was a scholar and an administrator, serving in the National University of Ireland Senate and as a member of the governing body of University College, Dublin. 'She pioneered the Irish language revival, was a member of the Executive Committee of the Gaelic League and President of the International Celtic Congress' (Newmann 203). Agnes was Professor of Irish Poetry at University College, Dublin; M.A. of the Old Royal, and D. Litt. *honoris causa* from the National University of Ireland. In 1929 Stephen Quinn called Agnes O'Farrelly 'Our Bilingual Poet'.
    The *Irish Monthly* published two of her poems in English in the issues of April 1925 and June 1929.

Biographical References:
Butler, Dame Columba. 'Agnes O'Farrelly and Aran'. *Capuchin Annual* (1952): 473-8.
Quinn, Stephen. 'Our Bilingual Poet'. *Catholic Bulletin* 19 (July 1929): 602-9.

Bibliography
Out of the Depths. Dublin: Talbot; and London: T. Fisher Unwin, 1921.

O'GRADY, Eleanor
Two poems by Eleanor O'Grady are included in Reverend J. J. Nesbitt's collection, *The Unique Reciter*. She is reported to have written *Select Recitations*, about which publishing information has not been found.

O'HANLON, Mary I.
Born: 25 March 1856, in Dublin
Died: April 1884, in Drumcondra
Married name: Mary I. Kelly

Mary was the daughter of a builder, Henry O'Hanlon, and began publishing her poetry at an early age. At age twenty-three she emigrated to India and the following year she married a hotel proprietor, Mr Richard Kelly, in 1880.

Mary O'Hanlon published poetry in the *Penny Dispatch*, and the *Weekly Freeman*. She may also have contributed poems to the *Bombay Gazette* while she was living in India.

O'HARA, Cassie M.

Cassie O'Hara lived near Ballymena, in Co. Antrim. She won the Tercentenary of St Teresa prize for 'Saint Teresa of Jesus; A Poem in Four Cantos'. Cassie O'Hara also wrote short stories.

Cassie was a regular contributor to the *Catholic Fireside*, and five of her poems were published in the *Irish Monthly*, January 1882 to March 1886.

Bibliography:
Clare's Sacrifice: a Tale for First Communicants. London: R. Washbourne, 1880.
Saint Teresa of Jesus; a Poem in Four Cantos. London: R. Washbourne, 1883.

O'KEEFE, Lena Lanigan
Pseudonym: L. L. O'K.

The *Irish Monthly* published three poems by Lena O'Keefe between June 1910 and July 1912.

O'LEARY, Ellen
Born: 22 October 1831, in Tipperary
Died: 16 October 1889, in Cork, and burried in Tipperary
Pseudonyms: Lenel, and Eily

Ellen's brother, John, was the Fenian selected by William Butler Yeats to personify the death of 'Romantic Ireland'. Ellen also took an active role in the Fenian movement, and it was through her work for her brother's paper, *The Irish People*, that she met Edward Duffy, a Roscommon man and a devoted member of the Fenian movement. There are conflicting reports as to whether it was Ellen or Mary, her half-sister, who was engaged to Edward Duffy, the good friend of O'Donovan Rossa and of John O'Leary. Duffy was again arrested in 1867, and died in solitary confinement at Millbank. Ellen O'Leary never married.

Ellen was a member of the St Vincent de Paul Society, and President of the Sacred Heart Society in Tipperary. The Society's first director was Father Shelly, and is referred to as *Soggarth aroon* in Ellen's poetry. Jessie Tulloch (see listing), in her memoir of Ellen, sadly informs the reader that Ellen was an inept seamstress. However, Tulloch also reports that Ellen continued to ply her needle on behalf of the poor, and that she derived great satisfaction from seeing her garments worn by needy locals. Jessie Tulloch implies that Ellen's lack of sewing skills made her handiwork easily recognisable.

In 1881 Ellen was elected a treasurer for the new Ladies' Land League. Ellen O'Leary lived in Tipperary, at her home 'Lady Lodge' until 1885, when she established a household with her brother at 40 Leinster Road, Rathmines.

Ellen was diagnosed with cancer of the breast and abdomen about 1885. An operation failed to fully contain the growth and she slowly declined. Ellen made a final round of visits to friends and family in 1889, before she died on 16th October 1889, in Cork, at the home of her nephew, John King. Her brother was in Paris visiting the dying J. P. Leonard, and was unable to return in time to attend Ellen's funeral. She is buried in the O'Leary plot, in the old cemetery, in Tipperary.

Her volume, *Lays of Country, Home and Friends*, was published posthumously and contains the commemorative poem, 'Ellen O'Leary', the final poem written by Rose Kavanagh (see listing).

Ellen O'Leary contributed to *The Irish People, The Gael, The Nation, Irishman,* and *Irish Fireside.* The *Irish Monthly* published five of Ellen's poems, March 1887 to May 1889.

Anthologized in: Brooke/Rolleston, *Cabinet* IV, Cooke, Graves, Sparling, Welsh, and Yeats.

Biographical References:

Mulholland, Rosa. 'Some Recollections of Ellen O'Leary'. *Irish Monthly* 39 (1911): 456-62.
Obituary. *Cork Examiner* (16 October 1889).
Obituary. *Nation* (26 October 1889).
Obituary. *United Ireland* (26 October 1889).
Obituary. *Nationalist* (26 October 1889).
Rolleston, T. W. Introduction. *Lays of Country, Home and Friends.* Dublin: Sealy, Bryers and Walker, 1891.
Yeats, W. B. 'Ellen O'Leary; 1831-1889'. *Poets and Poetry of the Century.* Alfred Miles, ed. Vol. 5. London: Hutchinson, 1892.
Tynan, Katharine. Obituary. *Boston Pilot* (9 November 1889).

Bibliography:
Lays of Country, Home, and Friends. T. W. Rolleston, editor. With portrait, memoir and introduction by Sir Charles Gavan Duffy. Dublin: Sealy, Bryers and Walker, 1891.

O'LEARY, Kate
Kate O'Leary was a resident of Graiguenamanagh, Co. Kilkenny. She was a regular contributor to the *Weekly Freeman, Irish Emerald, New Ross Standard*, and *Shamrock*.

Bibliography:
A Bresna from Bandon Hill. Wexford: privately printed, 1901.

O'MEARA, Kathleen
Born: 1839, in Dublin
Died: 10 November 1888, in Paris
Pseudonym: Grace Ramsey

Kathleen O'Meara was the daughter of a Tipperary man, but the family moved to Paris shortly after her birth. She claimed to have been related to Barry O'Meara, Napoleon's physician during his final years. Kathleen was a regular contributor to the *Irish Monthly*.

Anthologized in: *Birthday*.

Bibliography:
Frederic Ozanum; His Life and Works. Edinburgh: 1876. Another edition: 1878.
Iza; a Story of Life in Russian-Poland. London: Burns, Oates and Washbourne, 1877.
A Heroine of Charity. London: Burns, Oates and Washbourne, 1878. Another edition: [1912].
The Bells of the Sanctuary. London: Burns and Oates, 1879.
Henri Perreyve; and His Counsels to the Sick. Translated and with biographical sketch. 1881.
Madame Mohl; Her Salon and Her Friends. London: R. Bentley and Son, 1885. Another edition: Boston: Roberts Bros., 1886.
Queen by Right Divine; and Other Tales. London: Burns, Oates and Washbourne, 1885.
Thomas Grant; First Bishop of Southwark. Second edition: London: W. H. Allen and Co., 1886.
The Old House in Picardy. London: Bentley and Son, 1887. Another edition: 1897.

Narka; a Novel. 2 vols. London: Bentley and Son, 1888. Another edition: 1897.

The Blind Apostle and a Heroine of Charity. London: Burns and Oates, [1890].

The Ven. Jean Baptiste Vianney, Cure d'Ars. London: 1891.

Queen by Divine Right; Jeanne Rendu. London: Burns and Oates, [1912].

A Woman's Trials. London: Hurst and Blackett, n.d.

Are You My Wife? London: Tinsley, n.d.

A Salon in the Last Days of the Empire. London: n.d.

Life of Bishop Grant. London: n.d.

O'NEILL, Henrietta Bruce
Married name: Henrietta Boate

Henrietta Bruce O'Neill published her first volume under her maiden name. She later married Edward Wellington Boate, a prominent Irish journalist. Her second volume lists the author as Henrietta Boate, and the preface was written from Lower Gloucester Street, Dublin. She is reported to have written *Tales of the Sacred Heart* and *Early Doomed*, but publishing information has not been substantiated.

Bibliography:
Nugæ Canoræ. London: James McGlashan, 1847.
Carlo Marillo, and Other Poems. 1857.

O'REILLY, Mary Anne
Born: 1846

Anthologized in: Welsh.

O'REILLY, Miss
Born: Ballymorris, Co. Longford
Married name: Mrs B. Somers

Miss O'Reilly was a sister to the wife of John Burke, the genealogist. She was a close friend of Maria Edgeworth, to whom her volume of verse translations is dedicated.

Bibliography:
Selections from the Modern Poets of France; Translated into English Verse, with Biographical Notices. Dublin: 1848.

O'REILLY, Sister Amadeus
Born: 24 December 1864, at Cork
Pseudonyms: Shandonian, and John Romaine

She was the daughter of John Myles O'Reilly and her early years were spent in Cork, where she was educated in both convent and private schools. In 1882 she emigrated to America where she later joined the Franciscan Order in or about 1899.

Sister Amadeus contributed largely to American journals, although some poems by Miss O'Reilly appeared in the London *Weekly Budget* prior to her emigration.

ORR, Emily C.
Died: 16 February 1919

Emily Orr was the daughter of the Rev. Robert Orr, Methodist Minister, of Belfast, and graduated with Honours at the Royal University of Ireland, taking as subjects for her degree, History, Jurisprudence and Political Economy. The family home was 15 Malone Avenue, Belfast.

She entered the Wesley Deaconess Order in September 1903, and in 1904 was appointed Tutor in the Training College of that Order at Ilkley, in Yorkshire. She held this post until compelled through the failure of her health, to relinquish all work in 1918. She died in February 1919.

Emily Orr had prepared a volume of essays on Shakespeare, entitled *A Clown in Fairyland*, but she died before submitting the manuscript for publication. She published short sories and prose essays, most notably in *Flying Leaves*, the journal of the Wesley Deaconess Institute. She also published in *The Quest* and *The Catholic Belletin*. Of particular interest is her unpublished manuscript, "Spiritual Autobiography", which details her religious beliefs and experiences.

Bibliography:
A Harvester of Dreams. London: Burns, Oates and Washbourne, 1922.

O'RYAN, Julia M.
Born: 4 February 1823, in Cork
Died: 14 May 1887

Julia was a sister of Dr E. O'Ryan, a medical doctor and poet who was supportive of his sister's literary endeavours. She was a contributor to the *Irish Monthly*, with three poems published from April to

September 1874. Julia also wrote prose stories.

Anthologized in: Connolly.

Bibliography:
In Re Garland. London: Richardson, 1873.

O'SULLIVAN, E. C.
Married name: Mrs Denis O'Sullivan

Anthologized in: Graves *Book*.

Bibliography:
Harry Butters; Life and War Letters. Edited. 1918.
Mr Dianock. New York and London: John Lane Co., 1920.

P

PARKER, Sarah
Born: 15 May 1824, at Newry, Co. Down
Died: 1880, in Scotland
Married name: Sarah Douglas

Sarah Parker was known in Scotland as 'The Irish Girl'. She was born into an impoverished family that moved to Ayr while she was a child. Barely educated, she nonetheless began to write at an early age, and her first poems appeared in the *Ayr Advertiser*. Anna Maria Fielding (see listing), was among those who took an interest in Sarah's work and her welfare.

Unfortunately, an ill-advised marriage to a 'very intemperate' husband, resulted in a life-long state of poverty. An Irish poem she wrote in the July 1846 issue of *Dublin University Magazine*. She became a frequent contributor to *Chambers' Journal*.

Bibliography:
The Opening of the Sixth Seal, and Other Poems. Ayr: M'Cormich and
    Gemmell, 1846.
Miscellaneous Poems. Glasgow: Bowie and Glen, 1856. Another

revised edition: 1856.
Poems by Sarah Parker Douglas, 'The Irish Girl'. Printed for the author.
   Third edition: Ayr: 1863.

PARNELL, Catherine Maria Anna Mercer
Born: 13 May 1852
Died: 20 September 1910, at Ilfracombe, Devon, and buried there,
   in the Church of England's Holy Trinity Cemetery

Anna Parnell was the tenth of eleven children born to John Henry Parnell, an Anglo-Irish landlord, and his wife Delia Tudor Parnell, an American. Anna's brother, Charles Stewart Parnell, played an important role in her life and in Irish politics. The family was strictly Protestant and the study of Scripture occupied a prominent educational role. Anna was educated at home by a series of English nursemaids and governesses. She and her sister, Frances Isabel (see listing), were near in age and close friends throughout their lives.

Anna's experiences while growing up as the daughter of a Protestant landlord in post-famine Ireland sensitised her to the inequalities of social class. The death of her father in 1859, and the disregard exhibited in his will for the female members of her family, left Anna with a personal hatred of discrimination on the basis of gender. Anna's small annuity, £100 per year, was left as the responsibility of John Parnell Jr., reportedly the least competent of her brothers. Anna's income thereafter proved as unreliable as her brother. At the point when her brother's financial speculations had failed, he simply declined to pay her annuity and Anna was left destitute until her friends came to her aid.

Avondale, the family home, was rented out to pay her father's debts and the family moved to Dalkey. In 1860 the family moved again to Kingstown. She was nine when the American Civil War began, and with her maternal family's ties in America, Anna was deeply interested in the outcome. Her views were both abolitionist and Unionist in regard to the American conflict, and Anna began to view the position of the American slave and the native Irish peasant as parallels. Such views put her at odds with the prevailing Anglo-Irish support for the American Confederacy.

The family moved to Paris in 1865 where Anna studied art. She returned to Dublin at age eighteen, studying at the Royal Dublin Society Art School. Four years later she moved to London, furthering her studies at the South Kensington School of Design. She visited America and the maternal family home at Bordentown in 1879, but returned to Ireland when her brother became publically associated with the Land League. She became heavily involved in the Ladies' Land League, and remained so until the Ladies' organization was disbanded. Her distress over the part her brother played in the Ladies' League dissolution caused her to never again speak with Charles Stewart Parnell.

While Anna was living in London and assisting in Helen Taylor's 1885 campaign, Katharine Tynan developed a friendship with Anna. Following Charles Stewart Parnell's involvement in the O'Shea divorce case, and his subsequent fall from political power, she disassociated herself from her brother. Eventually Anna settled in Ilfracombe, Devon, under the name of Cerisa Palmer, to guard her privacy. On 20 September 1910 she drowned in unexpectedly rough seas around the Tunnel Baths.

Biographical References:
Cote, Jane McL. *Fanny and Anna Partnell.* Dublin: Gill and Macmillan, 1991.
Dickinson, Emily Parnell. *A Patriot's Mistake; Reminiscences of the Parnell Family, by a Daughter of the House.* London: 1905.
Hughes, Maria. 'The Parnell Sisters'. *Dublin Historical Record* 21.1 (March-May 1966): 14-27.
Obituary. *Irish Book Lover* 3 (November 1911): 57.

Bibliography:
Old Tales and New; In Verse. Dublin: Sealy, Bryers and Co., 1905.
The Tale of a Great Sham. Dana Hearne, ed. Dublin: 1986.

PARNELL, Frances Isabel
Born: 4 September 1848, at Avondale, in Co. Wicklow
Died: 18 July 1882, in Bordentown, New York, and buried in
      Cambridge, Massachusetts
Pseudonym: Aleria, Alena

Fanny Parnell was the daughter of John Henry Parnell, and his wife, the former Delia Tudor, of Boston. Fanny was also the sister of the politician, Charles Stewart Parnell. The eighth of eleven children, Fanny was close in age and in affection to her sister, Catherine Anna Parnell (see listing), and her childhood and early adolescence mirrored that of her sister. Fanny also received a small, unreliable annuity in her father's will. Frances, like Anna, never married.

In 1864 Fanny began to write poetry of a decidedly nationalistic persuasion, and she was the first Parnell to openly align herself with the cause of Irish independence. Her first poem, 'Masada', appeared in the May 1864 issue of *Irish People*. From 1869 to 1874 Fanny and her family lived in Paris with her mother's brother. Fanny worked at caring for the wounded soldiers until the Siege of Paris when she fled on foot with her mother and sister before the advancing army. Fanny returned briefly to Paris before moving permanently to the family's American home at Bordentown, in 1869, following the deaths of Fanny's maternal grandfather and uncle.

By 1880 Fanny was deeply involved in the New York branch of the Famine Relief Fund, and subsequently with the American branches of the Ladies' Irish National Land League. Her commitment to these organizations continued until failing health forced her resignation.

Fanny began to experience a mysterious and recurring fever in 1880. However, her health would be fully restored between episodes, until the next bout arrived. By late 1881 she was unable to continue her political involvements. Her death the following year was attributed to paralysis of the heart and occurred at Bordentown. Her body was carried to the Riverview Cemetery in Trenton, New Jersey, awaiting permission to have it shipped back to Ireland for burial. Charles Stewart Parnell refused the requests to have her body transported, a sentiment with which her family was evidently in agreement. A second funeral procession, which became an immense spectacle, then conveyed her from Trenton to Boston. Another funeral was held in Boston before Fanny was placed in the Tudor family vault in Cambridge.

Fanny's two volumes, *The Hovels of Ireland* and *Land League Songs*, were both published in America. Her poems appeared in the *Irish People*, *The Nation*, and the *Irishman*.

Anthologized in: Brooke/Rolleston, Cooke, Graves, Hoagland, Robinson, Sharp/Matthay, Sullivan, and Welsh.

Biographical References:
Cote, Jane McL. *Fanny and Anna Parnell*. Dublin: Gill and Macmillan, 1991.
Dickinson, Emily Parnell. *A Patriot's Mistake; Reminiscences of the Parnell Family, by a Daughter of the House*. London: 1905.
Hughes, Maria. 'The Parnell Sisters'. *Dublin Historical Record* 21.1 (March-May 1966): 14-27.
Leahy, Maurice. 'Fanny Parnell; Poet and Patriot'. *Ireland-American Review* 1.2 (1938-1939): 248-52.

PATTERSON, Annie Wilson
Born: c. 1870, at Lurgan, Co. Armagh

Died: 1934
Pseudonym: Niamh

Annie Wilson Patterson was educated at Alexandra College, Dublin, and at the Royal Irish Academy of Music. She was the first woman to earn a doctorate in music, being awarded the degree in 1889. Annie was also a Gold Medallist on the Organ, a Professor of Music, a journalist, lecturer, composer and poet. She held the position of Examiner in Music at the Royal University of Ireland, 1892 to 1895, and was re-elected in 1900. Annie Patterson was the originator of the *Feis Ceoil* movement for the Irish Music Festival. She lived primarily in Cork, at 43 South Mall. Among her numerous compositions were the Rallying Song of the Gaelic League, and two Irish operas. Most of her poetry was written for recitation.

Bibliography:
Schumann. Master Musicians Series. London and New York: 1899. Reissued: London: 1921. Another edition, revised with portraits: London: J. M. Dent and Sons; and New York: E. P. Dutton and Co., 1934.
The Story of Oratorio. The Music Story Series. 1902.
Chats with Music Lovers. n.p.: Music Lover's Library, 1905.
How to Listen to an Orchestra. London: Hutchinson and Co., 1913. Another edition: 1928.
The Profession of Music, and How to Prepare for It. London: Wells Gardner and Co., [1926].
Beautiful Song and the Singer.
Native Music in Ireland.
Irish Music in the Home.
Our National Musical Heritage.
Great Minds in Music.

PEACHY, Lucy A. M.
The December 1914 issue of the *Irish Monthly* contains a poem by Lucy A. M. Peachy.

PERRY, Jennie
The *Irish Book Lover*, April 1913, contains one poem by Jennie Perry.

PERSSE, Isabella Augusta
Born: 5 March 1852, at Roxborough, near Loughrea, in Co. Galway
Died: 22 May 1932, at Coole, near Gort, in Co. Galway
Married name: Lady Augusta Gregory

Several full-length biographies of Lady Gregory exist, and are included in the biographical reference listing. Her maiden name is sometimes given as Perse, but the general consensus and her own bookplate gives the spelling as Persse.

Augusta Persse was the daughter of Dudley and Frances Barry Persse, a wealthy Anglo-Irish Protestant couple of Roxborough House, Co. Galway. She was the youngest daughter in a family of sixteen children born to Dudley Persse during his two marriages. In 1879 she met her future husband, Sir William Gregory, while travelling in Italy. They married the following year in Dublin, on the 2nd March 1880. Sir William Gregory was a retired governor of Ceylon, and thirty-five years older than his new wife. Their home was Coole, an estate Sir William owned near Gort, Co. Galway. Coole was only a short distance from Roxborough, the Persse family home. In May 1881 their only child, Robert, was born. The following year Sir William died and his widow was never to remarry.

Lady Gregory began studying the Irish language, became proficient, and by 1890 she was collecting and translating folklore from the Coole area. She met W. B. Yeats in 1897. Their meeting was a catalyst for Lady Gregory's literary career, and for Yeats's dream of the Irish Literary Theatre. Lady Gregory, W. B. Yeats, and J. M. Synge became the three directors of the Abbey Theatre, with financial support from Miss A. Horniman, an Englishwoman. Lady Gregory was the aunt of Hugh Lane, the art dealer whose painting collection later created controversy.

Robert Gregory, a pilot in World War I, died on 23 January 1918, in Italy. Yeats immortalized Robert Gregory in his poems, particularly 'An Irish Airman Foresees His Death'. His mother was spared knowing his plane was erroneously shot down by Allied Forces.

By 1926 she was ill with cancer, and she underwent an operation in September of that year. She died six years later, in 1932. Coole had already been sold to the Department of Lands and Agriculture in 1927, although with the stipulation she be allowed to rent the property until her death.

Lady Gregory was known for her theatre work; she was playwright, actress and administrator to the Abbey Theatre. She was considered one of Ireland's prominent folklorists, both collecting tales and translating mythological tales. Lady Gregory was an enthusiastic member of the Gaelic League, assisting Douglas Hyde in founding the Kiltartan branch. She was one of the most successful and influential women of her times. Lady Gregory's translations of poetry and prose were abundant, but she wrote little original verse.

Anthologized in: Fitzhenry, Furlong/Hyde, and Hoagland.

Biographical References:
(a partial list of biographical volumes only, excluding periodicals):
Adams, Elizabeth. *Lady Gregory.*
Coxhead, Elizabeth. *Lady Gregory; A Literary Portrait.*
  Gregory, Anne. *Me and Nu; Childhood at Coole.*
  Kopper, E. A. *Lady Isabella Persse Gregory.*
  Saddlemyer, Ann. *In Defence of Lady Gregory, Playwright.*

Bibliography:
Arabi and His Household. 1882.
*Mr Gregory's Letter-Box; 1813-30.*Edited. London: Murray, 1898.
Ireland. Edited. London: Unicorn, 1901.
Cuchulainn of Muirthemne· Preface by W. B. Yeats. London: Murray, 1902.
Ulster. London: Murray, 1902.
Poets and Dreamers. Dublin: Hodges, 1903.
Gods and Fighting Men. London: Murray, 1904.
Drama Breithe Chríosta. Translated. Dublin: 1904.
Kincora. First version. Dublin: Abbey Theatre Publications, 1905.
A Book of Saints and Wonders. London: Murray, 1907.
The Kiltartan History Book. Dublin: Maunsel, 1909.
The Image: A Three-act Play. Dublin: Maunsel, 1910.
The Kiltartan Molière. Dublin: Maunsel, 1910.
The Kiltartan Wonder Book. Dublin: Maunsel, 1910.
Irish Folk-History Plays. First Series: Kincora, Grania and Dervorgilla. London: Putnam, 1912.
Irish Folk-History Plays. Second Series: The Canavans, The White Cockade, and The Deliverer. London: Putnam, 1912.
Our Irish Theatre. London: Putnam, 1914.
The Bogie Men. London: Putnam, 1915.
The Unicorn from the Stars, and Other Plays by W. B. Yeats and Lady Gregory. 1915.
The Kiltartan Poetry Book: Prose translations from the Irish. Dublin: Cuala Press, 1918.
The Golden Apple: A Play for Kiltartan Children. London: Murray, 1916.
The Dragon: A Wonder Play in Three Acts. Dublin: Talbot Press, 1920.
Visions and Beliefs in the West of Ireland. First and Second Series. London: Putnam, 1920.
Hugh Lane's Life and Achievement; with Some Account of the Dublin Galleries. London: Murray, 1921.
Mirandolina: A Comedy Translated and Adapted from La Locanciera of

Goldoni. London: Putnam, 1924.

Three Wonder Plays: The Dragon, Aristotle's Bellows, and The Jester. London: Putnam, 1923.

The Story of Brigit. London: Putnam, 1924.

Case for the Return of Hugh Lane's Pictures to Dublin. Dublin: Talbot Press, 1926.

On the Racecourse. Dublin: Talbot Press, 1926.

Three Last Plays: Sancho's Master, Dave, and The Doctor in Spite of Himself. London: Putnam, 1928.

My First Play: Colman and Guire. Mathews and Marrot, 1930.

Coole. Dublin: Cuala Press, 1931.

Ideals in Ireland. Unicorn, 1941.

Lady Gregory's Journals: 1916-1930. Lennox Robinson, ed. London: Putnam, 1946.

Four Plays. Vol. I: Damer's Gold, Hanrahan's Oath, The Full Moon, Travelling Man. London: Putnam.

Four Plays. Vol. II: The Wrens, McDonogh's Wife, The Bogie Men, Coats. London: Putnam.

Four Plays. Vol. III: The Workhouse Ward, The Jackdaw, Aristotle's Bellows, The Jester. London: Putnam.

Four Plays. Vol. IV: The Rising of the Moon, On the Racecourse, Shanwalla, The Image. London: Putnam.

PHILLOTT, Alicia C.

Alicia Phillott refers frequently to Ballymoney, Co. Antrim, in her poems.

Bibliography:
The Rectory Garden and Other Poems. London: 1866.

PIKE, Annie Margaret

The *Irish Monthly* published five poems by Annie Pike between May 1908 and January 1916.

Bibliography:
Playtime Rhymes; Verses for Children. London: Headley Bros., [1907].
Phelim the Blind and Other Verses. London: Headley Bros., [1913].
An Arab Chief, and Other Playtime Verses. Vancouver: McBeath Spedding, [1923].
Silver Bells and Cockleshells. London: Merton Press, [1926].

PIM, Sophia Soltau
Married name: Mrs Pim

Sophia Pim's volume contains a memoir written by a Bedford Pim, probably her husband.

Bibliography:
Job; a Poem, and Fugitive Pieces, with Memoir of the Author. London: Gee and Co., 1885.

PLUNKETT, Geraldine
Born: 1891
Married name: Geraldine Dillon

Geraldine was the daughter of George Nobel Plunkett, Papal Count and poet. She was a sister of Joseph Mary Plunkett, who was executed for his part in the 1916 Rising. Geraldine married Thomas Dillon, a chemistry professor at University College, Galway, and was the mother of the late Eilís Dillon, a noted writer, and grandmother of the contemporary poet, Eiléan Ní Chuilleanáin. Geraldine was also known as a painter.

Geraldine Plunkett wrote a single volume of poetry, and an introduction to her brother's volume, *Poems of Joseph Mary Plunkett* (Dublin: Talbot Press, 1919). The *Irish Review* published her poetry twice, in the June 1914 and September/November 1914 issues.

Bibliography:
Magnificat. Dublin: The Candle Press, 1917.

PONSONBY, Catherine
Catherine Ponsonby evidently emigrated to Scotland, or lived there for an extensive period of time. She was the editor of *The Christian Family Advocate* during 1852, and was a novelist.

Bibliography:
The Countess d'Auvergne; or, Sufferings of the Protestants in France in the Sixteenth Century. Edinburgh: 1841.
The Border Wardens; an Historical Romance. 3 vols. London: 1844.
The Desborough Family. 3 vols. London: 1845.
The Protégé. 3 vols. London: 1847.
Lays of the Lakes, and Other Poems of Description and Reflection. Edinburgh and Glasgow: 1850.
Confession not the Confessional. London: [1859].
A Night among the Mountains. Pleasant Stories for the Young Series, no. 7. [c.1860].

PONSONBY, Emily Charlotte Mary
Born: 17 February 1817
Died: 3 February 1877
Married name: Lady Ponsonby

Lady Ponsonby was the daughter of the Earl of Bessborough. She wrote mostly novels, and little poetry.

Bibliography:
The Discipline of Life. 1848.
Pride and Irresolution. 1850.
Clare Abbey; or, The Trials of Youth. 1851.
Mary Gray, and Other Tales and Verses. 1852. (Published anonymously).
Edward Willoughby. 1854.
The Young Lord. 1856.
Sunday Readings; Consisting of Eight Short Sermons Addressed to the Young. 1857.
The Two Brothers. 1858.
A Mother's Trial. 1859.
Katherine and her Sisters. 1861.
Mary Lyndsay. 3 vols. London: 1863.
Violet Osborne. 3 vols. London: 1865.
Sir Owen Fairfax. 3 vols. London: 1866.
A Story of Two Cousins. London: 1868.
Nora. 3 vols. London: 1870.
Olivia Beaumont and Lord Latimer. 3 vols. London: 1873.

POWER, Marguerite A.
Born: c. 1815
Died: July 1867
Pseudonym: Honoria

Marguerite A. Power was a niece of Marguerite Power, the Countess of Blessington, who was born in the late eighteenth century. Marguerite A. Power wrote novels and travel journals, in addition to poetry. She published verses in annuals, and she was 'one of the best poetesses of her day', in O'Donoghue's opinion (388). She also edited a periodical entitled *The Keepsake* from 1851 to 1857. Marguerite A. Power wrote several biographical sketches of her more famous aunt.

Anthologized in: Brooke/Rolleston.

Bibliography:
Evelyn Forester; a Woman's Story. London: 1856.
The Foresters; a Novel. 2 vols. London: 1858.
The Letters of a Betrothed. London: 1858.
Nelly Carew; a Novel. 2 vols. London: Saunders and Otley, 1859.
Virginia's Hand. London: 1860.
Sweethearts and Wives. 3 vols. Second edition: London: 1861.
Arabian Days and Nights; or, Rays from the East. London: 1863.
The Blessington Papers. Printed for private circulation, 1895.

PRESTON, May Frances
Born: 15 October 1844
Died: 16 May 1865
Pseudonym: M. F. P.

May Frances Preston was probably a native of Belfast.

Bibliography:
Memorial and Remains of M. F. P. William McIlwaine, D.D., editor.
   Belfast: privately printed, 1865.

PRICE, Mona
Dublin Magazine published thirteen poems by Mona Price between December 1923 and April/June 1931. She also wrote reviews and prose pieces.

PRINGLE, Miss
Pseudonym: Annagh

Bibliography:
The Dream of the King's Cupbearer. Dublin: Maunsel and Co., 1906.
   Another edition: 1907.

PUNCH, Helen
The *Irish Monthly* published eight poems between February 1921 and June 1934, by Helen Punch.

Bibliography:
The Sun, and Other Poems. London: printed for the author, 1928.

R

RAWLINS, Jennie L.
The *Irish Monthly* published two poems by Jennie Rawlins, in the May 1900 and September 1900 issues.

REDDIN, Mary Gertrude
Born: 1844, in Rathgar, Dublin
Died: 12 February 1917, at Loreto Abbey, Rathfarnham, Dublin,
     and buried in the Abbey cemetery
Name in religion: Sister Mary Gertrude, Mother Mary Gertrude
Pseudonym: M. R., M. G. R., and S. M. R.

Mary Gertrude Reddin was from Rathgar, but nothing more is known of her family. She entered the Loreto Abbey, Rathfarnham, on 30 May 1861, at the age of seventeen. She was professed on 27 October 1864, becoming a member of the Institute of the Blessed Virgin Mary, Irish Branch, commonly called the Loreto Order. She was a teacher for more than fifty years, before her death at age seventy-three.

Sister Mary Gertrude is described as 'a ripe scholar, a brilliant musician and a prolific authoress', in her *Irish Book Lover* obituary.

A Wreath of Wild Flowers, gives the author's names as M. and F. R. *Sunday Evening at Loreto*, is by M. G. R. Both volumes are bound with very similar cover designs, suggesting a companion-volume intent. The identity of F. R. remains a mystery.

Mary Gertrude Reddin was a frequent contributor to *The Annals of St Anthony*, *The Messenger of the Sacred Heart*, and *The Irish Rosary*.

Anthologized in: *Carmina Mariana*.

Biographical Reference:
Blake, Sister Mary. Personal letter. 15 January 1994.
Obituary. *Irish Book Lover* 8 (April-May 1917): 120.

Bibliography:
A Wreath of Wild Flowers; Poems. Dublin: W. Powell, 1875.
Sunday Evenings at Loreto; Poems. Dublin: M. and S. Eaton, 1881.
Memories; Poems. Dublin: 1887.
Nemesias, a Christian Drama.
The Little Golden Dove; a Play.
Diana or Christ; a Play.

The Coming of Conaill; a Play.
Eithne's Love; a Play.

RIORDAN, Joan
Joan Riordan published four poems in the *Catholic Bulletin*,
September 1912 to May 1914.

ROBERTSON-HICKS, Maude
The *Irish Monthly* published seven of her poems, April 1909 to April
1911.

ROBINSON, Agnes Mary Frances
Born: 1857
Died: 1944
Married name: Agnes M. F. Darmesteter

University Magazine printed five poems by Agnes Mary Frances
Robinson between the June 1879 issue and the Christmas 1880 issue.

ROBINSON, Mary
Red Hand Magazine, the September 1920 issue has a poem by Mary
Robinson.

ROCHE, Frances Maria
Born: c. 1817
Married name: Frances Maria Kelly
Pseudonym: De Rupe

Frances was the sister of Edmund Burke Roche, later Lord Fermoy. In
1834 she married James Kelly of Cahircon, Co. Clare, who was a
former M.P. for Limerick. The 'Rose', who co-authored Frances's lone
volume, was Rose Kirwan (see listing).

Bibliography:
Poems (by Rose and De Rupe). London: Longman, Brown, Green, and
    Longmans; and Dublin: James M'Glashan, 1856.

ROLT-WHEELER, Ethel
Ethel was the daughter of Joseph Wheeler from Westlands,
Queenstown, and Amina Wheeler, who was the daughter of William
Cooke Taylor, L.L.D., a noted author. Ethel seems to have preferred to
have her surname hyphenated, as Rolt-Wheeler.

She was a frequent contributor to many leading journals, including: *The Theosophical Review, Great Thoughts,* and *East and West.* Ethel belonged to the Irish Literary Society where she was a frequent lecturer. The *Irish Book Lover* carried reports of her lectures and reading, and published one of her poems in the February 1913 issue.

Anthologized in: Rhys.

Bibliography:
Verses. London: R. Brinsley Johnson, 1903.
The Year's Horoscope; Sonnets. The Brochure Series, No. 2. London: 1905.
Behind the Veil; Tales. London: David Nutt, 1906.
Famous Blue Stockings. London: Methuen and Co., 1910.
Ireland's Veils, and Other Poems. London: Elkin Mathews, 1913.
Women of the Cell and Cloister. London: Methuen and Co., 1913.
Ethel Rolt-Wheeler. John Gawsworth, ed. Richard's Shilling Selections from Modern Poets. London: 1937.

RONAYNE, M. Christine
Born: Youghal, Co. Cork
Died: January 1917
Name in religion: Sister M. Christine
Pseudonym: Caple Yland

M. Christine Ronayne was a member of the Loreto Convent at Fermoy. She was 'a prolific contributor of prose and verse to Catholic magazines' (Obituary 120). Equally at home in French and English, she published in both languages. Her obituary lists a total of five prose serials: Kilvara, The Forbidden Flame, A Steel King, A Modern Cinderella, and Sir Rupert's Wife.

Biographical Reference:
Obituary. *Irish Book Lover* 8.9-10 (April-May 1917): 120.

Bibliography:
Lord Clandonnell. London: Washbourne, 1914.

ROSS, Marian
Born: 1869, at Crossmolina, Co. Mayo
Died: 1893, in Belfast

Marian Ross was the daughter of a schoolmaster at Crossmolina, and a constant contributor to the *Weekly Irish Times* during the period from 1887-1892. She was a resident of Belfast when she died.

RUSSELL, Mary Agnes
Name in religion: Sister Mary Agnes

The *Irish Monthly* published seventeen poems by Sister Mary Agnes Russell, between August 1879 and January 1887.

RUTLEDGE, A. K.
Mrs Rutledge was the wife of a bank manager at Clifden, Co. Galway.

Bibliography:
Dream Mists. Dublin: 1911.

RYAN, Margaret Mary
Born: c. 1855, in Garrynor, Co. Tipperary
Died: 1915
Pseudonym: A. E., Alice Esmonde, M. M. R., and M. My. R.

Margaret was the sister of the Reverend Philip Ryan, P.P. of Mullinahone, and of the Very Reverend Dr John Ryan, P.P., of Ballin-garry, and Vicar-General of Cashel diocese. She was a constant contributor to the *Irish Monthly*, where ninety-five poems appeared from 1874 to 1904, usdually under the pseudonym of Alice Esmonde. Adding to the confusion, she occasionally published under the initials of her pseudonym, A. E., which is similar to the pseudonym of George William Russell (AE). Her only volume of verse lists the author by her true name, Margaret Mary Ryan.

Anthologized in: *Birthday*, *Cabinet* IV, and Robinson.

Bibliography:
Songs of Remembrance. Dublin: M. H. Gill and Son, 1889.

RYEMAN, Nora
The July 1901 issue of the *Irish Monthly* contains a poem by Nora Ryeman.

S

SALKELD, Blanaid
Born: 10 August 1880, in Chittagong, Pakistan
Died: 1959, in Dublin
Married name: Blanaid Salkeld
Pseudonym: B. S.

Blanaid Salkeld's father was employed by the Indian medical service in Chittagong. The family returned to Dublin while she was a child, and she lived there until her marriage. In 1902, she married an Englishman who worked for the Indian civil service in Bombay. At twenty-eight years of age Blanaid returned to Ireland where she joined the Abbey Theatre as an actress, using the stage name Nell Byrne. Her son, Cecil Ffrench Salkeld, became a noted artist and her granddaughter, Beatrice, was married to Brendan Behan. Blanaid wrote several verse plays, a substantial amount of poetry, and translations from the Irish and Russian languages. Her Russian translations include the work of V. Briusov, and Anna Akhmatova. Blanaid was a regular contributor to the *Dublin Magazine*, where twenty-one of her poems appeared between July 1933 and December 1959. Additional poems were published in: *Ireland To-Day*, December 1937; *Irish Writing*, November 1947 and July 1949; *Poetry Ireland*, July 1948, April 1951, June 1954; *The Bell*, December 1950. She contributed a variety of book reviews, essays and prose pieces to other Irish journals, including *Envoy*.

Bibliography:
Criticism and Courage. Tower Press Booklets, No. 6. Dublin: Maunsel, 1906.
Hello, Eternity! London: E. Mathews, Marrot, 1933.
The Fox's Covert. London: J. M. Dent, 1935.
The Engine Left Running; Poems. Dublin: Gayfield Press, 1937.
A Dubliner; Poem. Dublin: Gayfield Press, 1943.
Experiment in Error. Aldington: Hand and Flower Press, [1955].

SARGANT, Alice
Born: 1858

Bibliography:
The Crystal Ball; a Child's Book of Fairy Ballads. London: G. Bell and Sons, [1895].

The Fairy Fowk's Rade. London: E. Mathews, 1896.
Brownie; a Children's Play. London: J. M. Dent and Co., [1897]. Another edition, with music: [1898].
A Book of Ballads. London: E. Mathews, 1898.
Master Death, Mocker and Mocked; a Poem. London: J. M. Dent and Co., 1899.
Death of Oscar; a Chronicle of the Fianna, in 12 Cantos. Edinburgh and Dublin: N. Macleod, 1901.

SARGENT, Maud Elizabeth
Maud Elizabeth Sargent was a resident of New Ross, Co. Waterford.

Bibliography:
Shamrocks and Roses. London: 1908.

SCOTT, Margaret McComb
Bibliography:
Old-Time Happenings and Other Verses. Belfast: Printed at *The Witness* Office, 1921.

SCOTT, Rebecca
Rebecca was the youngest daughter of Joseph Scott, the owner of a large weaving factory in Castlefin, Co. Donegal. She was the granddaughter of William Scott, of Londonderry, who played a major role in the introduction of the weaving industry to Ireland about 1832. She wrote hymns and songs in addition to poetry. In 1880 she was awarded a £200 grant from the National Bounty Fund by Lord Beaconsfield. *Dublin University Magazine* published six of her poems, June 1875 to December 1876.

Bibliography:
A Glimpse of Spring: Gertrude's Dower and Other Poems. Dublin: 1870.
Echoes from Tyrconnel. Londonderry: Derry Sentinel Office, 1880.

SHACKLETON, Lydia
Born: 1828, in Ballytore

Lydia Shackleton was a Quaker.

Anthologized in: Armitage.

SHEKLETON, Mary
Born: 1827, in Dublin

Died: 1883, in Dublin

Mary Shekleton was the sister of Margaretta Shekleton, a prose writer. Mary was an invalid for much of her later life. She was a successful hymnist whose lone volume of poetry was published posthumously. Margaretta compiled her sister's poetry volume, and wrote the introductory memoir.

Bibliography:
Chosen, Chastened, Crowned. London and Edinburgh: Nisbet and Co.,
    1884.

SHERIDAN, Caroline Elizabeth Sarah
Born: 1809, in London
Died: June 1877
First married name: Lady Norton
Second married name: Lady Stirling-Maxwell
Pseudonyms: Libertas, and Pearce Stevenson

Caroline was a daughter of Thomas Sheridan, and the sister of Helen Selina Sheridan (see listing), who became Lady Dufferin. Caroline married George Chapple Norton in 1829, but he proved to be an unfortunate choice. Separated in 1836, George Norton cited Lord Melbourne as co-respondent in their divorce. Lord Melbourne and Caroline were cleared, but the scandal followed her throughout the rest of her life. George Norton refused to allow her to see her children for six years, until after the death of their youngest child. In responses to her estranged husband's cruelty, Caroline wrote articles and pamphlets to help change the child custody laws. Following Norton's death in 1869, she married Sir Stirling-Maxwell in 1877, but Caroline lived only a few months after this marriage.

George Meredith based his novel *Diana of the Crossways*, on Caroline Norton's troubled life. In it Meredith implies that she betrayed government secrets, an unsubstantiated claim. Her first publication, 'The Dandies Rout', was written when she was eleven years old.

Lady Norton contributed to the following periodicals: *Birthday, Cabinet* III, *The Court Magazine* (1832-4, J. Bull), *The English Annual* (1834-5), Hayes, *Fisher's Drawing-Room Scrap-book* (1846-9), *La Belle Assemblee* (1832-4, J. Bull), *The Keepsake* (1836), Lover, *Macmillan's Magazine* (1861-75), Mrs Sharp, Taylor, and Welsh.

Biographical References:
Acland, Alice. *Caroline Norton*. London: Constable, 1948.
Falvury, Paul. 'Reminiscent Sketches, XI; Caroline Norton, later Lady Stirling-Maxwell'. *Irish Monthly* 81 (December 1953): 494-5.
Hector, A. F. *Mrs Norton: Women Novelists of Queen Victoria's Reign — A Book of Appreciation*. London: Hurst and Blackett, 1897.
Perkins, Jane G. *The Life of Mrs Norton*. London: J. Murray, 1909.

Bibliography:
The Sorrows of Rosalie; a Tale, with Other Poems. London: J. Ebers and Co., 1829. Published anonymously.
The Undying One, and Other Poems. London: H. Colburn, 1830. Second edition: 1830. Another edition: 1853.
The Nudging One. 1830.
Poems. Boston: Allen and Ticknor, 1833.
The Wife and Woman's Reward. London: Saunders and Otley, 1835. Another edition: 1836.
A Voice from the Factories; in Serious Verse. London: John Murray, 1836.
The Separation of Mother and Child by the Law of 'Custody of Infants'. Considered. 1838.
A Plain Letter to the Lord Chancellor on the Infant Custody Bill. 1839. Another edition: New York: 1922.
The Dream, and Other Poems. London: Henry Colburn, 1840. Another edition, second: 1841.
Lines (on the 'Young Queen' Victoria). London: Saunders and Otley, 1840.
Letters: Dated from June, 1836 to July, 1841. London: privately printed, [c.1841].
The Child of the Islands; a Poem. London: Chapman and Hall, 1845. Second edition: 1846.
Fisher's Drawing-Room Scrap-Book; with Poetical Illustrations by Mrs Norton. London: The Caxton Press, 1847.
Aunt Carry's Ballads for Children. Adventures of a Wood Sprite. The Story of Blanche and Brutikin. London: J. Cundoll, 1847. Another edition: 1848.
Letters to the Mob. By Libertas. London: T. Bosworth, 1848. (Reprinted from the *Morning Chronicle*).
A Residence at Sierra Leone. Edited. 1849.
The Martyr; a Tragedy in Verse. London: 1849.
Tales and Sketches in Prose and Verse. London: 1850.
Love Not; a Song. [c.1850].
Stuart of Dunleath; a Story of Modern Times. 3 vols. London: George

Routledge and Sons, 1851. Another edition, 2 vols.: 1851. Another edition, the Parlour Library Series, vol. 90: 1853.

English Laws for Women in the Nineteenth Century. London: privately printed, 1854.

A Letter to the Queen on Lord Chancellor Cranworth's Marriage and Divorce Bill. London: 1855.

Remarks on the Law of Marriage and Divorce; Suggested by the Hon. Mrs Norton's Letter to the Queen. London: 1855. Second edition, with appendix: London: 1856.

The Centenary Festival; Verses on Robert Burns. London: 1859. (Reprinted from *The Daily Scotsman*). Another edition: The Burns Centenary Poems. 1859.

The Lady of La Garaye; a Poem. Cambridge: Macmillan and Co., 1862. Another edition: Cambridge and London, 1862. Another edition: 1863. Another edition: New York: Anson D. F. Randolph, [c.1865].

Lost and Saved; a Novel. 3 vols. London: Hurst and Blackett, 1863. Fourth edition: 1863. Another edition, 2 vols: 1863. Another edition: [1864]. Another edition: 1865.

Home Thoughts & Home Scenes. ('Crippled Jane'. London: Routledge, Warne and Routledge, 1865).

Old Sir Douglas. First serialised in *Macmillan's Magazine*, from January, 1866. Another edition. 3 vols. London: Hurst and Blackett, 1867. Another edition. 2 vols. Leipzig: Bernhard Tauchnitz, 1867. Another edition: 1868.

The Rose of Jericho. Edited. 1870.

Bingen on the Rhine; a Poem. London: John Walker and Co., [1888].

Some Unrecorded Letters of Caroline Norton in the Altschul Collection of the Yale University Library. Bertha Coolidge, ed. Boston: privately printed, 1934.

The English Bijou Almanack. Poetically illustrated. n.d.

SHERIDAN, Helen Selina
Born: 1807, in England
Died: 13 June 1867, in London
First married name: Lady Dufferin
Second married name: Countess of Gifford
Pseudonym: The Honorable Impulsia Gushington

Helen Selina Sheridan was the daughter of Thomas Sheridan, who was the son of Richard Brinsley Sheridan. She was the eldest of three daughters, and sister to both Lady Norton (see previous listing for Caroline Elizabeth Sarah Sheridan) and the Duchess of Somerset. She also had four brothers. When Thomas Sheridan was posted to South

Africa, Helen was the only one of the children to accompany her parents.

Following her father's death, Helen and her mother returned to London, stopping at St Helena on the way, where she recalled having watched the exiled Napoleon strolling in his garden. On 4 July 1825 she married Captain Price Blackwood, the heir to the Marquess of Dufferin and Ava. The match was approved by Helen Sheridan's mother. However, the Dufferin family disapproved, so the couple moved to Italy to avoid any further hostilities. Helen's son, Frederick Hamilton Blackwood, was born in 1826 and later became Lord Dufferin, a noted diplomat. After a two-year absence, Helen and her family returned to England, and thereafter they were frequently separated for long intervals as a result of Captain Blackwood's naval career. Her husband died in 1841, the result of an accidental overdose of morphine that had been hastily and incorrectly prepared by a chemist. She remained a widow for twenty-one years, until 1862, when she married the Earl of Gifford.

Lord Gifford was some twenty years younger than Helen, and had long adored her. Informed by his doctors that Lord Gifford was dying, Helen found she could not refuse his request that she marry him. Her son recalls that 'in justice to herself, to him and to his parents, she thought it necessary to obtain from the doctors a formal assurance that his recovery was impossible', an interesting insight into her character and the times in which she lived (Dufferin 93). Lord Gifford died within a few months, and Helen died five years later, of advanced breast cancer, in 1867.

Her son states that her early work was occasionally published under her sister's name, Caroline Norton, at the request of Helen's first husband. As the Countess of Gifford, she published one poem in the *Dublin University Magazine*, February 1865 issue. A play, 'Finesse; or, a Busy Day', was performed in the Haymarket in 1863.

Anthologized in: Brooke/Rolleston, *Cabinet* III, Cooke, Duffy, Graves, Lover, Robinson, Mrs Sharp and Yeats.

Biographical References:
Hamilton, C. J. *Notable Irishwomen*. Dublin: Sealy, Bryers and Walker, n.d.
Temple-Blackwood, Frederick Hamilton. 'A Sketch of My Mother'. *Songs, Poems and Verses by Helen, Lady Dufferin*. London: Murray, 1894.

Bibliography:
The Irish Emigrant. London: E. Hodges, 1840. A single sheet publication.
To My Dear Son, On His Twenty-First Birthday. Clandeboyne: privately printed, c. 1861.
Lispings from Low Latitudes. London: Murray, 1863.
Songs, Poems, and Verses. London: John Murray, 1894. Edited and a memoir by her son, the Marquess of Dufferin and Ava.
A Selection of the Songs of Lady Dufferin: Set to Music by Herself and Others. London: John Murray, 1895. Edited by her son.
Terence's Farewell. London: Ryle and Co., n.d.

SHERIDAN, Louisa Henrietta
Married name: Louisa Henrietta Wyatt
Pseudonym: L. H. S.

Louisa Henrietta Sheridan does not seem to have been related to the Sheridan family of literary fame. She was a frequent contributor to the annuals between 1829 and 1839.

Bibliography:
The Ladies' Offering. Illustrated by the authoress. 1830.
The Comic Offering. Edited. London: 1831.
The Diadem; a Book for the Boudoir. Edited. London: 1838.

SIGERSON, Dora Mary
Born: 1866, in Dublin
Died: 6 January 1918, in England, and buried in
Glasnevin Cemetery, Dublin
Married name: Mrs Clement Shorter

Dora Mary Sigerson was the eldest daughter of four children born to Dr George Sigerson and Hester Varian (see listing). Dora was also the sister of Hester Sigerson (see listing), and a niece of Ralph Varian and his wife, Elizabeth Willoughby Treacy (see listing). Dora Sigerson was a multi-talented woman who was proficient in sculpture, drawing, painting and poetry. She married Clement Shorter, editor of the *Illustrated London News*, in July 1895 and lived in London thereafter. Dora was a close friend of Katharine Tynan and the Furlong sisters, especially Alice Furlong (see listings).

Dora Sigerson was one of the most popular women poets of her day, and fervently nationalistic. There were several memorial poems written about her by poets of both genders. Katharine Tynan wrote in a biographical sketch that Dora Sigerson Shorter died 'of a broken heart', following the execution of the 1916 Rising leaders. While that presents a romanticized view, the executions did have a substantial impact on Dora, who felt the defeat of the Rising as an intensely personal loss.

Dora Sigerson was a frequent contributor to several magazines: thirteen poems appeared in the *Irish Monthly*, December 1888 to December 1917; one poem in the *Journal of the National Literary Society of Ireland*, 1902 issue; and one poem, posthumously, in *Studies*, March 1918. She also had work published in *Poetry Ireland*.

Anthologized in: Brooke/Rolleston, Brown, Cooke, Fitzhenry, Graves, Hoagland, Kyle, Rhys, Robinson, Sharp/Matthay, Tynan, Walsh, Walters, and Yeats.

Biographical References:
Hyde, Douglas. 'Dora Sigerson Shorter'. *Studies* 7.25 (March 1918): 139-44.
Lawlor, Bridget F. 'Dora Sigerson Shorter'. *Irish Monthly* 48 (February 1920): 100-6.
Memoriam Dora Sigerson, 1866-1923 (Died 6th January 1918). Poems by various authors. Privately printed, 1923.
Obituary. *Catholic Bulletin* 9 (February 1918): 64.
Obituary. *Irish Book Lover* 9 (Feb.-Mar. 1918): 86-7.
O'Brien, Deirdre. 'Dora Sigerson Shorter'. *Irish Monthly* 56 (August 1928): 403-8.

Bibliography:
Verses. London: E. Stock, 1893.
The Fairy Changeling and Other Poems. London and New York: J. Lane, 1897. Another edition: 1898.
My Lady's Slipper, and Other Poems. London: 1898.
Ballads and Poems. London: J. Bowden, 1899.
The Father Confessor: Stories of Danger and Death. London: Ward, Lock, 1900.
As the Sparks Fly Upward. London: Alexander Moring at the De La More Press, n.d. [c.1902].
The Woman Who Went to Hell, and Other Ballads and Lyrics. London: The De La More Press, [1902].
The Country House Party. London: Hodder and Stoughton, 1905.
The Story and Song of Black Roderick. London: Alexander Moring, 1906.
Collected Poems. Introduction by George Meredith. London: Hodder

and Stoughton, 1907.

Through Wintry Terrors. London: Cassell, 1907.

The Troubadour and Other Poems. London: Hodder and Stoughton, 1910.

New Poems. Dublin and London: Maunsel and Roberts, 1912. Third edition: 1921.

Madge Linsey and Other Poems. Dublin and London: Maunsel and Co., 1913. Another edition: 1916.

Do-Well and Do-Little. London: Cassell, [1913].

Comfort the Women; a Prayer in Time of War. Privately printed, [1915].

An Old Proverb . . . It Will Be All the Same in A Thousand Years. London: 1916.

Love of Ireland. Dublin and London: Maunsel, 1916. Another edition, with additional poems: privately printed, 1916. Another edition: 1921.

The Sad Years. With portrait and a memoir by Katharine Tynan, London: Constable, 1918. Another edition, illustrated: privately printed, 1918.

Sixteen Dead Men and Other Poems of Easter Week. New York: Mitchell Kennerley, 1919. (This is the American version of *The Tricolour*, with a short prose parable added as an introduction).

A Legend of Glendalough and Other Ballads. Dublin and London: Maunsel and Roberts, 1919. Another edition: 1921.

A Dull Day in London, and Other Sketches. London: Eveleigh Nash, 1920.

The Tricolour: Poems of the Revolution. (With portrait and a photo of the monument she sculpted to the 1916 Rising martyrs). Dublin: Maunsel and Roberts, 1922. Revised edition, edited by Dan Barry, with poems added from other volumes and the memoir by Katharine Tynan from *The Sad Years*: Cork: C. F. N., 1976.

Twenty-one Poems. London: Ernest Benn, [1926].

The Augustan Book of Modern Poetry: Dora Sigerson Shorter. London: Ernest Benn, [c.1930].

SIGERSON, Hester
Born: Dublin
Married name: Mrs Arthur Donn Piatt
Pseudonym: Uncle Remus (II)

Hester was one of four children of Dr Sigerson and Hester Varian (see listing). She was named for her mother, and she was the sister of Dora Sigerson (see listing). Hester Sigerson became Uncle Remus for the *Weekly Freeman*, following the death of Rose Kavanagh (see listing), and she remained on their staff for many years. Hester married Mr Arthur Piatt, the American Vice-Counsel for Dublin, about 1900.

Hester Sigerson was a frequent contributor to *The Lyceum*, *The Catholic Bulletin*, and the *Irish Fireside*. She also published in an American Paper, *The Providence Journal* of Rhode Island, and in *The Weekly Register*, a London paper.

Anthologized in: Yeats.

Bibliography:
The Golden Quest. Dublin: At the Sign of the Three Candles, 1940.

SKIDDY, Ellen Mary
Married name: Mrs E. M. Skiddy
Pseudonym: E. M. S.

Ellen Mary Skiddy was a contributor to the Cork *Southern Reporter and the Cork Examiner*. Her only volume was co-authored with her daughter, Mary Angela Skiddy (see listing).

Bibliography:
Miscellaneous Poems. Cork: 1866.

SKIDDY, Mary Angela
Mary Angela was the daughter of Ellen Mary Skiddy (see listing), and like her mother, Mary Angela Skiddy was a contributor to the Cork *Southern Reporter*, and the *Cork Examiner*. Mary is probably the Miss M. Skiddy whose work was anthologized in *Echoes from Parnassus*, a collection of local poetry from the Cork area, published in 1849.

Bibliography:
Miscellaneous Poems. Cork: 1866.

SKIDMORE, Harriet M.
Born: 1837
Died: 1904

Harriet Skidmore seems to have emigrated to America at some point during her life. Her only volume, *Beside the Western Sea*, was published in America.

Two of her poems were published in the *Irish Monthly's* issues of November 1881, and December 1898.

Anthologized in: Connolly.

SLATER, May Wilson
Pseudonym: May Shorsa

May Wilson Slater was a resident of Co. Meath.

Bibliography:
Love Letters of a Fenian; In Verse. Dublin: M. H. Gill, 1901.

SMITH, Bridie M.
Bridie M. Smith published one poem, an ode in memory of Father Meehan, which appeared in the *Breifny Antiquities Society Journal*, 1927-1933 edition. That same journal, in the 1923-26 edition, has a prose article about Castletara by Bridie.

Bibliography:
Cavan, Past and Present; The Official Guide. [1927].

SMITH, Charitie Lees
Born: 27 June 1841 at Bloomfield, Merrion, Co. Dublin
Married name: Charitie Lees Bancroft

Charitie was the daughter of Reverend Sydney Smith, D.D., rector of Aghalurcher, Co. Fermanagh. She was a popular hymnist.

Anthologized in: MacIlwaine

Bibliography:
Within the Veil; Verse. 1867.

SMITH, Frances Mary
The *Irish Monthly* published two of Frances Mary Smith's poems, in the October 1888 and January 1889 issues.

SMITH, Miss
Married name: Mrs Thomas Christian Scott

She was the daughter of a Mr Palmer Smith.

Bibliography:
Poems. Dublin: privately printed, 1889.

SMITH, Sara Trainer
Died: 1899

Sara Smith emigrated to America where her books were published. Her only publication in Ireland was a single poem in the March 1900 issue of the *Irish Monthly*.

SOLOMONS, Rosa J.
Bibliography:
Facts and Fancies. Dublin: W. M'Gee, 1883.

SPARROW, Alicia Jane
Born: Killabeg, Enniscorthy, Co. Wexford
Died: 30 September 1858
Married name: Alicia O'Neill
   Alicia was the daughter of Edward Sparrow and was married to a Mr W. P. O'Neill. She died 'at a comparatively early age', (O'Donoghue 364).

Alicia was a frequent contributor to many journals, including: *The Dublin University Magazine, The Book of Beauty, New Monthly Magazine, Athenaeum, Literary Aspirant*, and *The Knickerbocker or New York Magazine*. Marguerite A. Power (see listing) also published some of Alicia's poems in *The Keepsake*, during the period from 1851 to 1857.

SPRING-RICE, Lucy
Born: 9 November 1845
Died: 10 May 1884
Married name: Lucy Knox

Lucy was the daughter of Stephen E. Spring-Rice and she married Octavius Newry Knox on 23 August 1866. With her sister, Aileen, Lucy Spring-Rice ran a private press at Mount Trenchard, Foynes.

Bibliography:
Sonnets and Other Poems. London: 1872. Second edition: London: 1876.
Pictures from a Life, and Other Poems. London: 1884.

STEELE-NICHOLSON, Lola
Studies published two poems, March 1920 and March 1921, by Lola Steele-Nicholson. The *Irish Monthly* published three of her poems,

in issues from November 1920 to May 1921.

STEWART, Mary
Bibliography:
The Mirror of the Heart; or Lays of Loyalty, Patriotism, Chivalry, and Devotion, with Music and Sketches. Dublin: Hodges, Smith and Co., 1861.

STOCK, Sarah Geraldine
Born: 27 December 1838
Died: 29 August 1898, in North Wales

Sarah Stock was probably born in the North of Ireland. Her works indicate that she was married to Eugene Stock and lived a large part of her life in Africa, probably as a missionary. She was thoroughly familiar with the country of Uganda. Sarah translated from and into the Yoruban language and she wrote one volume in Welsh. Apparently she was best known as a hymnist and a writer of religious prose during her lifetime. C. Maud Battersby (see listing) wrote a memorial poem following Sarah's death.

Bibliography:
Lessons on Israel in Egypt and the Wilderness; For The Use of Sunday School Teachers. Reprinted from the *Church Sunday School Magazine.* London: [1874].
Steps to Truth. With E. Stock. [1878]. Another edition, entitled *Isise si Otito*, was a translation into the Yoruban language: [c.1909].
The Child's Life of Our Lord. London and Belfast: [1879].
Give Ye Them to Eat; Meditations for Sunday-School Teachers, Founded on the Miracle of Feeding the Multitude. London: W. Wells Gardner, [1879].
From the Call to the Glory; or, Some Names of Christ's People. London: Religious Tract Society, [1881].
Bible Stories from the Old Testament. London: Church of England Sunday School Institute, [1884].
Joy in Sorrow. Second edition: London: J. F. Shaw and Co., 1884.
The Brighter Day. With E. H. Tompson. London: J. E. Hawkins, [1889].
The Eastern Equatorial African Mission of the Church Missionary Society. London: Church of England, 1891.
Life Abundant, and Other Poems. London: J. F. Shaw and Co., 1892.
The Story of Uganda and the Victoria Nyanza Mission. London: Religious Tract Society, 1892. Second edition, revised and enlarged: 1894.
The Story of the Year, 1893-1894. London: Church of England

Missionary Society, 1894.

Missionary Heroes of Africa. London: London Missionary Society, 1897.

Suffer Little Children; Verse and Prose. London: Marcus Ward and Co., [1894].

STODART, Mary Anne

Mary Anne Stodart's writings are very religious and fiercely Loyalist. O'Donoghue states, 'There are 118 "Christian" epigrams by this writer in Major McGregor's *Epigrams from the Greek Anthology*' (440). In 1849 the two-volume anthology of poetry compiled by the National Board of Education in Ireland included her work in the second volume.

Bibliography:
Hints on Reading; Addressed to a Young Lady. London: 1839.

Every Day Duties; in Letters to a Young Lady. London: 1840. Another edition: London: 1858.

Scriptural Poems for Children. 1841.

Female Writers; Thoughts on Their Proper Sphere, and on Their Powers of Usefulness. London: 1842.

Principles of Education Practicably Considered; with an Especial Reference to the Present State of Female Education in England. London: 1844.

National Ballads, Patriotic and Protestant. London: 1841. Second edition: 1851.

Christian Epigrams. Translated from Greek and Latin. [c.1857].

STOPFORD, Miss A. St. G.
Pseudonym: A. St. G. S.

Miss A. St. G. Stopford was a resident of Ardbraccan, Co. Meath. The proceeds of her volume were 'given to the suffering poor of Ireland', according to the cover. She seems to have been related to Edward Adderley Stopford, the Archdeacon of Meath, and his daughter, Alice Stopford Green, the well-known historian.

Bibliography:
Sad Sounds from a Broken Harp, or a Faint Death-cry from Ireland. Second edition: Dublin: Grant and Bolton; and London: Francis John Rivington, 1847.

STOPFORD, Octavia
Bibliography:
Sketches in Verse, and Other Poems. Hull: privately printed, 1826.

SULLIVAN, Madge
The *Catholic Bulletin* published three of Madge Sullivan's poems in issues from January 1929 to May 1930.

SWAN, Caroline D.
Only one poem, in the *Irish Monthly's* August 1911 issue, is attributed to Caroline Swan.

SWEETMAN, Elinor Mary
Born: c. 1860

Elinor Sweetman was the third daughter of Michael James Sweetman of Lamberton Park, County Laois, and his wife, the former Miss Powell of Fitzwilliam Square, in Dublin. Her sisters were Mary and Agnes Sweetman, who both became writers. Elinor's sister, Mary Sweetman (see listing), published under the pseudonym M. E. Francis, while Agnes used her married name, Mrs Anthony Egerton Castle. Elinor was educated by governesses at home, then in Brussels and London. Her primary interest apparently was music, and Katharine Tynan notes, 'to that she has devoted the greater portion of her life' (*Cabinet* IV, 317).

Nine of Elinor Sweetman's poems were published in the *Irish Monthly*, from October 1889 to May 1894.

Anthologized in: *Cabinet* IV, Cooke, Graves, and Gregory.

Bibliography:
Footsteps of the Gods, and Other Poems. London: G. Bell and Sons, 1893.
Pastorals, and Other Poems. London: J. M. Dent and Co., 1899.
Psalms. London: 1911.
The Wild Orchard. London: Herbert and Daniel, 1911.

SWEETMAN, Mary
Born: 22 August 1859, at Killiney Park, Co. Dublin
Died: 9 March 1930, at Maes, Alyn, and buried in the
        Little Crosby Churchyard
Married name: Mrs. Francis Blundell
Pseudonym: M. E. Francis

Mary Sweetman was the second of four daughters born to Michael James and Margaret Sweetman. Margaret was the daughter and heiress of Michael Powell, of Fitzwilliam Square, Dublin. Mary was one of five children, four girls and a boy and she was so frail at birth that she was baptised immediately and given only the name Mary, 'it being considered not worth while to bestow more than one name upon a child who appeared to have no intention of remaining in this world' (Blundell 1). However Mary survived and the family moved when she was a few years old to Lamberton Park, Co. Laois, where their home was three miles from the parish church at Portlaoise. Three of the four Sweetman daughters were to become writers: Mary, Elinor (see listing) and Agnes.

Mary Sweetman credited her early governess, Miss Larkin, with instilling her love of literature. Agnes, Elinor and Mary founded two magazines, *The Ivy Home Magazine* and *The Ivy Home Library*, with the editorial offices of both these childhood ventures being ' "a little clearing in the shrubbery . . . hidden from the eyes of the grown-up world and completely overgrown with ivy" ' (Blundell 9). Mary wrote her first novel at the age of eight, *True Joy*, which was quickly destroyed. Mary's sisters tore up the manuscript when she refused to allow them to read it, on the grounds the story was far too mature. In 1873, the Sweetman family moved to Brussels, and the girls studied music, painting and languages. They stayed four years in Brussels before returning to Ireland when Mary was eighteen. The family's holiday excursions were to Switzerland, Ireland and Italy.

In Brussels, Mary began to correspond with the editor of the *Irish Monthly*, Father Matthew Russell, who became her literary mentor. She also met her future husband, Francis Nicholl Blundell, who was the second son of Colonel Blundell, of Crosby in Lancashire. Mary Sweetman's mother had been an heiress and had married well, so the match between Mary and Francis was forbidden by Mary's mother because of the financial inequality between the pair. Mary's mother expected a suitable match for her daughter, and Francis's prospects were dim. After two years of protest Mrs Sweetman became resigned to the match and her daughter was married to Francis Blundell on 18 November 1879. Coincidentally, Mary Sweetman's first publication in the *Irish Monthly* occurred on her wedding day. The couple married at Lamberton Park, then moved to a small cottage in Crosby, where they settled into a happy marriage, which proved to be unfortunately short. After four years of marriage, and three children, Francis Blundell died suddenly of heart failure. Mary never remarried, and lived with her husband's family while raising her children. Mary took up writing to help pass the time, and she went on to become one of the leading novelists of her day, publishing largely under her pseudonym. Writing became her consuming interest for the remaining forty-six years of her life. Mary died after a short illness, probably of pneumonia.

Although she published only prose volumes, her poetry appeared in the *Irish Monthly*. Her work was also published in *Green and Gold*.

Biographical References:

Blundell, Margaret. *An Irish Novelists' Own Story*. Dublin: Catholic Truth Society of Ireland, c.1935.

Francis, M. E. *The Things of a Child: Memoir*. Collins, 1916.

G. M. S. 'M. E. Francis.' *Irish Monthly* 58 (May 1930): 229-39.

Bibliography:

The Little Rosary of the Sacred Heart; Containing Short Meditations for Every Day in the Month, Especially Adapted for Children. Dublin: M. H. Gill, 1886.

Whither? 3 vols. London: Griffith and Farran, 1892. Another edition: 1893.

In a North Country Village. London: Osgood, McIlvaine and Co., 1893. Another edition: 1896.

The Story of Dan. London: Osgood and McIlvaine, 1894.

Town Mice in the Country: a Story of Holiday Adventure. London: Blackie and Son, 1894.

A Daughter of the Soil. The *Times* Novels Series. London: Osgood, McIlvaine and Co., 1895.

Frieze and Fustian. [1895]. London: Osgood, McIlvaine and Co., 1896.

Among the Untrodden Ways. Edinburgh and London: Blackwood and Sons, 1896.

Maime o' the Corner. [1897]. London and New York: Harper and Brothers, 1898.

Miss Erin. London: Methuen and Co., 1898.

The Duenna of a Genius. London and Cambridge, U.S.A.: Harper and Bros., 1898. Another edition: London: Thomas Nelson and Sons, 1907.

Yeoman Fleetwood. London: Longmans and Co., 1900.

Pastorals of Dorset. London: Longmans and Co., 1901.

Fiander's Widow. London: Longmans and Co., 1901.

North, South, and Over the Sea. London: George Newnes, 1902.

The Manor Farm. London: Longmans and Co., 1902.

Christian Thal. London: Longmans and Co., 1903.

Lychgate Hall. London: Longmans and Co., 1904.

Dorset Dear. London: Longmans and Co., 1905.

Wild Wheat. London and New York: Longmans, Green and Co., 1905.

The Lord's Ambassador, and Other Tales. London: Catholic Truth Society, 1905.

Father Anselm, and Other Stories. London: Catholic Truth Society, 1905.

Simple Annals. London: Longmans and Co., 1906.

Stepping Westward. London: Methuen and Co., 1907.

Children of Light and Other Stories. London: Catholic Truth Society, 1907.

Margery o' the Mill. London: Methuen and Co., 1907.

Hardy-on-the-Hill. London: Methuen and Co., 1908.

Madge Make-the-best-of-it. The St Nicholas Series. 1908.

Galatea of the Wheatfield. London: Methuen and Co., 1909.

Noblesse Oblige. London: John Long, 1909.

The Wild Heart. London: Smith, Elder, 1910.

The Tender Passion. London: John Long, 1910.

Gentleman Roger. London: and Edinburgh: Sands and Co., 1911.

Honesty. London: Hodder and Stoughton, [1912].

Our Alty. London: John Long, 1912. Other editions: 1914, 1921.

The Story of Mary Dunne. London: John Murray, 1913.

Molly's Fortunes. London: Sands and Co., [1913].

The Child's Book of Prayers in Time of War. London: R. and T. Washbourne, 1914.

Dark Rosaleen. London: Cassell and Co., 1915.

Penton's Captain. London: Chapman and Hall, 1916.

Little Pilgrims to Our Lady of Lourdes. London: Burns and Oates, 1917.

A Maid o' Dorset. London: Cassell and Co., 1917.

The Things of a Child. London: W. Collins, 1918.

Beck of Beckford. London: Allen and Unwin, 1920.

Rosanna Dew. London: Odhams, [1920].

Renewal. London: G. Allen and Unwin, 1921.

Many Waters. London: Hutchinson, [1922].

The Runaway. London: Hutchinson, [1923].

Lady Jane and the Smallholders. With Margaret Elizabeth Clementina Mary Blundell. London: Hutchinson and Co., [1924].

Young Dave's Wife. London: Hutchinson, [1924].

Cousin Christopher. London: T. Fisher Unwin, [1925]. Another edition: Dublin: Phoenix Publishing, n.d.

Golden Sally. With Agnes Mary Frances Blundell. London and Edinburgh: Sands and Co., 1925.

Napoleon of the Looms. London: Hutchinson and Co., 1925.

Tyrer's Lass. With Agnes Blundell. London: Sands and Co., 1926.

Idylls of Old Hungary. London: Sheed and Ward, 1926.

Mossoo; a Comedy of a Lancashire village. London: Hutchinson and
Co., [1927].
The Evolution of Ænome. London: Hutchinson and Co., 1928.
Wood Sanctuary. With Margaret Elizabeth Clementina Blundell.
London: G. Allen and Unwin, 1930.

SYNGE, Frances Mary
Born: 1842, at Glenmore, Co. Wicklow
Died: 1883
Married name: Frances May Owen

Frances Synge married the Reverend James Owen, of Cheltenham
College, in 1870. She published prose pieces on Keats, and
Washington, and the volume of poetry listed below contains essays
on Shakespeare, Browning, Wordsworth, and others. Her *Essays and
Poems* was posthumously published.

Bibliography:
Essays and Poems. London: privately printed, 1887.

T

TAINTER, Helen D.
Six issues of the *Irish Monthly*, February 1882 to May 1884, contain
Helen Tainter's poems.

TANE, Ethel
The *Irish Monthly* published ten poems, October 1876 to May 1886, by
Ethel Tane.

TATHAM, Emma
Bibliography:
The Sceptre of Tara and the Dream of Pythagoras and Other Poems.
London: Bath, [1854]. Second edition, revised and enlarged: [1854].
Fifth edition, with memoir by Reverend B. Gregory. London: 1872.

Bibliography:
On the Ocean of Time: Verses. London: Hodder and Stoughton, [1890].

TERESA, Sister Mary
Only one poem, in the September 1881 issue of the *Irish Monthly*, is
attributed to Sister Mary Teresa.

THOMPSON, Marie M.
Born: 1822
Died: January 1916, at Ravensdale, Co. Louth
Pseudonyms: Ethne, and Eithne

Marie Thompson's first name is frequently given as Mary, and her
pseudonym is reported as Ethne by the *Irish Book Lover*.
    Marie was a good friend and frequent correspondent of John
Mitchel. She was noted for writing historical ballads. Beginning in
1853, she was a frequent contributor to *The Nation*. Marie's work is
found in the *Celt*, during the period from 1857 to 1859. She was
ninety-four years of age at her death.

Bibliography:
Poems by Ethne of 'The Nation'. J. de L. Smyth, ed. Dundalk: Dundal-
    gan Press, 1915.

TRAVERS, Eva L.
Married name: Mrs Evered Poole
Eva Travers is listed as an Irish poet by O'Donoghue, with no further
information.

Bibliography:
Lonely? No, Not Lonely, and Other Poems. London: 1881. Second
    edition: London and Edinburgh: Nisbet and Co., 1881.
A Christmas and New Year's Greeting to Blue Ribbons. London: Morgan
    and Scott, [1882].
Evening Stars; or, the Promises of Christ for His Little Ones. London:
    Nisbet and Co., 1882.
The Life and Letters of a Soldier. Third edition, enlarged: London: J.
    Nisbet and Co., 1883.
*A Collection of Religious Tracts, Leaflets and Cards, by E. L. Poole, and
    Others*. Southampton: Gulch and Cox, [1884].
Golden Links in a Life Chain; a Tale. London: Nisbet and Co., 1886.
Lamps for Little Feet; a Series of Tracts for the Young. London: Morgan
    and Scott, [1886].
Lotta's Life Mistake. London: Nisbet and Co., 1887.
Jewel Series; Twelve Booklets for the Young. Stirling: Drummond's

Tract Depot, [1888-1893].

Drummond's Tract Depot; a Total of Twelve Tracts in Verse. Stirling: Drummonds, [1889].

Sunbeams for the Sick and Sorrowful. London: Nisbet and Co., 1889.

What Shall I Do? Thoughts for Young Enquirers and Disciples; Sunbeams from the Shepherd Psalm, in Two Parts. Stirling: Drummond's Tract Depot, [1889].

Left Alone with Jesus, and Other Poems. London: Nisbet and Co., 1890.

Four Strong Anchors. Stirling: Drummond's Tract Depot, [1890].

Rockholme Series of Tracts. No. 1-16. Stirling: Drummond's Tract Depot, [c.1890].

Flower Stories for our Little Folks. London: Religious Tract Society, [1891].

Goodnight. Thoughts about God; or Evening Readings for the Young. London: Nisbet and Co., 1891.

Helpful Messages; in Four Parts. Stirling: Drummond's Tract Depot, [1891].

His Troublesome Sister. London: Digby and Long, [1894].

TREACY, Elizabeth Willoughby
Born: c. 1830
Died: 1896
Married name: Mrs Ralph Varian
Pseudonyms: Finola, and Finnuala

Elizabeth Treacy was probably born in Co. Antrim. She married Ralph Varian, the poet and anthology editor from Cork, in 1871. She became the sister-in-law of Hester Varian Sigerson, and thus the aunt of Hester and Dora Sigerson (see listings for Hester Varian, Hester Sigerson and Dora Sigerson). All of her volumes of poetry were published under the pseudonym of Finola. She was living at Blackrock, Co. Cork, in 1893.

Elizabeth was a constant contributor to *The Nation* between 1850 and 1860. The July 1883 issue of the *Irish Monthly* also contains her poetry.

Anthologized in: MacDermott, and Varian.

Bibliography:
Poems by Finola. Belfast: John Henderson, 1851.
Never Forsake the Ship, and Other Poems. Dublin: 1874.
The Political and National Poems of Finola. Dublin: 1877.

TREACY, Ethna
The *Irish Monthly*, July 1925 issue, has a poem by Ethna Treacy.

TRENOR, Elizabeth
Bibliography:
Tales and Essays for Youth. Dublin: 1840.

TUCKEY, Mary B.
Mary Tuckey was a resident of Ferney, near Cork. She contributed poetry to the *Dublin Literary Journal*, from 1843 through 1845.

Bibliography:
The Wrongs of Africa; a Tribute to the Anti-Slavery Cause. Glasgow: 1838. Second edition: 1838.
The Great Exemplar; Religious Poetry. Dublin: Religious Tract and Book Society for Ireland, 1839. Other editions: 1840, [c.1850].
Harry and Willie. 1844.
Creation, or a Morning Walk. Dublin: 1845.
The Christian's Economy of Human Life. [1845].
Old James, the Irish Pedlar; a Tale of the Famine. Dublin: [1852].

TUFNELL, Ida
Born: Co. Dublin
Married name: Ida Peacock

Ida was the daughter of Dr Jolliffe Tufnell, a former president of the Royal College of Surgeons of Ireland. She married Captain P. L. Peacock, and her married name is frequently spelled as Peacocke. Ida contributed verse to the newspapers on an occasional basis.

Ida Peacock is credited with having published *Brought to Light; a Collection of Short Tales*, and *Caasga; a Romance*. Publishing information about these prose works has not been substantiated.

TULLOCH, Jessie
Died: 18 April 1913, in Tipperary
Pseudonym: J. T.

Jessie Tulloch may have been born in Scotland, but her father was a shopkeeper in Tipperary, and she was raised there. She sang in the St Michael's Church Choir and was known to be a particularly gifted singer. Jessie had a stationery shop at 1 James' Street, Tipperary, in 1889. Jessie was a good friend of Ellen O'Leary. She wrote a memoir of Ellen for the *Irish Monthly*, at the request of John O'Leary. 'She was an almost life-long friend of John and Ellen O'Leary' (IBL, Obit., 196).

Jessie Tulloch was a constant contributor to the *Irish Monthly*, where fifteen poems appeared during the period from June 1888 through March 1905. She also wrote biographical sketches and short stories. Her personal recollections of John O'Leary are found in the *Irish Monthly*, March 1910 issue. Jessie also contributed to *The Gael*, *The Irish Fireside*, *The Catholic Herald* and *The Boston Pilot*.

Biographical Reference:
Obituary. Irish Book Lover 4 (June 1913): 195-6.

TULLY, Elizabeth
The *Irish Monthly* published three poems by Elizabeth Tully, between April 1929 and September 1930.

TWIGG, Lizzie
Pseudonym: Eilís Ní Craoibín

The preface in her volume was addressed from St Kevin's House, Rutland Square, Dublin.

Bibliography:
Songs and Poems. Introduction by Very Reverend Canon Sheehan. Dublin: Sealy Bryers and Walker, 1905. Another edition: London: Longmans and Co., 1905.

TYNAN, Katharine
Born: 1858, in Dublin
Died: 2 April 1931, in London
Married name: Katharine Hinkson

Katharine Tynan's death certificate lists her as seventy-three years of age at death, indicating 1858 as the proper year of her birth. There are, however, alternate dates given by reference sources ranging from 1859 to 1861.

Katharine Tynan was the daughter of Andrew Cullen Tynan, and Elizabeth Reilly Tynan. Katharine was born in Dublin, one of twelve children. The family moved to Tallaght when Katharine was a young girl, and her father became a gentleman farmer. He and Katharine were devoted to each other. Her mother was an invalid who moved about in a bath chair and died before most of the children were grown. Katharine described her mother as, 'a large placid, fair woman, who became an invalid at an early age and influenced my life scarcely at all' (*Twenty-Five Years* 27). Katharine was the sister of Norah Tynan (see listing), who recalls Katharine liked to be served her breakfast in bed, and whose household duties were foregone so Katharine could concentrate on writing. Anna Johnston was a constant visitor, as were the Sigerson sisters and the Furlongs (see listings). Katharine gave lavish Sunday luncheons for her literary friends, and Norah remembers her sister was an enthusiastic member of the Ladies' Land League.

Sometime in the late 1860s, Katharine's eyes developed a chronic ulceration and while the medical specialists were able to successfully treat the ulcers, her eyesight was severely damaged. Katharine's own term for her vision was 'purblind', but it would probably translate to a severe myopia. Her vision problems enhanced a naturally introspective nature. While the fine details of the world were no longer available to her, colours were, so colour became a correspondingly important element of her work.

Katharine Tynan was educated at the Dominican Convent of St Catherine of Siena, in Drogheda, until age fourteen. She contemplated entering the convent, particularly after her sister Mary died of typhoid just prior to beginning her training as a novitiate in 1868. After Katharine completed her education and returned from the convent she became a constant companion to her father. Her first poem was published in 1878 and her father financed the publication of her first book, in 1885, *Louise de la Vallière and Other Poems*. Her popularity was established as the volume went rapidly into a second edition. She was earning a steady income of several hundred pounds annually before her marriage. The poets, Dora Sigerson and Frances Wynne (see listings), plus Sarah Atkinson, the historian and biographer, were among her close friends. For Rosa Mulholland (see listing), Tynan had an 'idealising passion' (*Twenty-Five Years* 105).

Through her literary connections, Katharine came to know the Yeats family. Her relationship with W. B. Yeats was mutually advantageous from a literary aspect, and a romantic relationship never developed. Katharine Tynan was a devout Catholic, and Yeats's Protestant background, coupled with his mysticism, would not have attracted her. In 1920, when her friendship with Yeats had apparently cooled, she sold his letters to an American dealer for £100. It was a decision which further estranged Yeats from Tynan.

In 1893, Katharine married Henry Albert Hinkson, an aspiring barrister and a classics scholar. She travelled alone to London for the wedding. They settled first in Ealing, where Katharine's five pregnancies resulted in three living children. The family moved briefly to Notting Hill, then returned to Ealing until their move to

Ireland in 1911, when Henry Hinkson was named a Resident Magistrate for Co. Mayo. Henry remained in that job until 1919. The Hinksons were firmly middle-class, and Katharine Tynan's work reflects her support for the British policies, as well as her dislike of the 1916 'rebellion'. Perhaps her social class, coupled with having lived in England for a lengthy period and her husband's magistrate position, may explain why she was not attracted to Irish Nationalism. Following the death of her husband in 1919, she relied upon writing as her source of income, and wandered throughout Europe with her daughter, Pamela. Katharine wrote travel articles, novels, poetry and short stories in astonishing quantities.

Katharine Tynan's first poem appeared in *Graphic*. The *Irish Monthly* published twenty-seven of her poems, beginning with the July 1880 issue. Eleven poems appeared in *Studies*, December 1913 to September 1922. Single poems are found in: *Dublin University Review*, August 1885 issue; the February 1883 issue of *Hibernia*; and the *Irish Review*, August 1913 issue. She also had work published in *Green and Gold*. She edited the revised edition of *The Cabinet of Irish Literature*, a four volume anthology, that had previously been compiled by Charles Read.

Anthologized in: *Birthday*, Brooke, Brown, Cooke, Graves, Gregory, Hoagland, Lynd, Morton, Paul, Rhys, Robinson, Mrs Sharp, Sharp/ Matthay, Sparling, Sullivan, Walsh, Walters, Welsh, and Yeats.

Biographical References:
O'Mahony, Norah Tynan. 'Katharine Tynan's Girlhood'. *Irish Monthly* 59 (June 1931): 358-68.
Rose, Marilyn Gaddis. *Katharine Tynan*. Irish Writers Series. Lewisburg, Pennsylvania: Bucknell UP, 1974.
Hinkson, Katharine Tynan. Autobiographies: *Twenty-Five Years; Reminiscences*. London: Smith, Elder and Co., 1913. *The Middle Years*. London: Constable and Co., 1916. *The Years of the Shadow*. London: Constable and Co., 1919. *The Wandering Years*. London: Constable and Co., 1922. *Life in the Occupied Area*. London: Hutchinson and Co., 1925.

Bibliography:
Louise de la Vallière and Other Poems. London: Kegan Paul and Co., 1885. Another edition: 1886.
Shamrocks. London: Kegan Paul, Trench and Co. 1887.
The Land I Love Best. London: Unwin Bros., 1890.
Ballads and Lyrics. London: Kegan Paul, Trench and Co., 1891.

(Dedicated to Rosa Mulholland).

A Nun, Her Friends and Her Order. London: Kegan Paul, 1891.

Irish Love Songs. Edited. The Cameo Series. London: T. F. Unwin, 1892.

Cuckoo Songs. London: Elkin Mathews, 1894.

A Cluster of Nuts: Being Sketches Among My Own People. London: Lawrence and Bullen, 1894. Another edition: 1895.

An Isle in the Water. London: A. and C. Black, 1895. Another edition: 1896. Another edition: London: Adam and Charles Black, 1904.

Miracle Plays: Our Lord's Coming and Childhood. London: J. Lane, 1895.

The Way of a Maid. London: Lawrence and Bullen, 1895.

The Land of Mist and Mountain. London: Unwin Bros.; and London: Catholic Truth Society, 1895.

A Lover's Breast-Knot. London: E. Mathews, 1896.

Oh, What a Plague is Love! London: A. and C. Black, 1896. Sixpenny edition: London: A. and C. Black, 1904.

The Wind in the Trees: a Book of Country Verse. London: G. Richards, 1898.

The Land I Love Best. London: Catholic Truth Society, 1899. Another edition: London: Gresham Press/Unwin Bros., 1899.

The Handsome Brandons: a Story for Girls. London: Blackie and Son, 1899.

The Dear Irish Girl. London: Smith, Elder and Co., 1899.

Led by a Dream. London: Catholic Truth Society, 1899.

The Queen's Page. London: Lawrence and Bullen, 1899. Another edition: New York: Benziger Bros., 1900.

She Walks in Beauty. London: Smith, Elder and Co., 1899.

A Daughter of Kings. London: Smith, Elder, 1900. Other editions: New York: Benziger Bros., 1905. London: Eveleigh Nash, 1905. London: Hodder and Stoughton, 1909.

A Daughter of the Fields. London: Smith, Elder, 1900. Another edition: London: Hodder and Stoughton, [1910].

The Adventures of Carlo. London: Blackie and Son, [1900]. Another edition, Pinnacle Library Series: London and Glasgow: Blackie and Son, 1932.

Three Fair Maids; or, The Burkes of Barrymore. London: Blackie and Son, 1901. Another edition: 1909.

Poems. London: Lawrence and Bullen, 1901. Another edition: 1910.

That Sweet Enemy. London: Archibald Constable, 1901. Other editions: Philadelphia: J. B. Lippincott, 1901. Constable's Sixpenny Series: London: Archibald Constable, [1908].

The Great Captain. London: Constable, [1901]. Another edition: New York: Benziger Bros., 1902.

The Golden Lily. London: Constable, [1901]. Another edition: New York: Benziger Bros., 1902.

A Union of Hearts. London: J. Nisbet and Co., [1901].

A Girl of Galway. London: Blackie and Son, 1902. Another edition: [1914].

The Handsome Quaker. London: A. H. Bullen, 1902.

A King's Woman. London: Hurst and Blackett, 1902.

The Cabinet of Irish Literature. Edited, with C. A. Read. Revised edition. 4 vols. London: Gresham Co., 1902.

Love of Sisters. London: Smith, Elder and Co., 1902.

A Red, Red Rose. London: Eveleigh Nash, 1903.

The Honourable Molly. London: Smith, Elder, 1903. Another edition, Newnes' Sixpenny Novels: [1907].

Julia. London: Smith, Elder, 1904. Other editions: 1905. Sixpenny Novel Series, no. 103: London: *Daily Mail*, [1910].

The French Wife. London: Hodder and Stoughton, 1904. Another edition: London: White and Co., 1904.

Judy's Lovers. London: White and Co., 1904.

Fortune's Favourite London: White and Co., 1905.

Luck of the Fairfaxes: a Story for Girls. London: Colins' Clear-Type Press, [1905].

Innocencies. London: A. H. Bullen; and Dublin: Maunsel and Co., 1905. Another edition: Chicago: A. C. McClurg, 1905.

Dick Pentreath. London: Smith, Elder, 1905.

For the White Rose. London: Constable, (1905). Another edition: New York: Benziger Bros., 1905.

The Adventures of Alicia. London: White, 1906.

The Story of Bawn. London: Smith, Elder, 1906. Another edition: Chicago: A. C. McClurg, 1907.

For Maisie: a Love Story. London: Hodder and Stoughton, 1906.

The Yellow Domino, and Other Stories. London: F. V. White and Son, 1906.

A Book of Memory: The Birthday Book of the Blessed Dead. London: Hodder and Stoughton, [1906]. Another edition: 1907. Later republished as: *A Little Book for John O'Mahony's Friends*.

A Little Book for John O'Mahony's Friends. Petersfield: Pear Tree Press, 1906. Another edition, with memoir of her sister's husband: Portland, Maine: Thomas B. Mosher, 1909.

A Little Book for Mary Gill's Friends. Petersfield: Pear Tree Press, 1906.

A Little Book of Courtesier. London: J. M. Dent and Co., [1906].

Her Ladyship. London: Smith, Elder, 1907.

A Little Book of Twenty-Four Carols. Portland, Maine: T. B. Mosher, 1907.

Twenty-One Poems by Katharine Tynan: Selected by W. B. Yeats. Dundrum: Dun Emer Press, 1907.

Ireland. Peeps at Many Lands Series. 1907. Another edition: London: A. and C. Black, 1927.

The Rhymed Life of St Patrick. London: Burns and Oates, 1907.

The Story of Our Lord for Children. Dublin: Sealy, Bryers and Co., 1907. Another edition, with coloured illustrations: London: Burns, Oates and Washbourne, 1923.

Peggy, the Daughter. London: Cassell and Co., 1907. Cassell's Sixpenny Novel Series: London: Cassell and Co., 1912.

Experiences: Poems. London: A. H. Bullen, 1908.

Men and Maids: or, The Lovers' Way. Dublin: Sealy, Bryers, 1908.

Father Mathew. The Saint Nicholas Series. London: Burns, Oates and Washbourne, 1908.

The Lost Angel. London: John Milne, 1908. Another edition: Philadelphia: J. B. Lippincott, 1908.

Mary Grey. London: Cassell, 1908. Other editions: 1909, and 1911.

Love of Sisters. London: Smith, Elder, 1908.

The House of the Crickets. London: Smith, Elder, 1908.

The Book of Flowers. With Frances Maitland. London: Smith and Elder, 1909.

Lauds. London: Enfield, 1909.

Kitty Aubrey. London: James Nisbet and Co., 1909.

Her Mother's Daughter. London: Smith, Elder and Co., 1909. Another edition: London: Murray, n.d.

Peggy, the Daughter. London: Cassell, 1909.

Cousins and Others. London: T. W. Laurie, 1909.

The House of the Secret. London: James Clarke and Co., 1910.

Betty Carew. London: Smith, Elder and Co., 1910.

Freda. London and New York: Cassell and Co., 1910.

New Poems. London: Sidgwick and Jackson, 1911.

The Story of Cecilia. London: Smith, Elder and Co., 1911. New York: Benziger Bros., 1911.

The Story of Clarice. London: James Clarke and Co., 1911.

Paradise Farm. New York: Duffield, 1911.

Princess Katherine. New York: Duffield, 1911. Another edition: London: Ward, Lock and Co., 1912.

Rose of the Garden. London: Constable, 1912. Another edition: Indianapolis: Bobbs-Merrill, 1913.

Heart o' Gold: or, The Little Princess. London: S. W. Partridge and Co., [1912].

The Unbeliever: a Romance of Lourdes. London: Burns, Oates and Washbourne, 1912.

Honey, My Honey. London: Smith, Elder and Co., 1912.
Irish Poems. London: Sidgwick and Jackson, 1913. Another edition: New York: Benziger Bros., 1914.
A Midsummer Rose. London: Smith, Elder and Co., 1913.
Twenty-Five Years: Reminiscences. London: Smith, Elder and Co., 1913.
A Misalliance. New York: Duffield, 1913.
The Squire's Sweetheart. London: Ward, Lock and Co., 1913.
Mrs Pratt of Paradise Farm. London: Smith, Elder, 1913.
The Wild Harp: an Anthology. Edited. London: Sidgwick and Jackson, 1913.
John Bulteel's Daughters. London: Smith, Elder, 1914.
Molly, My Heart's Delight. London: Smith, Elder, 1914.
The Daughter of the Manor. London: Blackie and Son, 1914.
The Flower of Peace. London: Burns and Oates, 1914. Another edition: New York: Charles Scribner's Sons, 1915.
A Shameful Inheritance. London: Cassell, 1914.
A Little Radiant Girl. London: Blackie, 1914. Reissued: London and Glasgow: Blackie, [1937].
Lovers' Meeting. London: T. W. Laurie, 1914. Another edition: London and Melbourne: Ward, Lock, 1932.
Men, Not Angels; and Other Tales Told to Girls. London: Burns, Oates and Washbourne, 1914.
Flower of Youth: Poems in War Time. London: Sidgwick and Jackson, 1915. Another edition: London: Sidgwick, 1917.
Countrymen All. Dublin and London: Maunsel and Co., 1915.
The House of the Foxes. London: Smith, Elder, 1915.
The Curse of Castle Eagle. New York: Duffield, 1915.
Since First I Saw Your Face. London: Hutchinson and Co., 1915.
Margery Dawe. London: Blackie and Son, 1916. Another edition: London and Glasgow: Blackie, [1934].
The Holy War: Poems. London: Sidgwick and Jackson, 1916.
The Web of Fraulein. London: Hodder and Stoughton, 1916.
Lord Edward. London: Smith, Elder and Co., 1916.
The Middle Years. London: Constable, 1916.
John-A-Dreams. London: Smith, Elder, 1916.
The West Wind. London: Constable and Co., 1916.
Late Songs. London: Sidgwick and Jackson, 1917.
The Rattle-Snake. London: Ward, Lock and Co., 1917.
Kit. London: Smith, Elder, 1917.
Miss Mary. London: John Murray, 1917.
Herb o' Grace: Poems in War-Time. London: Sidgwick and Jackson, 1918.

My Love's but a Lassie. London: Ward, Lock and Co., 1918. Another edition: 1932.

Miss Gascoigne. London: John Murray, 1918.

Katharine Tynan's Book of Irish History. Dublin and Belfast: Educational Co. of Ireland, [1918].

The Love of Brothers. London: Constable and Co., 1919. American edition: New York, Cincinnati, Chicago: Benziger Brothers, 1920.

The Man from Australia. London: W. Collins Sons, 1919. Novel Library Series edition: London: London Book Co., [1931].

The Years of the Shadow. London: Constable and Co., 1919. Boston: Houghton-Mifflin, 1919.

Denys the Dreamer. London: W. Collins Sons, 1920. Other editions: New York: Benziger Bros., 1921. London: Collins, 1930.

The House. London: W. Collins Sons, 1920.

Bitha's Wonderful Year. London: Humphrey Milford, [1921].

The Second Wife: Together with a July Rose. London: John Murray, 1921.

Sally Victrix. London: Collins, 1921.

Evensong. Oxford: Basil Blackwell, 1922.

The Wandering Years. London: Constable and Co., 1922. Boston: Houghton-Mifflin, 1922.

A Mad Marriage. London: Collins, 1922.

White Ladies. London: Eveleigh Nash and Grayson, 1922.

The House on the Bogs. London: Constable, 1922. Another edition: London and Melbourne: Ward, Lock and Co., 1922.

The Child at Prayer; a Book of Devotions for the Young. Compiled. London: Burns, Oates and Co., 1923.

Pat the Adventurer. London and Melbourne: Ward, Lock and Co., 1923.

They Loved Greatly. London: E. Nash and Grayson, 1923.

Mary Beaudesurt, V.S. London: Collins and Son, 1923.

The Golden Rose. London: E. Nash and Grayson, 1924.

Wives. London: Hurst and Blackett, [1924].

The House of Doom. London: E. Nash and Grayson, 1924.

Memories. London: E. Nash and Grayson, 1924.

Dear Lady Bountiful. London: Ward, Lock and Co., 1925.

Life in the Occupied Area. London: Hutchinson and Co., 1925.

Miss Phipps. London, Dublin and Melbourne: Ward, Lock and Co., 1925.

The Moated Grange. London: W. Collins Sons, 1926. Another edition, retitled: *The Night of Terror.* London: W. Collins Sons, [1932].

The Infatuation of Peter. London: Collins, 1926.

The Heiress of Wyke. London and Melbourne: Ward, Lock and Co., 1926.

The Briar Bush Maid. London and Melbourne: Ward, Lock and Co., 1926.

A Dog Book. London: Hutchinson and Co., [1926].

The Face in the Picture. London and Melbourne: Ward, Lock and Co., 1927.

Twilight Songs. Oxford: Basil Blackwell, 1927.

Haroun of London. London: Collins, 1927.

The Wild Adventure. London and Melbourne: Ward, Lock and Co., 1927.

The Respectable Lady. London: Cassell, 1927. Another edition: London: Collins, n.d.

Castle Perilous. London and Melbourne: Ward, Lock and Co., 1928. Another edition: 1929.

The House in the Forest. London and Melbourne: Ward, Lock and Co., 1928.

Lover of Women. London: W. Collins Sons, 1928.

A Fine Gentleman. London and Melbourne: Ward, Lock and Co., 1929.

The Most Charming Family. London and Melbourne: Ward, Lock and Co., 1929.

The Rich Man. London: W. Collins Sons, 1929. Another edition: 1930.

The River. London: W. Collins Sons, 1929. Another edition: London: Novel Library, [1934].

The Admirable Simmons. London: Ward, Lock and Co., 1930.

Collected Poems. London: Macmillan, 1930.

Grayson's Girl. London: W. Collins Sons, 1930. Another edition: London: Mellifont Press, [1952].

The Playground. London and Melbourne: Ward, Lock and Co., 1930.

Her Father's Daughter. London: W. Collins Sons, 1930.

Denise the Daughter. London and Melbourne: Ward, Lock and Co., 1930.

Philippa's Lover. London and Melbourne: Ward, Lock and Co., 1931.

A Red, Red Rose. London: Ward, Lock and Co., 1931.

Delia's Orchard. London and Melbourne: Ward, Lock and Co., 1931.

A Lonely Maid. London: Ward, Lock and Co., 1931.

The Forbidden Way. London: Collins Sons and Co., 1931.

The Augustan Books of Irish Poetry: Katharine Tynan. London: Ernest Benn, c.1931. Introduction by Pamela Hinkson.

The Other Man. London: Ward, Lock and Co., 1932.

The Pitiful Lady. London and Melbourne: Ward, Lock and Co., 1932.

An International Marriage. London and Melbourne: Ward, Lock and Co., 1933.

Connor's Wood. London: Collins, 1933.

Grayson's Girl. London: Collins, 1933.

The House of Dreams. London and Melbourne: Ward, Lock and Co., 1934.

A Lad was Born. London: Collins, 1934. Another edition, abridged: London: Melifont Press, [1945].

Maxims from the Writing of Katharine Tynan. Elsie E. Morton, ed. The Angelus Series. [1936].

Poems of Katherine [sic] Tynan. Edited by Monk Gibbon. Dublin: Allen Figgis, 1963.

TYNAN, Norah
Born: 1865
Died: 1932
Married name: Norah O'Mahony

Norah Tynan's name is frequently spelled as Nora, but the title pages of her volumes and her published pieces give the spelling as Norah.

Norah was the daughter of Andrew Cullen Tynan and Elizabeth Reilly Tynan. She was one of twelve children, and the younger sister of Katharine Tynan (see listing). Norah was educated by the Dominican nuns at the Siena Convent, Drogheda. She did not begin writing until after her marriage to John O'Mahony, on 29 April 1895. John O'Mahony was a Cork man who was on the staff of the *Irish Independent*, and was studying to be a barrister. He was called to the Bar in January 1899, four years after their marriage. Three sons were born to Norah and John, before John died of heart disease on 28 November 1904.

The O'Mahony's first home had been near Whitehall, but they moved to one of the Shamrock Villas, beyond Drumcondra Bridge in Northern Dublin, after John O'Mahony was called to the Bar. They had named their new home 'Shandon', commemorating John O'Mahony's Cork homeland. Following her husband's death, Norah and her children moved to Cooleen, adjacent to the Dominican Novitiate, in Tallaght.

Norah's first poem appeared in the *Irish Monthly*, the same year that she married. A total of thirty-five poems were published by the *Irish Monthly* between January 1904 and June 1931. Poems also appeared in the *Pall Mall Gazette*, and newspapers in Dublin and London. *The Social Review* published some of Norah's prose pieces.

Bibliography:
Una's Enterprise. Dublin: Browne and Nolan, 1907.
Mrs Desmond's Foster-Child. Dublin: Browne and Nolan, 1912.
The Fields of Heaven. The Little Books of Georgian Verse Series, No. 4, 1915.
The Secret of Yellow Meadows Farm. Dublin: Browne and Nolan, n.d.

U

UNIACKE, Mary
Pseudonym: M. U.

Bibliography:
The Doll's Pic-Nic. London: 1860.

V

VARIAN, Hester
Born: 1828, in Co. Cork
Died: 15 April 1898, and buried in Glasnevin Cemetery
Married name: Mrs Hester Sigerson

Hester was the daughter of Amos Varian, and sister to Ralph Varian. She became the wife of Dr George Sigerson, and the mother of Hester Sigerson and Dora Sigerson (see listings). Hester also had two sons, William Ralph Sigerson, who died in 1864 while still a child, and George Patrick, who died in 1901 at age thirty-six. Both sons are buried with Hester and George Sigerson in Glasnevin Cemetery.

Hester was a frequent contributor to the *Harp, Cork Examiner, Irish Fireside, The Gael, Young Ireland* and the *Irish Monthly*.

Anthologized in: *Cabinet* IV, and Varian.

Bibliography:
A Ruined Race; or, the Last Macmanus of Drumroosk. London: Ward and Downey, 1889.

VARIAN, Mary
Mary appears to have been a relative of Ralph Varian, in whose anthology, *Harp of Erin*, her verse appears.

Anthologized in: Varian.

VEREKER, Katherine
Title: Lady Vereker

Bibliography:
Daireen and Other Poems. London: Jarrold and Sons, 1901.

VERNER, Jane
Born: 1820
Died: 1900, in America
Married Name: Jane Mitchel
Pseudonym: Mary

Jane Verner was familiarly called Jenny. She was probably born in Armagh and was educated at Miss Bryden's School for Young Ladies in Newry. Her marriage to John Mitchel took place when she was fourteen years of age. Jane Verner wrote for *The Nation,* under the pseudonym of Mary, but it is difficult to ascertain which poems were hers, as several other authors used that same pseudonym in *The Nation.* She emigrated first to Australia before moving to America, where she settled in the New York area.

VILLIERS, Jane Anne
Married name: Jane Anne Tuthill

Jane was the wife of Jackson V. Tuthill.

Bibliography:
Songs of Past Hours. London: Saunders and Otley, 1852.

W

WADDELL, Helen Jane
Born: 31 May 1889, in Tokyo, Japan
Died: March 1965, and buried in Magherally Churchyard, Co. Down

Helen Waddell was the daughter of a Presbyterian missionary, Reverend Hugh Waddell, an Ulsterman living in Tokyo. The family returned to Belfast when Helen was two years of age, although her father did not receive permission to accompany them. A short time later, Helen's father arrived to find his wife had died of typhoid and Helen was stricken with the same disease. In 1893, Hugh Waddell married Martha Waddell, his cousin. He died in 1901, leaving Martha in charge of her ten stepchildren.

Helen was educated in Belfast at Victoria College, and at Queen's University, Belfast. In 1911 she received a B.A. degree in English, and the following year she earned an M.A. degree for her thesis entitled 'Milton, the Epicurist'. After the completion of her Master's degree, until she entered Oxford University in 1919, Helen tended her stepmother. Martha Waddell was both an invalid and probably an alcoholic, so the relationship between Helen and her stepmother was difficult. Martha seems to have been excessively strict and ungrateful for Helen's efforts. During this period Helen wrote a series of children's Bible stories for a Presbyterian weekly publication, this being the type of writing Martha favoured. Although she did not complete her doctorate at Oxford, Helen's area of specialization was medieval French literature, and she was the only female recipient of the A. C. Benson Medal of the Royal Society of Literature.

Helen accepted a position teaching Latin at Somerville College in 1920, and this was the beginning of a series of teaching jobs. She was the Casell Lecturer for St Hilda's College in 1921 and taught at Bedford College the following year. Thereafter, she supported herself through free-lance work: grading exams, lecturing, writing, and a brief foray into journalism. Helen Waddell became the first female member of the Royal Society of Literature, and in 1932 she was the first woman elected to the Irish Academy of Letters. Her first honorary D. Litt. was from the University of Durham, and two further honorary D. Litt. degrees were awarded in 1934 by Queen's University, Belfast, and by Columbia University. She was assistant editor of *The Nineteenth Century Journal* from 1938 until she retired in 1945.

Although she died of pneumonia in 1965, Helen suffered with a progressive neurological disorder for over fifteen years prior to her death. Her condition caused her to stop writing by 1950, and during the final ten years of her life she recognized no one, family or friend. It is possible from the symptoms recorded, to hazard the guess that she may have suffered with Alzheimer's disease.

Helen Waddell was best known as a scholar, although she also wrote children's stories, plays, a novel, and poetry. Her original poetry was not published until 1935. However verse translations were among her first works. She was published in the *Dublin Magazine*.

Biographical References:
Blackett, Monica. *The Mark of the Maker; a Portrait of Helen Waddell.*
    London: Constable and Co., 1973.

Corrigan, Felicitas. *Helen Waddell: a Biography*. London: Victor Gollancz, 1986.

Bibliography:
Lyrics from the Chinese. London: Constable, 1913.
The Spoiled Buddha; a Play in Two Acts. Dublin: Talbot; and London: T. Fisher Unwin, 1919.
The Wandering Scholars. London: Constable, 1927. Another edition, revised and enlarged: 1932. Another edition: 1949. Pelican Books edition: Harmondsworth: Penguin, 1954.
A Book of Mediaeval Latin for Schools. London: Constable, 1929. Another edition: 1931.
Mediaeval Latin Lyrics. Translated. London: Constable, 1929. Another edition: 1933. Penguin Classics edition: Harmondsworth: Penguin, 1952.
The History of the Chevalier des Grieux and of Manon Lescaut. Translated from French. Constable, 1931. Another edition: 1950.
Manon Lescaut. 1931.
The Abbe Prevost. 1931. London: Constable, 1933.
Peter Abelard. London: Constable, 1933. Another edition: New York: Henry Holt and Co., [1947].
Beasts and Saints. Translated from Mediaeval Latin. London: Constable and Co., 1934.
New York City. Newtown: Gregynog Press, 1935.
The Desert Fathers. Translated from Latin. London: Constable, 1936.
A French Soldier Speaks. Translated from French. London: Constable, 1941.
Epitaphium Damonis. Lament for Damon. Translated. London: Constable, 1943.
Poetry in the Dark Ages. W. P. Ker Memorial Lecture, delivered at University of Glasgow, 28 October 1947. Glasgow: Jackson, 1947.
Stories from Holy Writ. London: Constable, 1949.
Brother Ass and Brother Lion. Extract from Beasts and Saints [1934]. 1951.
The Princess Splendour and Other Stories. London: Longmans Young Books, 1969.

WALKER, Mary Grace
Pseudonym: M. G. W.

Mary Grace Walker published one poem in the *Irish Monthly*, May 1901 issue.

Bibliography:
Teena Rochforth-Smith. By M. L. R. Smith. With memoir and memorial lines by M. G. W. 1883.
To F. J. Furnivall; New Year, 1885. [London: 1885].

WALSH, Helena
Born: 1878, in Maghera, Co. Derry
Died: 27 February 1952, in Galway, and buried in the
New Cemetery, Rahoon
Married name: Mrs Thomas Concannon

Helena Walsh was the daughter of Louie Walsh, District Justice in Letterkenny. She was educated at the Loreto College, Coleraine, and in Dublin, Rome, Berlin and Paris. She married Thomas Concannon in 1906, and moved to Galway shortly thereafter. Helena was fluent in the Irish langruage. She was a member of Dáil Éireann from 1933 to 1938.

Helena won the *Tailteann* Gold Medal twice. The majority of her writings are history and biography, with emphasis on Catholic perspectives. She focused on women writers and the history of Irish women for several of her volumes. Helena had both M.A. and D.Litt. degrees. She was a strong supporter of the Irish language and culture.

Biographical Reference:
Macken, Mary M. 'Musings and Memories'. *Studies* 42 (March 1953): 90-7.

Bibliography:
The Sorrow of Lycadoon. Iona Series. Dublin: Catholic Truth Society, 1912.
A Garden of Girls; or, Famous Schoolgirls of Former Days. London: Longmans, Green and Co., 1914.
The life of St Columban. Dublin: Catholic Truth Society, 1915.
Women of 'Ninety-eight. Dublin: Gill and Son, 1919.
Daughters of Banba. Dublin: Gill and Son, 1922. Another edition: 1930.
Defenders of the Ford; Pages from the Annals of the Boys of Ireland from the Earliest Ages Down to 1798. Dublin: Gill and Son, 1925.
Makers of Irish History. Dublin: Talbot Press, [1925].
The Defence of Our Gaelic Civilisation, 1460-1660; An Irish History for Junior Grade Classes. Fallon's New Secondary School Series. Dublin: Browne and Nolan, [1926].
Ireland's Fight for the Mass. Dublin: Office of the *Irish Messenger*, 1928.

The Poor Clares in Ireland, A.D. 1629-A.D. 1929. Dublin: Gill and Son, 1929.

At the Court of the Eucharistic King; The Story of the Franciscan Convent of Perpetual Adoration, Drumshanbo . . . and its Foundresses. Dublin: Gill and Son, 1929. Another edition, retitled: *At His Feet; The Story of the Foundation of the Franciscan Convent of Perpetual Adoration, Drumshanbo, Co. Leitrim.* Dublin: Gill and Son, 1948.

St Paschal Baylon, Patron of Eucharistic Congress. Dublin: *Irish Messenger* Office, 1930.

White Horsemen; The Story of the Jesuit Martyrs. London: Sands and Co., 1930.

St Patrick; His Life and Mission. London: Longmans, Green and Co., 1931.

Irish Nuns in Penal Days. London: Sands and Co., 1931.

The Jesuits in Ireland. Dublin: *Irish Messenger* Office, 1932.

Blessed Oliver Plunkett. Dublin: 1935.

The Queen of Ireland; an Historical Account of Ireland's Devotion to the Blessed Virgin. Dublin: Gill and Son, 1938.

The Cure of La Courneuve; l'Abbé Jean Edouard Lamy. Dublin: Gill and Son, 1944.

The Irish Sisters of Mercy in the Crimean War. Dublin: *Irish Messenger* Office, [1950].

Père Gailhac; Founder of the Religious of the Sacred Heart of Mary. Dublin: *Irish Messenger* Office, [1950].

Poems. Dublin: Gill and Son, 1953.

WALSH, Mrs Honor
The *Irish Monthly* twice published poems by Mrs Honor Walsh, in the September 1903 and November 1909 issues. Mrs Walsh also wrote short stories. Her volume, *The Story-Book House*, was published in America.

WEBB, Deborah
Born: 1837, in Dublin

Deborah was one of four children born to the Quaker family of Richard and Hannah Webb. Her father was a printer and the author of a biography of John Brown the abolitionist. Deborah Webb's brother, Alfred, became a Nationalist M.P. and she has said her family was 'much interested in literature, and in all reforms and good causes, especially that of the negro slave, and our house was a resort . . . particularly of abolitionists and escaped slaves' (Armitage 289).

Deborah Webb was educated for two sessions at the London

Bedford Square Ladies' College. In 1862, after the death of her mother, she resigned her membership of the Society of Friends. A family friend, William Lloyd Garrison had introduced her to spiritualism, and she remained interested in religious alternatives for the rest of her life. She was an ardent supporter of Irish Nationalism and of equal rights for women. Her best known work is the ballad, 'John Brown's March'. Between January 1888 and August 1912, six of her poems appeared in the *Irish Monthly*.

WEST, Elizabeth Dickinson
Born: c. 1840
Married name: Mrs Edward Dowden
Pseudonym: E. D. W.

Elizabeth Dickinson West was the daughter of John West, Dean of St Patrick's Cathedral, Dublin. While studying at Alexandra College in 1867 she met Edward Dowden, Professor of English at Trinity College and noted literary critic. Professor Dowden had married the previous year, a woman about ten years older than himself and the marriage was apparently unhappy. Elizabeth West and Edward Dowden formed a long-lasting relationship, intellectually and emotionally, which culminated in their marriage in 1895, three years after the death of his first wife. His collection of love poems, *A Woman's Reliquary*, was written for Elizabeth. When she was in her 70s Elizabeth published fragments of letters she received from Edward Dowden during the period before their marriage, 1869 to 1892.

Anthologized in: Cooke, Graves, Gregory, and MacIlwaine.

Bibliography:
Verses by E. D. W. Dublin: 1876.
Verses, Part 2. Dublin: 1883.
Iphigeneia in Tauris. Translated from J. W. von Goethe. Temple Dramatists, 1906.
Poems; by Edward Dowden. Edited. 1914.
Letters of Edward Dowden and His Correspondents. Edited with H. M. Dowden. 1914.
Fragments from Old Letters E.D. to E.D.W.; 1869-1892. Edited. London: J. M. Dent; and New York: E. P. Dutton, 1914.

WETHERELL, Mrs Dawson Bruce
Pseudonym: C. C. V. G.

She was the wife of Robert Hurd Wetherell and a frequent contributor to *The Dublin Family Magazine* in 1829.

Bibliography:
Bunyan's Pilgrim's Progress. Converted into an Epick Poem. Parsonstown, King's Co.: 1824. Second edition: 1844.
The Four Ages of Life; Translated from General Count Paul Philippe De Ségur. Dublin: 1826.
Tales of Many Climes. Part I. Dublin: 1832. (Part II was never published).
The Anatomy of the Affections. Dublin: 1841.
Lays of the Troubadours. London: W. Purves; and Parsonstown: Shields and Sons, 1847.

WHATELY, B.
Married name: Mrs George Wale

Miss Whately appears to have been the daughter of Richard Whately, the Archbishop of Dublin. She married George Wale in 1860. Her sister, Elizabeth Jane Whately was a successful prose writer.

Bibliography:
Songs of the Night. Published under her maiden name. Dublin: 1858. Second edition, published anonymously: 1860. Third edition, published under her married name: 1861.

WHEELER, Edith
Edith Wheeler was living at Thornhill Gardens, Marlboro Park, Belfast, in 1902.

The *New Ireland Review* published one poem by Edith in June 1909.

Bibliography:
My Wedding Day; a Gift Book Designed by E. Wheeler, with Selections from Various Authors. Edinburgh and London: George Waterston and Sons, [1902].
A Nice Little Supper; a Dialogue. London: Joseph Williams, [1905].
A Woman's Way; a Play in One Act. London: Joseph Williams, [1906].
A Bouquet; a Play in One Act. London: Joseph Williams, 1907.
A Discord; a Duologue. London: Joseph Williams, 1907.
In Wonderland; a Fairy Operetta for Children in Two Acts, Founded on Lewis Carroll's Book, 'Alice in Wonderland'. London: Joseph Williams, [1908]. Adapted and with lyrics by Edith Wheeler.

The Sentence; a Play in One Act. London: Joseph Williams, [1908].

WHITE, Agnes Romilly
Born: 1872
Died: 1945

The *Irish Monthly* published twelve poems between May 1896 and December 1903, by Agnes Romilly White. Another poem by Agnes is found in *The New Ireland Review*, March 1902 edition. Agnes wrote two novels; *Gape Row* and *Mrs Murphy Buries the Hatchet*, both set in Dundonald, a suburb of Belfast. She also wrote several short stories.

Bibliography:
Gape Row. London: Selwyn and Blount, [1934]. Reprint: Belfast: White Row Press, 1988.
Mrs Murphy Buries the Hatchet; a Novel. London: Selwyn and Blount, 1936.

WHITE, Elizabeth
Born: 16 August 1868, Castle Caulfield, Co. Tyrone
Died: 7 December 1891
Pseudonym: Lillie White

Lillie was the daughter of Reverend Robert White, and lived most of her life in Maghera, near Banbridge in Co. Down, where her father was Rector. She was a delicate child whose health continued to be of concern throughout her life. Lillie was educated at home, with brief periods of study at art schools in Dublin and Belfast. She began writing at an early age and some of her verses have a notation stating they were written at the age of sixteen.

She sent an unsolicited manuscript of poems to W. B. Yeats in 1868 for his opinion, inadvertently becoming the first poet ever to do so. Yeats responded with a letter dated 30 January [1889], calling her poems 'musical and pleasant' (*Letters* 130). He suggested that she submit her verses to Reverend Matthew Russell, editor of the *Irish Monthly*, for possible publication. The following day Yeats wrote to Father Russell about Lillie and her poems, calling her work, 'somewhat artless but musical and sincere and having often really pretty phrases' (*Letters* 132). Yeats then tells Russell of his suggestion that Lillie send her work to the *Irish Monthly*. That same day, in a letter written to Katharine Tynan, Yeats provides a more extensive report:

I got, did I tell you, a bundle of verses, for an opinion on them, from
a stranger the other day. Some lady in Co. Down. I spent a long time
trying to say some thing pleasent [sic] about them, without saying
to[o] much. They were not very good — though sincere and
musical. You I suppose often get such letters. It was my first (*Letters*
135).

Prior to requesting Yeats's critical opinion Lillie White had published
her poems only in the Banbridge *Chronicle*. The 4th of March, and
24th of June 1882 issues of that newspaper carry her poems. Father
Russell did accept a short story, which appeared in the same issue of
the *Irish Monthly* as her obituary. 'More White Lillies' was posthumously published in Volume 25 of the *Irish Monthly*, Lillie having
already died of consumption, at the age of twenty-three.

She was a contributor to the *Irish Monthly* issues of August and
September 1893. Her poems were published in typescript and bound
for private circulation.

Biographical Reference:
Russell, Matthew. 'Lillie White; A Memento of a Short Life'. *Irish
Monthly* 21 (Sept. 1893): 473-80.

Bibliography:
Poems, by Lillie White. Typescript intended for private circulation: c.
1889.

WHITE, Harriet
Pseudonym: Harriet

Harriet White lived at Cashel, Co. Tipperary, and she was probably
related to John Davis White, the founder of the Cashel *Gazette*, and
the poet Newport Benjamin White.

Bibliography:
Verses, Sacred and Miscellaneous. London: 1853.

WHITE, Ida L.
Pseudonym: Ida

Ida was the wife of George White, the editor and founder of the
Ballymena Observer. O'Donoghue states, 'To judge from her poems,
her later life has been a stormy one, and she appears to hold very
advanced opinions' (478).

Ida's opinions included supporting women's rights and being a Republican. Kate Newmann reports, in the *Dictionary of Ulster Biography* that Ida was 'exiled in Paris . . . imprisoned in Holloway and made a public attack on the Tzar of Russia' (266).

Bibliography:
Lady Blanche, and Other Poems, by Ida. London: Hamilton Adams; and
 Belfast: C. Aitchison, 1875.
The Three Banquets, and Prison Poems. London: 1890.

WHITEFORD, Isabella
Born: Ballycastle, Co. Antrim

Isabella Whiteford emigrated to Newfoundland at a young age.

Bibliography:
Poems. Belfast: 1860.

WILLISON, Mabel
A single poem by Mabel Willison appeared in the July 1921 *Irish Monthly*.

WILSON, Florence Mary
Born: c. July 1874, in Lisburn, Co. Antrim
Died: 7 November 1946, at Bangor, Co. Down, and
 buried in Newtownards Road Cemetery, Bangor
Married name: Mrs Frederick Hugh Graham Wilson

Florence Mary Wilson was reared on Mill Island in Lisburn, where she was the daughter of the Island Spinning Company's mill manager. She attended the Friends' School in Lisburn as a day student. Florence married Frederick Hugh Graham Wilson in 1898. Her husband was a solicitor with offices in Bangor and Belfast. The Wilsons had nine children, four sons and five daughters. She was a close friend of Alice Milligan (see listing), and of Alice Stopford Green.

Florence was a poet, essayist, historian, artist and archaeologist. She was a frequent contributor to *T. P.'s Weekly, Irish Homestead, Northern Whig,* and the *Ulster Guardian.* The *Irish Review* published one poem by Florence Wilson in the November 1911 issue, and she also had work published in the *Dublin Magazine.*

Anthologized in: Gregory

Bibliography:
The Coming of the Earls and Other Verse. Poetry Booklets: Number 4.
 Dublin: The Candle Press, 1918.

WILSON, Mary
Dublin University Magazine published a poem by Mary Wilson in
April 1876.

WINTER, Mary
Psesudonym: M. W.

Bibliography:
Alton Park; or, Conversations on Religious and Moral Matters. 1830.
The Ideal Confidant; a Poem. Dublin: 1836.
Hermann and Dorothea. Translation of Goethe. Dublin: 1833. Other
 editions: 1849, and 1850.
The Ice-bound Ship, the Sleeping Beauty, and Other Poems. T. R. and A.
 Winter, eds. London: 1860.
*A Fair Exchange is No Robbery; a Drama or Charade for Drawingroom
 Acting.* Dublin: Gill and Son, 1881.
Where There's a Will There's a Way; or, The Old Family Name. Dublin:
 Hodges, Figgis and Co., 1886. An old-fashioned Irish comedy in
 three acts. Written in 1853, but not published until 1886.

WOLFE, Ffrida
Ffrida Wolfe's family was from Kildare. She was the granddaughter of
Reverend Thomas Romney Robinson, the noted Armagh Observat-
ory astronomer and writer.

Bibliography:
Vanities; Poems. Vigo Cabinet Series, No. 67. London: Elkin Mathews,
 1909. Another edition: 1910.
The Orange Cat, and Other Verses. London: Sidgwick and Jackson,
 1910.
Roundabout Ways; Verses. London: Sidgwick and Jackson, 1912.
How to Identify Oriental Rugs. With A. T. Wolfe. London: T. Fisher
 Unwin, 1927.
The Very Things; Readable Rhymes for Children. London: Sidgwick and
 Jackson, 1928.
The Cardinal, and Other Poems. London: Ernest Benn, 1930.

WOLSELEY, Mrs C.
Mrs Wolseley was the wife of an Archdeacon of Glendalough, and a

member of the Brooke family. She contributed poetry to *Dublin University Magazine's* issue of February 1852.

WRIGHT, A. M.
Pseudonym: A. M.

A. M. Wright was a frequent contributor to *The Nation*, after 1860. She published exclusively under her initials.

Bibliography:
Little Star, and Other Poems. Bath: 1864.

WRIGHT, Gertrude
Gertrude was a daughter of the Rector of the Parish of Desartlyn, Moneymore. Her volume is dedicated to her paternal grandmother, Mary Harkness, and her maternal grandmother, Anna Despard. The dedication was written from Erenagh, Lands of Desartlyn, Moneymore although Gertrude lived in The Cottage, Moneymore.

Bibliography:
Voices from Erenach. Belfast: University Book Publishing House (Allen, Son and Allen), 1886.

WYNNE, Catherine Adelaide
Pseudonym: C. A. W.

Bibliography:
Fragments Collected from the Manuscripts of C. A. W. Edited by Reverend F. R. Wynne. Dublin: Steam Printing Co., 1868.

WYNNE, Frances Alice
Born: 1863, at Collon, near Drogheda, Co. Louth
Died: 9 August 1893, in London
Married name: Mrs Henry Wynne

Frances was the daughter of a Reverend Wynne and she was born and reared in Collon. In 1892 she married her cousin, Mr Henry Wynne, and moved to London where they settled at Southampton Row. They moved to an East End curacy when her husband became Reverend Henry Wynne. Frances died in childbirth after about eighteen months of marriage, although the son she bore survived her.

Katharine Tynan (see listing) and Frances Wynne were very close friends. In her memoir of Frances Wynne, Tynan describes her as a woman 'who was greatly loved by children, and the poor, and animals, and by her social inferiors' (ii). Father Matthew Russell, editor of the *Irish Monthly*, was lavish in his praise of Frances's work.

Frances Wynne contributed to *Longman's Magazine*, *Irish Monthly*, and the *Spectator*. Fifteen of her poems appeared in the *Irish Monthly* between July 1887 and October 1890.

Anthologized in: Brooke/Rolleston, *Cabinet* IV, Graves, Rhys, and Welsh.

Biographical References:
Hinkson, Katharine Tynan. 'Frances Wynne: a Memory'. *Whisper!* London: Elkin Mathews, 1893.
Russell, Matthew. 'Our Poets, No. 27; Frances Wynne'. *Irish Monthly* 20 (March 1892): 130-6.
Russell, Matthew. 'The Late Mrs Frances Wynne'. *Irish Monthly* 21 (October 1893): 554-7.

Bibliography:
Whisper! and Other Poems. London: Kegan Paul, 1890. Another edition, with memoir by Katharine Tynan: The Vigo Cabinet Series, No. 35. London: Elkin Mathews and John Lane, 1893. Another edition, with Tynan memoir from 1893: London: Elkin Mathews, 1908.

Bibliographical note: Several sources incorrectly list the following two volumes as being written by this author: *The True Level* (Dublin: Gill, 1947), and *Eastward of All* (Dublin: Sheed and Ward, 1945). Neither of these two books were written by Frances Alice Wynne; they were written by another woman, another Frances Wynne, who was a prose writer from Northern Ireland.

WYNNE, Frances Alice
Born: 1863, at Collon, near Drogheda, Co. Louth
Died: 9 August 1893, in London
Married name: Mrs Henry Wynne

Frances was the daughter of a Reverend Wynne and she was born and reared in Collon. In 1892 she married her cousin, Mr Henry Wynne, and moved to London where they settled at Southampton Row. They moved to an East End curacy when her husband became Reverend Henry Wynne. Frances died in childbirth after about eighteen months of marriage, although the son she bore survived her.

Katharine Tynan (see listing) and Frances Wynne were very close friends. In her memoir of Frances Wynne, Tynan describes her as a woman 'who was greatly loved by children, and the poor, and animals, and by her social inferiors' (ii). Father Matthew Russell, editor of the *Irish Monthly*, was lavish in his praise of Frances's work.

Frances Wynne contributed to *Longman's Magazine*, *Irish Monthly*, and the *Spectator*. Fifteen of her poems appeared in the *Irish Monthly* between July 1887 and October 1890.

Anthologized in: Brooke/Rolleston, *Cabinet* IV, Graves, Rhys, and Welsh.

Biographical References:
Hinkson, Katharine Tynan. 'Frances Wynne: a Memory'. *Whisper!* London: Elkin Mathews, 1893.
Russell, Matthew. 'Our Poets, No. 27; Frances Wynne'. *Irish Monthly* 20 (March 1892): 130-6.
Russell, Matthew. 'The Late Mrs Frances Wynne'. *Irish Monthly* 21 (October 1893): 554-7.

Bibliography:
Whisper! and Other Poems. London: Kegan Paul, 1890. Another edition, with memoir by Katharine Tynan: The Vigo Cabinet Series, No. 35. London: Elkin Mathews and John Lane, 1893. Another edition, with Tynan memoir from 1893: London: Elkin Mathews, 1908.

Bibliographical note: Several sources incorrectly list the following two volumes as being written by this author: *The True Level* (Dublin: Gill, 1947), and *Eastward of All* (Dublin: Sheed and Ward, 1945). Neither of these two books were written by Frances Alice Wynne; they were written by another woman, another Frances Wynne, who was a prose writer from Northern Ireland.

WYSE, Marie Studolmine Bonaparte
Born: 1833, in Waterford
Married name: Princess Marie Studolmine Bonaparte Rattazzi
Pseudonyms: Vicomte d'Albeno, Camille Bernard, Baron Stork, and Louis de Kelmar

Marie was the daughter of Sir Thomas Wyse, M.P. for Tipperary and later for Waterford. He also served as Lord of the Treasury in Lord

Melbourne's government. William Charles Bonaparte Wyse, her brother, was also a poet. Marie was twice married; the first marriage in 1850, and the second in 1863. She wrote plays and novels, and founded several journals. Marie ran her own theatre company where she performed the leading roles of plays she had written for herself.

Marie was a contributor to French journals after she moved to Paris. Apparently none of her volumes were published in English, although she is reported to have written occasional poems in that language. Her volumes were published generally in French.

Y

YOUNG, Ella
Born: 1865, in Fenagh, Co. Antrim
Died: 1951, in California, U.S.A.

Born in 1865, to an Ulster Presbyterian family, Ella Young became an ardent Nationalist. In the 1880s, the Young family relocated to Rathmines and Ella was educated in Dublin, where she obtained a university degree in political science and law. She was a member of the Hermetical Society. In 1912 she was running guns for the IRA from Temple Hill, Co. Wicklow. Ella moved to Achill for part of World War I. Returning to Dublin, she shared a house with Olive Agnes Fox (see listing) and continued her I.R.A. gun-running activities. She was blacklisted as a result of the 1916 Rising, and hid in Connemara for about three years until 1919. She stayed in Dublin throughout the Civil War. In 1925 she travelled about America before eventually settling in the San Francisco Bay area, where she lectured at the University of California.

A single poem by Ella Young is found in the *Red Hand Magazine*, September 1920 issue. She also had work published in the *Irish Review* and the *Dublin Magazine*.

Anthologized in: Æ, Cooke, Fitzhenry, Graves, and Welsh.

Bibliography:
The Coming of Lugh. Dublin: Maunsel and Co., 1905. Another edition: 1909.

Poems. Tower Press Booklet No. 4. Dublin: Maunsel and Co., 1906.

Celtic Wonder Tales. Dublin: Maunsel, 1910. Another edition: Dublin: Talbot Press, 1923.

The Rose of Heaven. Colm O'Loughlin, 1918. Another edition, illustrated by Maud Gonne: Dublin: The Candle Press, 1920.

The Wierd of Fionavar. Dublin: Talbot Press; and London: T. Fisher Unwin, 1922.

The Wonder-Smith and His Son. London: Longmans, 1927.

The Tangle-Coated Horse and Other Tales. Edited. Dublin: Maunsel, 1929.

YOUNGE, Marianne
Died: 1 May 1917, at Rathdowney, Queens Co.
Pseudonym: M. A. Rathkyle

Green and Gold published seven of Marianne Younge's poems posthumously, between the March 1921 issue and the September-November 1922 issue.

Bibliography:
Farewell to Garrymore. Dublin: Sealy, Bryers and Walker, 1912.

INDEX OF MARRIED NAMES,
NAMES IN RELIGION
AND PSEUDONYMS

CAMPBELL, Nancy (Maude, Nancy)
CARBERY, Ethna (Johnston, Anna Isabel)
CHAVASSE, Móirín (Fox, Olive Agnes)
CHEAVASA, Móirín (Fox, Olive Agnes)
CHEAVASSA, Mrs Claud de (Fox, Olive Agnes)
CHEAVASSE, Móirín (Fox, Olive Agnes)
CHESSON, Mrs W. H. (Hopper, Nora)
CHESTER, Harriet Mary (Goff, Harriet Mary)
CHRISTABEL (McCarthy, Mary)*
CLARIBEL (Barnard, Charlotte Alington)*
CLARKE, Mrs Charles Marion (See Doak, Marion)
CLIATHNA (Irwin, Mary Jane)
CLIODHNA (Irwin, Mary Jane)
COLLEEN (O'Doherty, Margaret T.)
COLUM, Mrs Padraic (Maguire, Mary)
CONCANNON, Mrs Thomas (Walsh, Helena)
CONNOLLY, Mrs Hope (Knight, Olivia)
CONYNGHAM, Elizabeth Emmet Lenox (Holmes, Elizabeth Emmet Lenox)
CORRY, Mrs Thomas (Corry, Helen M.)
COUNTESS OF CORK AND ORRERY (Boyle, Emily Charlotte)
CRAIK, Dinah (Mulock, Dinah Maria)
CRAWFORD, Mrs Abraham (Crawford, Sophia)
CUMMINGHAM, Mrs Jane (Cummingham, Jane)
D. L. (Hartnett, Penelope Mary)
D. M. L. (Large, Dorothy M.)
D'ALBENO, Vicomte (Wyse, Marie Studolmine Bonaparte)
DARMESTETER, Agnes M. F. (Robinson, Agnes Mary Frances)
DAVENPORT, Mary (Devenport, Mary)
DE BURGH, Emma Maria (Hunt, Emma Maria)
DEHAN, Richard (Graves, Clotilde Inez Augusta Mary)
DE RUPE (Roche, Frances Maria)
DILLON, Geraldine (Plunkett, Geraldine)
DONOVAN, Mrs J. F. (Keon, Grace)
DOWDEN, Mrs Edward (West, Elizabeth Dickinson)
DOWNING, Mary (McCarthy, Mary)
DRAKE, Miriam (Doak, Marion)
DUFFERIN, Lady (Sheridan, Helen Selina)
E. D. W. (West, Elizabeth Dickinson)
E. K. (Keary, Elizabeth)
E. L. L. (Fallon, Mrs Garnett)
E. M. H. (Hamilton, Elizabeth Mary)

*Note: The 'Claribel' of James Stephens' 'Reminiscences' was Mary McCarthy Downing whose actual pseudonym was 'Christabel'. Stephens was in error regarding Mrs Barnard's pseudonym.

H. K. (Kierman, Harriet)
H. M. C. (Goff, Harriet Mary)
HALL, Mrs S. C. (Fielding, Anna Maria)
HAMILTON, Eliza Mary (Hamilton, Elizabeth Mary)
HARRIET (White, Harriet)
HENRIETTA (Nethercott, Henrietta)
HERBERT, Jean (Leslie, Mary Isabel)
HICKSON, Agnes (Mahony, Agnes)
HIME, Mrs Maurice Charles (Apjohn, Rebecca Helena)
HINKSON, Katharine (Tynan, Katharine)
HOBHOUSE, Violet (McNeill, Violet)
HODGES, Mrs John F. (Benn, Miss)
HONORIA (Power, Marguerite A.)
HUTTON, Mary Anne (Drummond, Mary Anne)
IDA (White, Ida L.)
INGLIS, Catherine H. (Mahon, Catherine Hartland)
IRISH MOLLY (Cowan, Charlotte)
J. E. L. (Leeson, Jane Eliza)
J. M. M. (Black, Josephine Macauley)
J. T. (Tulloch, Jessie)
JOBLING, Charlotte (Cowan, Charlotte)
JOHNSTON, Harriet (Allen, Marriet)
KANE, Edward (Knox, Kathleen)
KATE (Downing, Ellen Mary)
KEELING, Elsa (D'Esterre, Elsa)
KELLY, Mrs E. C. (O'Callaghan, Miss)
KELLY, Frances Maria (Roche, Frances Marie)
KELLY, Mary Anne (Kelly, Mary Eva)
KELLY, Mary I. (O'Hanlon, Mary I.)
KELLY, May (Kelly, Mary)
KELMAR, Louis de (Wyse, Marie Studolmine Bonaparte)
KIELY, Anne (Keilly, Anne)
KILBROOK, T. B. (Boylan, Teresa C.)
KNOX, Lucy (Spring-Rice, Lucy)
L. G. C. (Condon, Lizzie G.)
L. H. S. (Sheridan, Louisa Henrietta)
L. L. O'K. (O'Keefe, Lena Lanigan)
L. N. F. (O'Connell, Ellen Bridget)
LA TOUCHE, Mrs (La Touche, Maria)
LANE, Temple (Leslie, Mary Isabel)
LENEL (O'Leary, Ellen)
LIBERTAS (Sheridan, Caroline Elizabeth Sarah)
LITTLE, L. M. (Little, Elizabeth Mary)

LITTLE, Lizzie M. (Little, Elizabeth Mary)
LIZZIE (Condon, Lizzie G.)
LOCKE, Mary (Cooney, Mary)
M. (O'Doherty, Margaret T., or Large, Dorothy M.)
M——— COOTEHILL (Madden, Mary Anne)
M. E. M. (Martin, M. E.)
M. F. D. (McCarthy, Mary)
M. F. P. (Preston, May Frances)
M. G. R. (Reddin, Mary Gertrude)
M. G. W. (Walker, Mary Grace)
M. J. I. (Irwin, Mary Jane)
M. J. P. H. (Hughes, Mary Jane Patricia)
M. L. (Large, Dorothy Mabel)
M. L. D. (Dawson, M. L.)
M. M. D. (McDonagh, Mary)
M. McD. (McDermott, Mary)
M. M. R. (Ryan, Margaret Mary)
M. My. R. (Ryan, Margaret Mary)
M. R. (Reddin, Mary Gertrude)
M. T. P. (O'Doherty, Margaret T.)
M. U. (Uniacke, Mary)
M. W. (Winter, Mary)
MacDOWELL, Maeve Cavanagh (Cavanagh, Maeve)
MacMANUS, Anna (Johnston, Anna Isabel)
MacMANUS, Mrs Seumas (Johnston, Anna Isabel)
MACLEOD, Fiona (Pseudonym of a male poet, William Sharp)
MAGRATH, Mary Elizabeth (McGrath, Mary Elizabeth)
MARGUERITE (O'Doherty, Margaret T.)
MARKIEVICZ, Constance (Gore-Booth, Constance)
MARY (Downing, Ellen Mary, or Verner, Jane)
MAUREEN (Garvey, Maura)
MEADE, John (Gyles, Althea)
MEARS, Amelia (Garland, Amelia)
MEDA (Gibbons, Margaret)
MERVA (Kilgallen, Mary)
MESSAGER, Mrs Andre (Davis, Miss)
MILLAIS, Ruth (Mulholland, Rosa)
MITCHEL, Jane (Verner, Jane)
MOI-MÊME (Coveney, Mary)
MOLLAN, Mrs Helen (Cromie, Helen C.)
MONTGOMERY, Lady (Montgomery, Mrs Alfred)
MORTON, May (Morton, Mary Elizabeth)
MOTHER AUGUSTINE (McKenna, Ellen)

Note* A poetic reference to 'Rose' is probably a reference to Rose Kavanagh. Rose as the pseudonym of an author is probably a reference to Rose Kirwan.

SISTER MARY JANE PATRICIA (Hughes, Mary Jane Patricia)
SISTER MARY STANISLAUS (MacCarthy, Mary Stanislaus)
SKIDDY, Mrs E. M. (Skiddy, Ellen Mary)
SKORPIOS, Antares (Barlow, Jane)
SKRINE, Mrs W. C. (Higginson, Agnes Nesta Shakespeare)
SOLMS, Marie Studolmine Letizia de (Wyse, Marie Studolmine Bonaparte)
SOMERS, Mrs B. (O'Reilly, Miss)
SPERANZA (Elgee, Jane Francesca)
STARR, Sydney (Gallagher, Fanny)
STEVENSON, Pearce (Sheridan, Caroline Elizabeth Sarah)
STIRLING-MAXWELL, Lady (Sheridan, Caroline Elizabeth Sarah)
STOCK, Baron (Wyse, Marie Studolmine Bonaparte)
STORMY PETREL (Kenny, Annie M.)
TEMPLE, Hope (Davis, Miss)
THOMASINE (Knight, Olivia)
THOMPSON, Mary (Thompson, Marie M.)
TINY (Monck, Mary C. F.)
TOKE, Emma (Leslie, Emma)
TOWNSBRIDGE, Elizabeth (Murphy, Katharine Mary)
TUTHILL, Jane Anne (Villiers, Jane Anne)
UNA (McMullen, Mary Anne)
UNCLE REMUS (I) (Kavanagh, Rose)
UNCLE REMUS (II) (Sigerson, Hester)
VARIAN, Mrs Ralph (Treacy, Elizabeth Willoughby)
VERSCHOYLE, Mrs W. H. F. (Letts, Winifred M.)
VON RANKE, Clara (Graves, Clara)
WALE, Mrs George (Whately, B.)
WHEELER, Ethel Rolt (Rolt-Wheeler, Ethel)
WHITE, Lillie (White, Elizabeth)
WILDE, Lady (Elgee, Jane Francesca)
WILHELM (Dunn, Mary)
WILSON, Mrs F. H. G. (Wilson, Florence Mary)
WILLS, Mrs Katharine (Gorman, Katharine Elizabeth)
WYATT, Louisa Henrietta (Sheridan, Louisa Henrietta)
WYNNE, Mrs Henry (Wynne, Frances Alice)
X? (Humphreys, Cecil Francis)
YLAND, Caple (Ronayne, M. Christine)